Observations upon the Topography and Climate of Crowborough Hill, Sussex

Charles Leeson Prince

BIBLIOLIFE

The Observatory, Crowborough Hill, Sussex.

OBSERVATIONS

UPON THE

TOPOGRAPHY AND CLIMATE

OF

CROWBOROUGH HILL, SUSSEX,

BY

C. LEESON PRINCE,

MEMBER OF THE ROYAL COLLEGE OF SURGEONS; LICENTIATE OF THE
SOCIETY OF APOTHECARIES; FELLOW OF THE ROYAL ASTRONOMICAL AND
ROYAL METEOROLOGICAL SOCIETIES; MEMBER OF THE BRITISH ASTRO-
NOMICAL ASSOCIATION, THE SCOTTISH METEOROLOGICAL SOCIETY; THE
SELBORNE SOCIETY; VICE-PRESIDENT OF THE TUNBRIDGE WELLS PHOTO-
GRAPHIC SOCIETY, &C.

SECOND EDITION.

---

*Ex tempestatibus verò optimæ æquales sunt, sive frigidæ, sive calidæ, pessimæ
quæ maximè variant.*—CELSUS.

Lewes:

FARNCOMBE & CO., PRINTERS.

1898

INTRODUCTORY REMARKS.

HE first edition of my little monograph, upon the climate of Crowborough Hill, having been several years out of print, I have been induced at the requests of many friends and correspondents to prepare a second. It has been very gratifying to be able to state, that as a result of the free distribution of the first edition, the main object I had in view, when writing it, has been so successfully accomplished. It may be said that some fifty years ago the district around Crowborough Hill was scarcely known beyond the area of its own immediate neighbourhood.

A great transformation has come over the scene, during the last twenty years, as it is now rapidly becoming one of the most favoured health resorts in the South of England; nor can this be a matter for surprise when we take into consideration the remarkable purity of the air on the Hill, abounding as it does in ozone and other valuable atmospheric constituents.

Another point of value is its considerable elevation above the level of the sea; moreover, its actual distance from the coast is only twenty-one miles, which renders it a most conveniently accessible resort for invalids emerging either from London or any of our coast towns.

We frequently have a most refreshing breeze from the Channel when the wind current emanates from a

B

S.E , a S., or S.W. direction , and it is found to be absolutely pure and free from the smoke and dust of densely populated towns.

Until I came to reside here, in the spring of 1872, the respective conditions of temperature of the locality were wholly unknown ; but the observations which I then commenced, and have continued to the present time, have afforded important information upon this vital subject, much to the surprise of the uninitiated strangers who were ever alluding to the *fancied* bleak and dreary atmosphere of Crowborough Hill.

It is a subject for congratulation to find that its climatic advantages, and splendid position, have become fully recognised by so many eminent members of the medical profession, and especially in a report by a Committee of the Royal Medical and Chirurgical Society of London upon "The Climates and Baths of Great Britain," of which Dr. W. M. Ord is Chairman and Dr. A. E. Garrod, Secretary (published by Macmillan & Co., 1895).

By a careful perusal of this valuable work invalids can obtain such information, respecting various health resorts, as will enable them to decide upon one which would appear to satisfy their requirements.

Although during the last decade a large number of residences have been, and are being erected at the present moment, yet the number is scarcely sufficient to meet the demand for the class of house more commonly required.

Much, of course, depends upon the site, and the amount of land available for annexation to it, but the one desire appears to be that it shall be as near the higher ground as possible.

The actual elevation of the Government Stone, above the level of the sea, is 796 feet.

Few indeed are the invalids who do not quickly derive benefit from even a short sojourn in the immediate neighbourhood. The very equable temperature of the day and night, and the comparatively high temperature of the latter, is a subject to which I shall particularly allude when treating of the respective tables in reference thereto.

Among the suggested improvements I may mention that preparations for gas illumination are progressing, and we also hear that a good water supply will be carried to the summit of the Hill at an early date, which will be a great boon to many of the inhabitants who, by the increase of population, may not be sufficiently supplied by local wells and public springs, although up to the present time the latter have been of the greatest public service.

The dry seasons, of which we have had so many during the last five years, have proved beyond all doubt that a good water supply is essentially a great public necessity.

In addition to the building of many houses, an important hotel will doubtless be erected in the course of the ensuing summer (preparations for which are in actual progress), which will be of such a description as to afford superior accommodation to the many persons who may require a short sojourn here to enjoy the splendid view and delightful air, which may be obtained at the golf links, situated to the south of the plateau of the Hill.

A large preparatory school for boys has been conducted for several years at " The Grange," and I think there cannot be in this county a more health-giving and appropriate site for such an establishment, which is situated within an area of upwards of six acres. A large football and cricket ground, as well as a gymnasium, are attached; while the view of the surrounding country from the Belvedere of the house is unequalled in the South of England.

As I formerly occupied "The Grange" (my former observatory), I can assert from personal observation that considerably more than one hundred parish churches can be seen from this Belvedere, on a clear day, with the aid of a three-inch telescope.

In the former edition I gave a long list of such churches and various objects which were visible; and although I have not the advantage of so extensive a view from my present Observatory, yet I think it expedient to repeat these particulars on the following pages, as possible assistance to any future observations which may be taken in reference thereto In this new edition I shall exclude all reference to former observations taken at Uckfield with the exception of some general references relating to the character of the several months of the year

A long series of observations upon the temperature and rainfall of that place may be found in the two editions of my work on "The Climate of Uckfield." I have also issued a pamphlet which contains a full report of the rainfall of Uckfield during the long period of fifty consecutive years.

In conclusion, I will remark that with respect to the various tables of temperature, &c., which will be found in the following pages, the greater number will refer to continuous observations during the last 24 years. There will be also those which extend over eleven years only, viz , from 1874 to 1884, both inclusive, as I consider they will be sufficient to convey a fair amount of information respecting the various meteorological investigations to which they refer.

In the first edition of my work on "The Climate of Uckfield" I gave a chapter upon prognostics of changes in the weather derived from ancient, modern and local observations.

This chapter was omitted in the second edition of the said work, and as some regret was expressed at the omission, I purpose reprinting the same, with some additions, which I gave on this subject at the end of my translation of the Phenomena and Diosemeia of Aratus.

C. L. P.

CHAPTER I.

GEOLOGY — TOPOGRAPHY — TEMPERATURE DEPENDENT
UPON SOIL AND ELEVATION — WATER SUPPLY —
BOTANY — EXTENSIVE VIEWS.

Y the district of Crowborough is meant that portion of the county which is situated upon and around Crowborough Hill. The highest point is situated nearly 800 feet (796) above the mean level of the sea; and commands the most extensive panoramic view in the South of England. With respect to its geological character, it will be desirable to give an account of the Weald of the South-East of England, and for this purpose I will quote the excellent description of the same given by W. Topley, Esq., in his work on the "Agricultural Geology of the Weald," very nearly in the centre of which Crowborough Hill is situated: "The Weald may be described, in general terms, as consisting of a central undulating region of great extent, within which nearly every variety of soil occurs. The beds underlying this tract are the lowest of the series (Hastings Beds); they dip or incline outwards in all directions, and pass under the next division of the Weald Clay, which forms a flat country passing all round the Hastings Beds, excepting where it, like all other divisions, is cut off by the coast line. This Clay passes under the Lower Greensand, which is always associated with rising ground, and generally with a steep slope or 'escarpment.' The soils on this formation are generally light, it passes under the Gault, which forms a narrow zone of clay underlying the lighter sand of the Upper Greensand. The highest bed of the cretaceous series is the Chalk, which overlooks the inner country in a fine escarpment, passing completely round the district, broken only by narrow valleys through which the rivers escape. The crest of the chalk escarpment is, in Kent and Surrey, a tolerably uniform flat, varying in height from 500 to nearly 900 feet. In Sussex and Hants it is more varied in outline, the highest point is Butser Hill, south of Petersfield, 882 feet. The Lower Greensand country is generally of much less elevation than the Chalk, but in the western part of Surrey it attains the height of 967 feet at Leith Hill. The highest point in the central country is Crowborough Hill, in Ashdown Forest. The chief characteristic of the climate of the district is an excessive rainfall. This is partly attributable to the height of the country, and partly to its proximity to the Southern Coast, which has a rainfall varying from 40 inches in Cornwall and Devon, decreasing eastwards to 30 inches in Hants, and 29 inches at Hastings."

Again, at page 20, Mr. Topley says, in reference to the Hastings Beds, upon which Crowborough is immediately situated. " Most people who are personally unacquainted with the Weald have an idea it is all, or chiefly, a stiff soil. This is true of the Weald Clay flat, but not of the inland and upland country of which we have now to speak. Considerably more than half is light sand. Indeed, the name until lately used for the rocks of this district has been ' Hastings Sands.' This was misleading, as they contain somewhat thick beds of clay. Another erroneous notion, commonly held, is that the Weald is a valley, we frequently read of the ' Valley of the Weald.' Again this is true of the Weald Clay, but wholly false if the term ' Weald ' includes, as of course it does, the central area. Whenever the Hastings Beds crop out from under the Weald Clay they do so with gently rising ground, not a steep slope. This rise continues towards the centre of the country until the ground attains heights considerably over the average elevation of the Lower Greensand. These chief points are Crowborough Hill, Brightling Down, Fairlight Down, all in Sussex; Goudhurst, in Kent."

ROWBOROUGH has been formed into a new ecclesiastical district, within the parish of Rotherfield, and forms the principal part of its western side. The parish itself is bounded to the S.W, W., and N. by the parishes of Buxted, Withyham and Frant, and to the eastward by Mayfield. Tunbridge Wells, Mayfield and Uckfield are each distant about seven miles from Crowborough.

Situated upon high ground, the district is exposed occasionally to high winds, but these are, for the most part, less in force that at points situated 150 or 200 feet lower. The strong S.W. and N E are frequently more disposed to sweep round the hill than to pass over its summit. The temperature, as may be ascertained by subsequent tables, is remarkably equable and conforms probably to that of other localities of equal altitude and latitude It is a general but very erroneous idea to suppose that, in severe weather, the hill tops are colder than the valleys. As an instance of this I will quote the quaint remarks of Gilbert White* upon this subject in a letter to the Hon Daines Barrington.

" On the 10th, at eleven at night, though the air was perfectly still, Dollond's glass went down to *one degree below zero !* This strange severity of the weather made me very desirous to know what degree of cold there might be in such an exalted situation as Newton. We had, therefore, on the morning of the 10th written to Mr. ——, and entreated him to hang out his thermometer, made by Adams , and to pay some attention to it morning and evening, expecting wonderful phenomena in so elevated a region at two hundred feet or more above my house. But behold ! on the 10th, at eleven at night, it was only down to 17°, and the next morning at 22°, when mine was at 10° ! We were so disturbed at this unexpected reverse of comparative local cold, that we sent one of my glasses up, thinking that of Mr. —— must, somehow, be wrongly constructed But, when the instruments came to be confronted, they went exactly together ; so that, for one night at least, the cold at Newton was eighteen degree less than at Selborne ; and, through the whole frost, ten or twelve degrees , and indeed, when we

* Ed. 1789, Letter 62, p 296

came to observe the consequences we could easily credit this ; for all my laurustines, bays, ilexes, arbutuses, cypresses, and even my Portugal laurels, and (which occasions more regret) my find sloping laurel hedge were scorched up ; while at Newton the same trees have not lost a leaf! "

In this county, especially, the variations of climate would appear to be dependent upon the numerous local elevations, undulations and depressions which are found to exist at places nearly adjacent. The general character of the soil, too, has an important influence. Some varieties, as the gravelly and sandy loam, absorb heat from the sun's rays with remarkable rapidity, and radiate the same at night to an equal or even greater degree, causing thereby a large diurnal range of temperature—a serious disadvantage to any locality. Other soils in the county have a less amount of sand, as the Ashdown series of the Hastings Beds, which are not so sensitive, and enjoy a far more equable temperature. Again, there are some clay soils which by their close retention of moisture and less radiating properties are, for the most part, cold, damp and but slightly affected by the sun's rays, except in periods of unusual drought.

Although the temperature of the air on elevated ground is frequently colder at *mid-day* than that of the valley, yet the relatively warm temperature of the former position, at *night*, is an ample compensation. On cloudless nights, when radiation is at its maximum in the valley, the temperature on the hill will be from 10° to 12° higher.

One of the most striking features of the annual temperature on high ground is the small daily range, or the difference between the highest temperature during the day and greatest cold during the night, and subsequent tables will prove, I think, that in point of equability of temperature Crowborough will compare very favourably with the most popular health resorts in the kingdom. Of what vital importance this condition of the air is to the invalid, labouring under any chronic disease of the respiratory organs, I need not enter upon. Let it suffice to say that cases of endemic consumption are rare.

The climate appears to be more especially applicable to many diseases of the respiratory organs, as well as to those arising from nervous depression, general languor and debility of the system, whether arising from dyspepsia, hysteria, residence in foreign climates or remittent and typhoid fever. In all these cases it will be found, for the most part, that the delightful and extensive scenery, the open, airy and vivifying atmosphere, abounding in ozone, together with a numerous retinue of natural attractions in the vicinity, all contribute to secure to the visitor that measure of health which generally follows the due co-operation of an active body with a cheerful and contented mind

The numerous springs which rise to the surface *in ordinary seasons*, at many points on the Hill, render the water supply abundant, and of good quality. Upon occasion of unusual drought some of the artificial wells become exhausted, but the two chief public springs are never known to fail.

The average depth of the wells is from twenty to thirty feet—some much less—and they yield, for the most part, a sufficient quantity for domestic purposes It would be a comparatively easy undertaking to establish water works upon the upper ground, having a reservoir sufficiently large to ensure to all a constant supply of the needful element. There are also some strong chalybeate springs oozing from various slopes on the waste lands, which could be made available for medicinal purposes, as they contain a large proportion of the ferruginous salts.

The subsequent meteorological tables will, I trust, be found useful both for present and future data of information. The observations have been carefully taken with duly certified instruments placed four feet above the surface of the ground and comprise an unbroken series of eleven and twenty-four years respectively. Those taken by fully exposed instruments are, I believe, unique, for so long a series, in this country. The protected instruments were placed in a "Stevenson's Stand," as that particular form of enclosure is the one recognised by the Meteorological Societies of England and Scotland. The results obtained are useful by way of comparison with instruments placed under similar circumstances. This stand, however, is not so efficient as it ought to be. In the first place its cubical contents are much too small, and secondly, although it is provided with a double louvre boarding laterally, yet snow will sometimes pass through the interstices and completely cover up the thermometers.* The trees which appear to flourish the most luxuriantly are the several varieties of the coniferæ, as well as the oak, beech, holly, and sycamore. I will not attempt the botany of the district, which differs but little from that in the neighbourhood of Tunbridge Wells, but I will mention a few somewhat rare plants which may be found here, viz.,

* For some further remarks upon this subject see next chapter.

Drosera rotundifolia, cuscuta europæa, gentiana pneumonanthe, genista pilosa and tinctoria, campanula
hederacea and rotundifolia, hypericum elodes, malaxis
paludosa, cotyledon umbilicus, ulex nana, polygala
(three varieties), lysimachia nemorum, mentha pulejium,
erythræa pulchella, solanum dulcamara, anagallis tenella,
bartsia odontites, hyoscyamus niger, myosotis palustris,
vinca minor alba, symphytum officinale, habenaria bifolia,
listera ovata, &c. The following ferns may also be found,
viz., Polypodium vulgare, aspidium filix mas (two varieties), A. filix fæmina (two varieties), Lastræa oreopteris,
and dilatata, polysticum angulare, osmunda regalis,
blechnum boreale, asplenium adiantum nigrum, ruta
muraria, botrychium lunaria, cystopteris fragilis and
scolopendrium vulgare.

I have previously mentioned the extensive view which
Crowborough Hill commands; and I think that, so far
as I can learn, it is probably the most extensive in the
South of England, if not in the Kingdom; in proof of
which I purpose giving a list of the various parish
churches and other objects which, on clear days, were
seen from my old Observatory, together with their
respective bearings, the Tower on Saxonbury Hill being
taken as the zero point.

I need, perhaps, scarcely remark that a telescope of
moderate power will be required to identify the more
distant points, but many can be seen with a good opera
glass when their exact direction is known. It is not
usually a very easy matter to identify an object twenty
or thirty miles distant, and I will therefore describe the
method which I have adopted for this purpose and found
most satisfactory.

Our first care must be to ascertain, with great exact-
ness, our own position on the ordnance map, and to
enable us to accomplish this preliminary, the following
construction is employed, which, if accurately worked
out, will establish the precise point at once :—

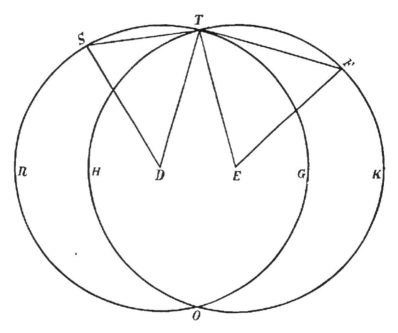

The letters S. T. F. in the above diagram refer to
three objects which were easily seen from my former
Observatory, viz., Saxonbury Tower, Ticehurst Church
and Fuller's Needle, and the method of proceeding will
be as follows :—

Let the angular distance of the observer's station
between Saxonbury and Ticehurst be 22°, and that
between Ticehurst and Fuller's Needle 29°. Join S. T.

and T. F. Then upon the base S. T. describe an isosceles triangle S. D. T., having the angle at its apex D = 44° (*i.e.*, twice 22°). And upon the base T. F describe an isosceles triangle T E. F., having the angle at the apex E = 58° (*i.e.*, twice 29°). Also with the centre D and radius D. S. or D. T. describe the circle S. R. O. G., and with centre E. and radius E. T. or E. F. describe the circle H. O. K. F. These will obviously intersect at O., and this intersection will show, with great accuracy, the observer's position on the map.

In proof of the truth of this construction let us refer to Euclid 3, XX., where we find that "The angle at the centre of a circle is double of the angle at the circumference, upon the same base, that is, upon the same part of the circumference." Hence the point at which S. T. subtends an angle of 22° must be on the circumference of the circle S. R. O. G., and for the same reason the point at which T. F. subtends an angle of 29° must be on the circumference of the circle H. O. K. F. These, though, are one and the same point which can therefore only be at O., where the circles intersect, and thus must represent the observer's *exact* position with reference to the three above mentioned objects.

Having thus ascertained the various angles required, and proved by actual observation that they are correct, we take a copy of the same upon tissue paper, on the same scale as our map, and place it over the three selected objects on it; then making a fine puncture through the point marked O., such puncture will mark our true position. The next step will be to ascertain, as nearly as possible, either our meridian line, or to select some conspicuous land object as our zero point; and mark it *as such* upon our map. Then from the observer's position, on the said map, we describe a circle of not less than twenty inches in diameter which shall be graduated into 360°. We now drive a strong pin into the point " O " which marks our Station, and loop over it a thread which shall be long enough to reach to the border of our map. The most important instrument now required is a good theodolite, which must be adjusted upon Saxonbury Tower, which we make our zero point. Having done this we may turn it upon an unknown object, and having taken its reading upon the theodolite, must refer to the same degree of azimuth on the map. Then taking the thread in our hand and stretching it through the same degree, on the map circle, to the edge of the map, we look carefully along the thread, and shall doubtless find the church or any other object for which we are seeking. It was by this means that I was able to identify all the points mentioned in the subjoined list, which were previously unknown to me.

<hr />

UCH churches and other objects mentioned in the subjoined list have all been seen on favourable occasions from the Observatory Some are visible only when the atmosphere is unusually clear, as sometimes occurs at intervals between showers; others under different conditions of light and shade, while a few can be seen during the winter months, *only*, when the foliage is absent.

Starting, then, from Saxonbury Tower, I commence the identification of distant objects by proceeding towards the South, West, and North, until the circle has been completed, the degrees and minutes refer to the distance of the several objects from Saxonbury.

						° ´
Saxonbury Tower				..	..	0 0
Goudhurst Church					...	1·48
Sissinghurst Do	...	...	.		...	6·48
Noviciate, Wadhurst		...	...		...	9·6
Wadhurst Castle	..	...	...		...	13·40
Markcross Church	...	...	...		...	13 56
Hemsted House	...	...	...			14 21
Wadhurst Church	...	...	...		...	14 30
Bestbeech Hill, Wadhurst	...	...			...	14·54
Benenden Church	...	...	...		...	16 38
Markcross Orphanage		...	...		...	17·50
St Augustine's, Ticehurst	...		...		...	19 42
Highgate Church, Hawkhurst		.		..	20 47
Ticehurst Do.	..	.	...		...	21 59
Stone Do.	.	..				25·26
Lydd Do.	...	...	...		.	26 52
Sandhurst Do.	...	.	.		.	27·21
Stonegate Do.	...	..	..			28·21
Hurst Green Village...		.	.			29 10
Rotherfield Church	..	...	...		.	29·14
Iden Do.	...	...	..		...	30·21
Bodiam Do.	..	...	..		..	30·22
Pennybridge Orphanage		...	...		...	31·18
Northiam Church	..	...	...		...	31·29

C

				° ′
Silverhill Windmill ..	...	..	...	32·21
Etchingham Church ..	...	...	...	33·3
Salehurst Do ..	...	..	..	35·31
Robertsbridge Village	..	...	...	37·20
Burwash Church	..	..	...	39 51
Rotherfield Rectory ...	...	..	..	40 24
Brede Church...	...	...	..	42·10
Convent Tower, Mayfield	...	..	..	44·41
Sedlescombe Church...	...	...	...	44·42
Mayfield Do. ..	...	...	...	45·13
Mountfield Do ...	...	...	..	45 25
Rotherhurst ..	..	...	...	45·28
Pett Church ...	...	...	...	45·32
Burwash Common Church ..		...	...	48 42
Fairlight Down Do	.	..	..	48 57
Fuller's Needle	..	...	...	51 5
Brightling Observatory	...	...	...	52·15
Fuller's Folly...	.	...	...	55 31
Dallington Church ..	..	.	..	58·47
Heathfield Tower	...	...	..	70·38
Martello Tower No. 67	...	...	...	86·58
Hailsham Church	...	..	...	..	90·3
Possingworth House, Waldron	...	...	90·18
Christ Church, Eastbourne ...	...	...	91·29
Waldron Do ...	.	..	..	92·25
St. Saviour's Do., Eastbourne	...	...	93·35
Hadlow Down Do. ...	...	...	...	94·31
Meads Do., Eastbourne	...	...	95·14
Willingdon Do. ...	...	..	.	95 26
Polegate Do. ...	...	..	.	95·40
Chiddingly Do. ...	...	..	...	99·28
Dicker Do. ...	...	...	...	99·53

				$\overset{o}{}\overset{\backprime}{}$
Arlington Church	...	..	...	... 103·13
Wilmington Do.	.	...	..	... 103·53
East Hoathly Do	..	...	...	... 107·30
Alfriston Do	...	...	...	... 108 53
Chalvington Do.	..	...	. .	... 108·57
Berwick Do	...	...	...	... 109·22
Rype Do.	...	...	...	... 110·21
Selmeston Do.	...	..	...	... 111·25
Alciston Do.	...	...	...	... 112·20
Firle Tower	..	.	.	... 118·31
Laughton Place	.	...	...	... 119·21
Framfield Church (Roof)		...	...	... 120·8
High Cross, Framfield		.	...	.. 120·28
Little Horsted Church		...	...	... 129 43
Buxted Do.		...	...	... 130 11
Horsted Place (Tower)		...	...	... 130 29
Ringmer Church		..	...	... 131 0
Uckfield Do.	...	...	...	... 134·53
The Castle Keep, }		. .	...	... 136·48
St. John's Church, } Lewes			...	... 136·52
St. Ann's Do }		.	. .	... 137·40
Hamsey Do.	...	. .	.	.. 138·58
Offham Do.	..	.	.	... 142·18
Maresfield Do.	..	.	...	... 146·36
Plumpton Do.	...	...	...	.. 153 30
Newick Do	...	..	. .	... 154·12
Fletching Do.	..	...	...	... 161·3
Ditchling Do.	. .	...	...	... 161 50
Maresfield Do. (on Forest)	...		...	.. 162·37
Keymer Do	.	...	...	.. 163·28
Devil's Dyke House	...	. .	.	... 163 38
Forest Lodge, Maresfield (Trees at Gate)			...	165·42

20

Bramber Church	...	... 169·47
Hurstpierpoint Do. ...	. .	... 170·7
Burgess Hill Church	... ...	... 171·45
Searles, Fletching ...	... ..	.. 171·47
Chanctonbury Ring ...	... ...	... 174 48
Henfield Village	..	... 175·10
Hayward's Heath Asylum ...	..	.. 177·48
,, ,, Church ..	.	... 181·14
Cowfold Monastery Do.	... ...	... 183 25
Cowfold Church ..	... .	. 185·10
Lindfield Do. ..	... ..	. 185·26
Dane Hill Do.	...	. 186·45
Broadwood's Tower, Surrey	..	206 22
West Hoathly Church	... .	209 25
Selsfield Lodge ..	.. ..	. 213·40
Turner's Hill Village	.. ...	.. 218·10
Leith Hill (Tower) ...	... ...	. 220·0
Burstow Church ...	. ...	.. 229·48
Eastgrinstead Do .		... 234·30
Redhill Do. ..	.. .	... 239·42
Ashdown House ...	... ..	... 239·54
Hammerwood Church .	...	... 252·45
Hartfield Do.	... ...	... 260·15
Crockham Hill Do	. .	.. 272·45
Markbeech Do	.. ..	. 274 35
Knockholt Beeches	... ...	. 282·35
Ide Hill Church ..	... ...	... 284·19
Hildenborough Do. .	. .	307 15
Langton Green Do. ...	. . .	.. 310·13
Shipbourne Do. ...	.. ...	... 311·12
Speldhurst Do. ...	.. ..	... 311·54
Plaxtol Do. ...	... ...	312 19

			° ᾿
Bidborough Church ...	...	..	... 313·48
Platt Do. ...	...	. .	.. 314·2
Southborough Church	...	...	. . 318·28
,, St Thomas Do.	...		... 319·48
Horley Down Do., Tunbridge Wells			. 321·24
West Peckham Do....	...	..	... 321 58
Rusthall Do. ...	...	.	... 323·10
Mereworth Do. ..	.	...	.. 323·31
Hadlow Do. . .	..	. .	.. 323·34
East Peckham Do. .	..	...	. . 325·37
St. John's Do., Tunbridge Wells			... 326 48
Huntingdon's Do , Do			.. 328·0
Trinity Do , Do.			... 329·30
Eridge Do. ...	...	..	. 332·32
Broadwater Do., Tunbridge Wells			... 333·25
St. James's Do., Do.			. 333·42
Eridge Castle (Flag Staff) .			336·12
Pembury Church .	.	...	... 339·15
Linton Do.	...	...	. 341·57
,, Place ...	...	..	. . 342·38
Leeds Church...	.	.	... 345·22
Frant Do. ...	...	...	... 347 20
Sutton Vallance Do. ..	...	...	. 348·49
Ulcombe Do. ..	...	.	351·1
Saxonbury Lodge ...	...	.	.. 351·30
Staplehurst Church ...	...	. .	356·25
Edgerton Do. ...	.	.	. 357·41
Headcorn Do. . .	...	. .	. 357·48

CHAPTER II.

O much difference is found to exist in the climatology of places situated not far distant from each other, that it may be as well to enquire what is meant by the term "Climate," as it affects the mental and physical condition of any community; and the following appear to be the more important influences, viz., the condition of atmosphere with respect to its pressure, temperature, rainfall, humidity and prevalent winds; its general freedom from noxious exhalations; its transparency as it affects radiation from the earth's surface; the amount of radiation itself being dependent, in a great measure, upon the nature of the soil, lastly, there is its electrical condition, which is doubtless a very important element, but extremely difficult of detection both as to its volume and specific character.

It will thus be seen what a field for enquiry lies open to those who seek to obtain all possible information with respect to the above-mentioned subjects, and how much care and patience are required for the several investigations.

In commencing a series of meteorological observations upon the summit of Crowborough Hill, the enquiry could not fail of being especially interesting, inasmuch as it would relate to the highest inhabited spot in this county, and also that no observations of a similar nature had ever been attempted, in the South of England, at so great an elevation above the sea.

During the first year of my residence I commenced observations of a similar kind to those which I had conducted for so many years at Uckfield. In the following year a considerable discussion arose, among our most eminent English meteorologists, respecting the particular form of thermometer-stand which should be employed for the reception of self-registering thermometers, but without any very satisfactory result It was, however, thought desirable, upon the whole, to adopt a form of stand known as "Stevenson's stand," which is, I believe, the form of stand at present recognised and adopted by the Meteorological Societies of England and Scotland.

The endless varieties of opinion expressed upon this subject induced me to commence a series of observations from self-registering instruments placed upon an open stand, without any protection whatever, a representation of which is given on the following page.

The thermometers are here exposed to every influence from radiation and wind. I attached additional interest to their indications, in the first place, because of their almost unique character, and secondly, because I had an impression that they would show, in a faithful manner, the temperature to which vegetation was actually exposed both by day and by night. In addition to the usual maximum and minimum thermometers, I also placed upon the stand another thermometer, having its bright bulb secured in vacuo, to register the heating power of the sun's rays.

SELF-REGISTERING INSTRUMENTS UPON AN OPEN STAND.

With the exception of some observations made in Scotland in the years 1861-62, and which are embodied in a paper by Alexander Buchan, Esq., "On the Meteorological Conditions which determine the profitable or unprofitable culture of farm crops in Scotland," published in the " Quarterly Report of the Scottish Meteorological Society," for June, 1862, I am not aware that any records of temperature, from exposed instruments, have been published. In the course of his paper, Mr. Buchan remarks, " The distinguishing peculiarity of the observations depends on the three-fold conditions under which the instruments were placed, viz., their bulbs not blackened, their height (four feet) from the ground, and their full exposure to sun and weather. Naked bulbs were preferred to blackened bulbs, inasmuch as observations made with unblackened bulbs furnish results more uniform, reliable and comparable with each other, than could otherwise be the case " For information respecting local climatology, and its adaptation as a health resort, or for any particular agricultural requirements, I hold that observations as to temperature should be conducted with fully exposed instruments in preference to those placed in a " Stevenson's stand," or any other device for protecting them against the influence of any source of radiation. The comparative tables of mean highest temperature in the open air and in the shade respectively, (tables 15 and 16) for eleven years, will show that the former gives a *mean* of 5°·6, in the three summer months, above the latter, which constitutes a difference sufficient to decide whether, or no, certain cereal crops can be cultivated. There are several other points connected with the subsequent tables which I trust will be of some interest and use, both to the meteorologist and agriculturist, as exhibiting the variations in temperature indicated by the two methods of instrumental position.

Both sets of instruments have been placed four feet above the ground, which, of course, renders their indications fairly comparable. It appears quite certain that, even then, fully exposed thermometers do not register so high a temperature as that to which vegetation is exposed, on account of the sun's rays being considerably deflected from the bulbs themselves , nevertheless they give a near approximation thereto, and, moreover, it is satisfactory to know that all kinds of crops are really subject to a higher temperature than the thermometers register. It should be duly considered that observations taken from instruments which are completely protected from the direct rays of the sun are not only absolutely useless, but positively misleading, when we know that during the important summer months they register perhaps a temperature of 10° lower than that to which plants have been exposed to, and influenced by, during their period of growth and maturation.

The table which gives the mean highest temperature in the sun's rays will probably be the most valuable to the agriculturist, and is altogether superior to the results shown by reference to the table of mean temperature, which, alone, will not inform us whether a certain crop will, or will not, grow to perfection in any given locality. The mean daily highest temperature, and the mean monthly temperature, as shewn by protected instruments, are wholly unable to indicate the actual summer temperature by which growing crops have been influenced. The true night temperature, to which most plants have been exposed, can only be ascertained by reference to the terrestrial radiation thermometer, placed upon the surface of short grass, and the exposed minimum thermometer placed four feet above it.

It is, however, possible, if not probable, that the terrestrial radiation instrument may show a lower temperature than that to which growing crops have been exposed when they have attained the height of a foot, or more—but a *very* approximately true condition of night temperature could be ascertained by adopting the results of the mean of these two thermometers; indeed, I cannot suggest any better method of obtaining the information sought for.

A competent knowledge of the average *night* temperature of any locality is of far more importance in respect
of the healthy condition both of animal and vegetable
life than is generally supposed ; and will often explain
the reason, more particularly, why the latter flourish
more freely in some situations than others, whatever care
may have been taken in each instance.

Before considering the following tables of temperature
I will just remark that all the instruments were obtained
from Negretti and Zambra of Holborn, and having been
duly examined at Kew Observatory, I received a certifi-
cate of their excellence.

TABLE 1 gives the highest temperature in the open air
   in each month and year, as observed from a self-
   registering thermometer having a bright bulb and
   the graduation on the stem.

TABLE 2 gives the highest temperature in the shade
   (Stevenson's stand) in each month and year. The
   thermometer is a counterpart of the preceding.

TABLE 3 gives the lowest temperature in the open air
   at night in each month and year.

TABLE 4 gives the lowest temperature in the stand at
   night, in each month and year.

TABLE 5 gives the monthly and yearly mean temperature in the open air at four feet above the ground.

TABLE 6 gives the monthly and yearly mean temperature in the shade at four feet from the ground.

TABLE 7 gives the monthly and yearly mean daily range
   of temperature in the shade.

TABLE 8 gives the mean temperature of the several
   seasons in the open air and in the shade.

28

TABLE 9 gives the monthly and yearly rainfall, on Crowborough Hill, in inches.

TABLE 10 gives the rainfall of the several seasons.

TABLE 11 gives the number of days in each month and year when rain fell to the amount of ·01 inch and upwards during the twenty-four hours ending at 9 a.m.

TABLE 12 gives instances of heavy rains from May 1st, 1872, to December 31st, 1897, wherein the amount exceeded 1 inch in depth during any twenty-four hours ending at 9 a.m.

TABLE 13 gives the prevalent direction of the wind at 9 a.m., daily, in each month and year referred to, eight points of the compass.

TABLE 14 gives the number of days in each year when the principal direction of the wind was from the following eight points of the compass respectively.

TABLE 15 gives the mean monthly and yearly highest temperature in the open air.

TABLE 16 gives the mean monthly and yearly temperature in the shade.

TABLE 17 gives the highest temperature of solar radiation (in Vacuo) in each month and year (bright bulb).

TABLE 18 gives the lowest temperature of terrestrial radiation upon the surface of short grass in each month and year.

TABLE 19 gives the mean monthly and yearly lowest temperature of radiation upon short grass.

TABLE 20 gives the monthly mean temperature of the dew point.

TABLE 1.
Highest Temperature in the Open Air in each Month and Year.

Year	Jan	Feb	March	April	May	June	July	Aug	Sept	Oct	Nov	Dec	Absolute
1874	51·2	55·2	69·0	73·6	77·4	81·0	89·4	82·8	76·2	67·6	63·2	50·2	89·4
1875	52·4	52·8	57·6	74·0	78·6	83·0	78·4	82·2	80·0	65·2	58·2	50·0	83·0
1876	52·6	57·0	58·0	66·0	72·0	84·0	92·4	92·0	72·2	72·0	63·0	53·0	92·4
1877	51·4	57·0	61·4	62·0	68·8	84·7	84·2	80·4	69·4	65·5	61·1	50·0	84·7
1878.	54·0	59·5	60·0	66·5	74·0	90·5	87·2	79·7	79·0	72·1	50·3	50·2	90·5
1879	47·4	54·0	65·0	64·2	73·5	76·5	82·6	82·8	76·2	68·0	57·4	50·0	82·8
1880	54·0	57·0	65·0	70·5	81·2	81·0	83·2	82·0	84·0	71·5	55·1	56·5	84·0
1881	50·0	52·7	64·5	66·5	77·2	81·5	97·4	82·5	76·0	64·0	60·6	58·0	97·4
1882	49·6	57·2	67·7	68·4	78·8	78·8	80·0	83·4	73·8	69·9	59·4	52·4	83·4
1883	51·0	57·4	58·6	73·6	77·2	83·6	80·6	84·2	77·0	70·2	56·7	52·8	84·2
1884	54·4	55·0	65·8	66·7	84·4	85·3	87·7	95·2	83·6	68·8	61·2	52·4	95·2
1885	47·7	55·0	60·6	74·5	73·6	83·5	90·0	86·0	76·0	69·3	58·0	52·0	90·0
1886	48·0	46·2	65·2	76·0	75·6	80·6	90·0	85·1	88·0	77·7	59·1	50·0	90·0
1887	50·0	54·6	59·6	71·0	73·0	87·0	93·4	93·5	71·5	65·8	57·2	50·5	93·5
1888	58·4	52·0	54·8	68·8	76·4	87·0	76·0	83·0	81·0	68·6	59·4	52·6	87·0
1889	54·2	61·8	60·3	68·4	85·0	89·0	83·8	85·0	83·5	63·7	60·0	50·9	89·0
1890	53·1	53·0	64·1	69·0	80·2	79·4	84·0	82·4	80·5	70·8	58·0	42·7	84·0
1891	51·1	68·0	62·0	68·0	80·5	83·4	82·0	79·5	83·0	69·5	57·0	53·0	83·4
1892	50·0	54·1	63·0	75·6	80·5	85·0	79·0	87·0	74·2	61·0	59·7	54·0	87·0
1893	47·0	56·8	67·8	83·1	79·0	94·0	86·0	92·2	84·1	68·0	56·6	53·2	94·0
1894	51·0	55·0	66·6	74·5	73·0	84·0	85·5	79·0	79·0	67·7	61·2	51·4	85·5
1895	49·0	48·2	68·0	69·0	82·5	84·0	83·6	85·0	86·4	73·2	62·0	53·0	86·4
1896	49·6	58·3	69·2	67·4	82·0	84·5	89·2	79·0	76·0	68·0	54·0	50·5	89·2
1897	46·0	61·0	63·0	72·0	73·0	87·8	86·4	86·7	73·5	69·6	61·0	55·0	87·8
Absolute	58·4	68·0	69·2	83·1	85·0	94·0	97·4	93·5	88·0	77·7	63·2	58·0	97·4

TABLE 2.

Highest Temperature in the Shade in each Month and Year.

Year.	Jan.	Feb.	March.	April.	May.	June.	July.	Aug.	Sept.	Oct.	Nov.	Dec.	Absolute.
1874	50·2	52·6	63·4	71·8	73·4	75·6	86·8	78·4	73·4	63·2	61·0	50·0	86·8
1875	49·7	47·1	54·0	76·8	74·2	77·5	72·4	77·6	75·7	62·6	55·1	50·1	77·6
1876	50·4	53·0	55·8	64·6	66·0	78·7	85·0	87·5	66·8	67·7	59·4	51·6	87·5
1877	51·3	54·4	63·0	61·4	61·2	77·4	79·0	75·5	63·6	62·0	56·5	50·0	79·0
1878	49·6	54·1	56·0	60·2	67·0	82·3	80·5	72·3	73·8	66·8	49·6	49·7	82·3
1879	47·4	50·0	62·0	56·1	66·8	68·0	77·0	75·3	68·0	64·0	52·2	48·4	77·0
1880	53·0	54·3	60·7	61·4	76·1	73·6	77·0	76·2	80·0	66·8	52·5	53·6	80·0
1881	48·1	50·0	60·8	62·6	72·7	75·9	91·5	76·0	72·0	58·4	58·0	50·0	91·5
1882	48·8	53·8	64·0	62·0	71·1	71·4	74·4	77·8	68·4	66·0	56·6	51·2	77·8
1883	50·2	52·0	52·6	68·2	72·6	78·2	76·0	79·1	72·4	65·0	52·3	51·2	79·1
1884	50·8	51·0	62·0	61·6	78·6	78·5	80·2	88·9	79·0	63·3	57·8	51·2	88·9
1885	46·9	53·2	56·2	70·8	68·1	78·4	84·1	78·3	71·0	60·0	56·0	53·0	84·1
1886	47·2	42·0	61·5	69·5	71·1	74·0	83·0	80·6	83·0	73·7	57·0	49·5	83·0
1887	47·5	51·1	55·0	65·0	67·0	81·0	86·8	84·3	66·2	62·5	52·8	50·0	86·8
1888	58·4	47·5	50·4	61·0	70·8	80·0	63·8	78·0	74·9	64·2	55·0	51·0	80·0
1889	50·8	57·1	56·5	65·0	79·2	80·6	78·0	79·3	77·1	58·5	57·0	49·4	80·6
1890	51·0	48·2	60·0	62·0	74·5	74·4	76·0	76·8	75·0	69·2	55·5	39·5	76·8
1891	49·0	66·6	58·8	63·6	75·8	78·4	78·0	74·0	78·5	64·7	53·6	52·0	78·5
1892	49·4	51·0	60·0	73·5	77·0	78·0	73·3	78·2	69·2	56·0	54·2	51·6	78·2
1893	47·4	54·0	62·8	78·0	74·0	88·0	82·0	87·0	78·8	63·0	55·6	51·4	88·0
1894	48·8	50·0	62·0	70·5	70·4	77·2	80·6	75·2	69·7	62·2	58·8	51·0	80·6
1895	48·6	43·0	61·0	63·0	77·3	78·3	76·8	77·0	82·7	68·9	59·2	52·6	82·7
1896	47·5	54·0	65·0	61·0	74·4	79·9	82·8	72·0	71·1	63·5	50·0	47·7	82·8
1897	44·3	54·6	57·8	67·0	69·8	82·2	79·0	82·0	68·0	64·5	58·8	52·5	82·2
Absolute	58·4	66·6	65·0	73·5	79·2	88·0	91·5	88·9	82·7	73·7	61·0	53·6	91·5

TABLE 3.
Lowest Temperature in the Open Air in each Month and Year.

Year	Jan.	Feb	March	April	May	June	July	Aug	Sept	Oct	Nov	Dec	Absolute
1874	27.8	22.0	16.2	32.2	31.2	37.0	47.2	43.8	41.0	33.0	25.2	18.2	16.2
1875	19.6	20.4	24.0	29.2	36.2	43.0	43.2	44.0	44.2	32.6	23.8	19.0	19.0
1876	14.7	20.4	22.2	26.8	29.8	38.4	44.6	40.0	39.2	30.3	25.2	26.2	14.7
1877	27.2	21.8	21.6	29.7	27.1	40.0	40.8	42.2	34.6	30.0	30.0	26.2	21.6
1878	25.0	26.5	20.3	23.3	34.0	42.0	43.4	46.1	39.0	28.0	26.4	18.5	18.5
1879	17.5	20.0	26.4	21.8	26.7	39.0	43.0	44.7	35.3	28.8	21.0	15.4	15.4
1880	17.2	28.0	28.5	31.2	32.0	33.3	44.2	45.0	38.0	26.6	23.8	24.5	17.2
1881	8.0	28.0	21.2	24.0	29.0	33.7	43.0	40.7	42.8	27.1	29.0	27.0	8.0
1882	21.0	24.1	21.2	29.8	33.3	38.4	45.0	43.1	37.2	33.0	26.1	21.2	21.0
1883	26.2	25.1	24.2	28.8	38.1	37.0	41.0	45.0	40.0	33.0	28.0	23.4	19.0
1884	27.5	25.7	26.5	27.0	33.0	40.1	41.0	45.0	41.6	31.0	24.4	27.0	24.4
1885	21.0	24.0	26.9	27.0	29.8	40.5	43.2	41.2	30.5	31.0	26.6	19.5	19.5
1886	19.5	20.2	19.3	30.0	29.0	38.0	44.0	42.8	39.5	37.7	31.0	19.2	19.2
1887	14.0	22.2	18.3	25.0	31.4	40.0	41.1	41.6	36.4	26.0	24.0	20.1	14.0
1888	18.3	15.2	19.2	24.0	31.2	40.3	36.2	42.2	39.5	25.5	27.7	24.4	15.2
1889	21.2	16.2	19.3	28.3	37.0	44.0	44.4	43.0	34.8	36.0	23.3	21.0	16.2
1890	25.3	23.1	12.0	27.8	33.3	35.0	40.4	39.0	38.0	24.4	8.6	13.0	8.6
1891	15.1	26.8	20.8	28.0	28.0	37.4	41.5	39.0	42.0	28.5	28.6	23.0	15.1
1892	19.0	14.0	18.2	23.9	27.9	36.0	45.0	42.7	39.0	29.8	33.3	22.7	14.0
1893	14.8	27.0	25.0	29.7	37.2	38.4	47.0	43.3	36.3	28.2	26.0	22.5	14.8
1894	7.1	21.1	28.9	35.0	29.3	41.2	46.0	43.0	36.0	34.0	34.3	23.7	7.1
1895	18.4	10.4	21.2	31.2	35.1	39.0	45.5	42.8	45.3	26.0	29.6	28.2	10.4
1896	29.0	22.6	30.6	28.6	31.5	46.5	45.2	42.0	39.7	31.0	24.6	23.0	22.6
1897	20.3	27.8	30.5	29.0	32.0	40.7	47.0	48.0	36.2	37.1	28.2	26.1	20.3
Absolute	7.1	10.4	12.0	21.8	26.7	33.3	36.2	39.0	30.5	24.4	8.6	13.0	7.1

TABLE 4.

Lowest Temperature in the Shade in each Month and Year.

Year.	Jan	Feb.	March.	April.	May.	June.	July.	Aug	Sept.	Oct	Nov.	Dec.	Absolute
1874.	27·8	22·0	18·2	33·0	31·0	37·2	47·6	43·2	40·4	34·0	25·2	17·6	17·6
1875.	22·3	22·1	26·6	31·6	38·2	44·4	45·3	45·6	45·4	37·0	26·0	20·4	20·4
1876.	16·8	23·6	23·0	28·6	31·0	39·3	48·6	42·6	41·0	32·1	28·6	29·4	16·8
1877.	29·4	23·3	23·8	32·0	29·3	41·0	42·8	45·0	36·7	32·8	32·0	28·0	23·3
1878.	26·6	27·5	22·7	25·1	36·0	43·0	46·3	47·8	40·6	30·0	28·4	19·3	19·3
1879.	18·8	22·2	27·3	24·5	28·4	40·4	45·0	45·0	37·0	30·6	22·4	17·6	17·6
1880.	19·6	30·0	30·2	32·6	33·3	35·5	45·6	47·6	40·2	27·6	25·7	26·3	19·6
1881.	9·0	26·2	22·6	25·6	32·0	35·5	45·0	43·4	45·2	27·5	30·2	28·8	9·0
1882.	24·4	26·8	26·4	31·6	35·0	39·8	46·5	44·5	40·0	34·5	28·6	24·6	24·4
1883.	27·7	32·0	21·1	30·0	30·1	38·6	43·5	46·4	42·2	35·0	30·0	25·7	21·1
1884.	28·0	27·5	29·0	29·0	35·4	42·0	43·3	44·0	37·0	32·7	25·8	28·8	25·8
1885.	22·8	26·3	28·6	29·2	32·0	40·0	45·6	43·0	32·5	32·2	28·0	21·8	21·8
1886.	20·8	23·2	20·8	31·7	31·0	39·1	45·0	44·2	41·0	39·2	33·2	21·6	20·8
1887.	16·5	25·0	21·1	27·4	33·0	42·3	44·0	45·3	39·0	28·0	27·1	22·5	16·5
1888.	21·0	18·2	21·8	26·2	33·4	41·9	37·0	43·8	41·2	28·0	28·0	25·8	18·2
1889.	23·7	18·2	21·8	31·0	36·8	45·8	47·6	44·5	37·5	36·0	25·2	23·0	18·2
1890.	27·9	24·7	15·8	29·8	35·7	38·0	42·6	41·1	40·0	27·3	11·3	14·8	11·3
1891	18·3	27·0	23·3	29·4	29·5	39·5	43·2	44·2	43·2	30·0	30·3	24·8	18·3
1892	21·8	16·2	19·9	26·0	29·8	37·0	45·8	44·5	40·3	32·1	33·5	24·2	16·2
1893.	18·2	28·1	27·0	32·1	39·0	41·2	48·1	45·0	38·2	29·5	27·0	23·6	18·2
1894.	8·0	22·8	29·5	36·4	31·0	42·6	47·8	45·0	37·5	35·8	35·3	25·0	8·0
1895.	20·0	12·8	22·4	33·0	35·2	40·0	47·0	44·0	46·1	27·3	30·7	29·0	12·8
1896.	30·0	23·8	31·4	30·0	33·0	47·2	46·2	43·0	42·0	32·8	25·6	22·8	22·8
1897.	21·2	28·5	31·4	30·0	32·1	41·6	48·2	48·8	37·3	38·2	29·3	27·6	21·2
Absolute	8·0	12·8	15·8	24·5	28·4	35·5	37·0	41·1	32·5	27·3	11·3	14·8	8·0

TABLE 5.

The Monthly and Yearly Mean Temperature in the Open Air.

Year.	Jan	Feb	March	April	May	June	July	Aug.	Sept	Oct	Nov.	Dec.	Mean.
1874	40.8	39.2	43.0	50.1	51.0	58.4	65.0	60.2	58.3	51.8	42.5	32.0	49.3
1875	41.8	34.4	39.5	46.9	54.8	57.9	59.1	63.1	60.6	48.6	41.6	36.6	48.7
1876	35.5	39.4	40.4	47.3	49.3	58.5	65.1	63.2	56.6	52.5	43.2	42.5	49.4
1877	41.4	42.5	40.3	45.4	49.1	61.5	60.7	62.1	53.9	49.3	44.8	39.0	49.1
1878	38.7	41.2	41.9	48.4	55.4	60.9	64.3	63.1	58.0	51.9	38.3	32.5	49.5
1879	30.6	37.0	41.1	44.7	49.1	57.5	58.7	61.1	56.9	50.9	38.2	32.0	46.4
1880	33.0	41.8	46.3	47.8	54.0	57.7	62.8	64.3	60.6	47.6	41.6	41.7	49.9
1881	30.4	36.9	43.4	45.9	54.1	58.9	65.7	60.2	57.1	45.6	47.0	38.4	48.6
1882	38.2	41.5	46.5	48.7	54.7	57.6	60.8	60.6	56.0	51.1	42.5	39.1	49.8
1883	39.3	41.6	36.8	48.1	53.3	59.1	61.0	63.2	58.6	50.7	42.8	38.1	49.3
1884	41.3	41.4	44.6	46.0	55.1	58.5	64.5	67.5	61.6	49.4	41.0	38.6	50.8
1885	34.5	42.1	41.3	47.9	51.0	60.0	63.9	61.0	56.5	46.8	42.9	37.7	48.7
1886	34.4	33.1	39.2	47.2	53.9	58.8	63.5	63.0	60.6	53.8	43.1	35.0	48.8
1887	34.3	37.8	39.0	44.1	50.5	60.8	66.3	63.8	55.0	45.9	39.9	35.2	47.7
1888	36.6	33.5	37.2	43.6	52.4	58.2	58.9	60.0	58.0	47.4	45.8	40.0	47.6
1889	36.1	35.5	39.7	45.7	57.5	62.4	62.0	61.4	57.4	49.3	43.1	35.3	48.7
1890	40.8	37.6	42.6	46.2	55.2	56.6	60.3	60.8	61.0	50.5	41.7	28.2	48.4
1891	33.4	40.9	39.3	44.3	51.5	61.1	61.2	60.0	59.8	51.0	42.2	40.0	48.7
1892	34.9	37.8	37.8	47.8	54.7	57.4	59.7	62.4	56.5	45.6	44.8	33.9	47.9
1893	31.8	40.0	47.2	53.0	58.5	61.5	63.7	65.9	57.8	51.7	40.1	39.6	50.9
1894	36.9	39.5	45.5	51.6	50.0	58.5	62.0	61.0	55.3	49.6	45.6	39.9	49.6
1895	32.0	28.7	42.1	48.1	56.6	60.4	62.7	63.1	64.6	47.6	46.5	39.3	49.2
1896	39.0	40.2	45.7	49.1	54.8	63.0	65.7	60.8	57.1	46.9	40.2	38.2	50.0
1897	34.7	42.1	44.5	46.3	51.8	61.3	64.8	62.8	56.3	53.1	45.4	41.1	50.3
Mean	36.2	38.5	41.8	47.2	53.2	59.4	62.6	62.2	58.0	49.5	42.7	37.3	49.0

D

TABLE 6

The Monthly and Yearly Mean Temperature in the Shade

Year	Jan	Feb	March	April	May	June	July	Aug	Sept	Oct	Nov	Dec	Mean
1874	40·1	38·3	41·9	49·0	49·2	56·8	63·8	58·6	56·9	50·6	41·7	31·2	48·1
1875	41·1	33·5	38·4	45·6	52·9	56·1	57·7	60·8	58·9	47·2	41·3	36·4	47·5
1876	35·3	38·9	39·3	45·8	47·2	56·3	63·3	62·2	55·3	51·8	43·9	42·3	48·4
1877	41·9	41·8	39·3	44·5	47·1	59·4	58·7	60·0	52·3	48·3	44·9	39·1	48·1
1878	38·4	40·4	40·2	46·4	53·1	58·5	61·6	60·6	56·2	50·6	37·8	32·2	48·0
1879	30·7	36·3	39·9	42·4	46·5	54·9	56·3	58·7	55·0	49·6	36·7	32·2	44·9
1880	32·8	41·0	44·5	45·6	51·0	55·6	59·5	62·0	59·0	46·6	41·2	41·5	48·3
1881	30·2	36·6	42·1	44·1	51·9	56·2	63·5	57·9	55·2	44·2	46·9	38·4	47·2
1882	38·3	40·5	45·3	46·9	52·4	55·2	58·3	58·4	54·2	49·9	42·0	39·1	48·3
1883	39·2	40·7	35·5	45·9	51·5	56·9	58·6	61·5	56·2	49·6	42·3	38·1	48·0
1884	41·2	40·8	43·0	43·5	52·9	56·6	61·9	65·2	58·7	48·3	40·8	38·6	49·3
1885	34·5	41·7	39·4	45·9	48·4	57·6	61·9	58·2	54·6	44·8	42·0	37·8	47·2
1886	34·3	32·3	37·9	45·2	51·8	56·2	60·9	60·7	58·1	52·3	43·4	35·0	47·3
1887	34·1	37·3	37·8	42·5	50·2	58·8	64·1	62·0	51·2	44·7	40·0	35·6	46·7
1888	36·6	32·8	36·0	41·7	50·5	55·9	56·4	57·6	56·0	46·3	44·7	40·1	46·2
1889	35·9	35·2	38·8	44·1	55·4	60·0	59·4	58·9	55·7	47·9	42·9	36·1	47·5
1890	40·9	36·6	41·5	44·5	53·1	54·5	57·3	58·7	58·8	49·0	41·5	28·4	47·0
1891	33·6	40·5	38·4	42·6	49·8	59·0	59·4	58·2	58·4	50·3	41·9	40·4	47·7
1892	34·8	37·2	36·3	46·4	53·1	55·2	57·4	60·1	55·0	44·4	44·4	35·9	46·6
1893	33·5	39·5	45·8	51·8	55·9	59·7	61·4	63·8	55·6	50·2	39·7	39·8	49·7
1894	36·2	39·2	43·6	50·1	48·2	56·3	59·8	58·7	53·4	48·9	45·3	39·2	48·2
1895	31·8	27·4	40·6	45·9	53·9	59·2	59·9	59·0	62·3	45·8	45·9	39·0	47·5
1896	38·6	38·9	44·1	46·9	52·4	60·3	62·3	58·0	55·4	45·5	39·3	37·9	48·3
1897	33·9	41·3	43·0	44·4	49·9	59·4	62·3	60·4	54·2	51·4	43·8	40·7	48·7

TABLE 7.

The Monthly and Yearly Mean Daily Range of Temperature in the Shade.

Year	Jan	Feb	March	April	May	June	July	Aug.	Sept.	Oct.	Nov.	Dec.	Mean.
1874	9.4	9.9	13.4	16.8	19.0	19.1	21.4	16.8	14.6	11.7	10.5	8.4	14.2
1875	7.3	7.0	9.6	14.4	15.3	14.8	12.4	13.7	12.8	9.6	8.1	6.0	10.8
1876	8.1	8.0	11.8	12.3	15.2	15.8	17.8	17.6	12.9	8.9	9.2	5.8	11.9
1877	9.0	9.3	11.6	12.1	13.6	17.6	15.4	13.4	12.3	12.4	9.8	8.6	12.1
1878	7.0	7.6	11.2	14.6	13.8	16.2	15.8	13.7	15.3	11.0	8.3	7.6	11.8
1879	6.9	8.6	12.2	13.0	15.4	13.8	13.6	12.9	13.4	11.3	8.4	9.4	11.6
1880	8.0	11.2	14.4	14.2	18.1	15.9	19.3	15.0	14.3	12.2	10.2	8.8	13.0
1881	8.1	7.8	13.8	13.9	17.4	15.9	15.6	14.6	12.5	11.0	9.3	7.4	12.5
1882	8.2	9.3	14.4	15.2	17.2	15.7	16.9	15.4	14.0	10.8	9.5	8.0	12.8
1883	7.8	10.3	12.9	16.0	17.6	19.0	15.6	16.7	14.2	11.2	11.1	7.7	13.4
1884	8.4	9.0	12.8	13.7	17.8	17.7	17.7	20.2	13.7	12.1	8.2	7.2	13.2
1885	6.3	9.3	13.5	15.5	14.1	17.2	18.4	17.4	14.6	11.1	8.1	8.6	12.8
1886	8.8	7.0	11.2	13.5	16.1	18.0	17.8	15.7	13.8	11.5	9.0	9.5	12.7
1887	7.8	10.0	13.4	15.9	18.5	19.1	21.3	19.0	14.2	12.6	8.1	8.0	14.0
1888	9.1	7.2	10.0	14.0	17.8	15.3	13.0	14.5	13.7	13.6	7.1	7.8	12.0
1889	8.6	9.6	13.3	13.9	16.0	17.6	15.7	16.0	15.1	13.0	8.2	7.9	13.0
1890.	9.0	9.6	13.4	14.7	18.2	16.4	14.6	15.9	15.7	13.9	9.8	6.6	13.1
1891	8.6	14.2	12.0	15.6	17.6	17.8	16.8	15.6	14.4	11.4	9.6	9.2	13.6
1892	9.6	9.8	13.4	18.8	18.4	16.3	14.0	14.5	12.9	11.2	7.2	10.4	13.2
1893	7.0	9.3	14.8	20.0	18.6	18.9	15.5	17.0	14.0	11.6	9.4	10.4	14.0
1894	8.6	9.3	13.2	14.2	14.6	14.6	13.8	12.4	11.6	10.2	7.8	7.4	11.5
1895	7.6	9.4	11.9	13.0	17.9	19.3	14.6	14.1	17.1	11.6	8.2	7.7	12.7
1896	7.6	10.4	11.6	13.6	19.0	16.1	17.3	16.2	10.8	10.4	8.8	7.8	12.5
1897	6.2	8.8	10.8	12.6	17.0	15.0	17.4	14.0	13.0	11.6	12.3	9.0	12.4
Mean .	8.1	9.2	12.4	14.6	16.8	16.8	16.3	15.5	13.7	11.5	9.0	8.1	12.6

TABLE 8.—Mean Temperature of the Seasons.

Year	In the Open Air				In the Shade.			
	Winter	Spring.	Summer	Autumn	Winter.	Spring	Summer	Autumn
1874	40 2	48 0	61 2	50 8	39 6	46 7	59 7	49 7
1875	36 0	47 0	60 0	50 2	35 2	45 6	58 2	49 1
1876	37 1	45 6	62 2	50 7	36 8	44 1	60 6	50 3
1877	42·1	44 9	61 4	49 3	42 0	43 6	59 3	48 5
1878	39 6	48 5	62 7	49 4	39 3	46 5	60 2	48 2
1879	33 3	44·9	59 1	48 6	33·0	42 9	56 6	47·1
1880	35 6	49 3	61 6	49 9	35 3	47 0	59 0	48 9
1881	36 3	47 8	61 6	49 9	36 1	46·0	59 2	48 7
1882	39 3	49·9	59 6	49 9	39 0	48 2	57 3	49 0
1883	40 0	46 0	61·1	50 7	39 6	44 3	59 0	49 3
1884	40 2	48 5	63 5	50 6	40 0	46 4	61 2	49 3
1885	38·4	46·4	61 6	48 7	38 2	44 4	59 2	47 1
1886	35 1	46 7	61 7	52 5	34 8	44 7	59 2	51 8
1887	37 5	44 5	63 6	46·9	35 4	43 5	61 6	45 3
1888	35 1	44 4	59 0	50 4	35 0	42 7	56 6	49 0
1889	37·2	47 6	61 9	49 9	37 1	46 1	59·4	48 8
1890	37 9	48 0	59 2	51·1	37 8	46 3	56 8	49 7
1891	34·2	45 0	60·7	51 0	34 2	43 6	58 8	50·2
1892	37 5	46 7	59 8	48 7	37 4	45 2	57 6	47 9
1893	35 9	52 9	63 7	47 8	36 3	51 1	61 6	48 5
1894	38·7	49 0	60 5	50 2	38 4	47·3	58·2	49 2
1895	33·5	48 9	62 1	52 9	32 8	46·8	59 3	51·3
1896	39 5	49 8	63·1	48 1	38 8	47 8	60 2	46 7
1897	38·3	47 5	62 9	51 6	37 7	45 8	60 7	49 8
Mean	37 4	47 4	61·4	49 9	37 0	45 7	59 1	48 8

The Difference in the Mean Temperature of the Seasons
under these two conditions was as follows :

	Winter	Spring	Summer	Autumn
In the Open Air	37·4	47 4	61 4	49 9
In the Shade	37 0	45·7	59·1	48 8
Excess of Temperature in the Open Air	0 4	1 7	2 3	1·1

* Including the previous December in both instances.

TABLE 9

The Rainfall on Crowborough Hill in Inches

Year	Jan	Feb	March	April	May	June	July	Aug	Sept	Oct	Nov	Dec	Mean
1871	2·89	2 34	1 65	4·77	0 72	4 76	3 40	1 64	4 03	2 98	0·70	2 24	32·12
1872	7·46	2 80	2 91	1 05	4 92	4·26	2 89	1 89	2 10	6 01	7 39	6 68	50 36
1873	4 16	2 30	2 52	0·83	1·69	3·47	2·84	3·76	3 53	5 90	3 33	1 19	35 52
1874	2 64	2 45	1 21	2·73	0·82	2 48	1 60	3 08	3 67	5 12	3 36	3 60	32 76
1875	5 00	1·44	1·14	1·24	1·83	3·72	6·01	2·16	2 07	5 54	5 53	1 94	37 42
1876	1 60	4·56	3 51	3 22	1 25	1 61	0 85	4 63	5 59	1 34	3 25	9 02	40 43
1877	9·18	2·82	3·01	2 92	2·44	1 07	3·37	4·23	1·41	3 95	9 04	2 91	46 35
1878	1 98	2 42	1 89	4 05	5 29	2 51	1·01	5 37	1 81	3 96	5 32	2 73	38 34
1879	3 74	4·72	1 30	4 93	3 70	3 87	4·71	6·56	3·95	1·08	1·31	1 28	41 15
1880	0·47	4 22	1 41	2 12	0 28	2 52	3 82	0 89	3·95	7 95	4 69	3 93	36 25
1881	2·01	4 20	3 30	0 53	1 57	2 64	1·88	5·75	3 52	3·52	5·79	4 49	39 20
1882	2 04	2 22	1 85	4 00	1 08	2 86	4·78	1 88	3 88	8 30	4 54	3 75	41 18
1883	3 16	4·94	1 28	1·84	2 56	2 25	2 86	1 38	4·49	3 16	5 35	1·78	35 05
1884	3·82	2·19	2 48	1 27	0 84	1 67	2 40	1 22	4·90	1·48	1 24	4·65	28 16
1885	3·39	4·97	2 06	1·53	2 89	0 94	0 47	0 61	5 07	4·45	4 13	1·37	31 88
1886	4·87	0·67	3 11	2 28	4 18	0 95	3 46	2·08	1 22	4·07	4 33	5·95	37·17
1887	3 23	0·76	1 86	1·82	2 05	1 09	0 64	3 26	4 24	1 61	5 87	2 80	29 23
1888	1 14	1 87	4 58	·84	1 66	4 31	6 76	3·11	1 20	2·49	5 35	2·93	37 24
1889	1·34	3 23	2 44	3·27	1 72	0 57	4 30	4 00	1·38	8 09	1 84	2·70	34 88
1890	3 87	1 12	2 88	3 00	1 62	3 26	4 19	4 02	0·85	1·71	4 27	0·74	31 53
1891	3·38	0 00	4 06	0 59	3 88	2 18	3 62	5 79	1·52	9 28	3 73	4·34	42 37
1892	1 33	1·77	1 65	1 42	1 47	2 99	2 30	4 63	2 82	6·19	3 66	2·97	33·18
1893	2 67	4 51	0 53	0 05	0 47	1 20	3 71	0 87	3 68	4·73	3 05	2·82	28·29
1894	5·50	2 48	1 74	2·28	1·48	2 18	5 53	2 31	4 04	5·30	6·23	3 00	42 07
1895	2 73	0 53	2 14	2 27	0 06	0 24	3 56	3 08	0 64	4·02	6·18	4 20	29·65
1896	1·64	0 36	3 24	0 92	0·39	3·45	1 11	2 11	8·01	5 64	1 73	4 95	33 55
1897	3 09	3 04	5 06	2 20	1 66	1 78	1·45	3 14	3 27	0·36	1 73	4 14	30 92
Mean	3 27	2 55	2 40	2 18	1 94	2 40	3 09	3 09	3 22	4 38	4·18	3·45	36·15

TABLE 10.

The Rainfall of the Seasons in Inches.

Year	Winter	Spring	Summer.	Autumn.
1871	9·76	7·14	9 80	7·71
1872	12·50	8 88	9·04	15 50
1873	13·14	5·04	10·07	12·76
1874	6 28	4 76	7·16	12·15
1875	10 04	4·21	11 89	12 94
1876	8·10	7·98	7 09	10·18
1877	21·02	8 37	8 67	14 40
1878	7·31	11 23	8 89	11 09
1879	11·19	9·93	15·14	6·34
1880	5·97	3 81	7·23	16 59
1881	10 14	5·40	10 27	12 83
1882	8·75	6 93	9 52	16·72
1883	11·85	5 68	6 49	13 00
1884	7·79	4·59	5 29	7·62
1885	13·01	6·48	2 02	13·65
1886	6 91	9·57	6 49	9 62
1887	9 99	5·73	4 99	11 72
1888	5 81	8 08	14 18	9·04
1889	7·50	7 43	8·87	11·31
1890	7 69	7 50	11·47	6·83
1891	4·12	8·53	11·59	14 53
1892	7 44	4·54	9 92	12 67
1893	10 15	1·05	5·78	11 46
1894	10 80	5·50	10·02	15 57
1895	6 26	4 47	6·88	10·84
1896	6·20	4 55	6 67	15 38
1897	11·08	8·92	6·37	5·36
Average	9 29	6·52	8·65	11 77

Number of days in each month and year when rain fell to the amount of ·o1 of an inch and upwards during any 24 hours ending at 9 a.m.

Year.	Jan.	Feb	March	April	May.	June	July	Aug.	Sept	Oct.	Nov	Dec	Mean.
1873	17	7	14	13	11	10	9	14	12	19	14	7	147
1874	11	9	11	10	8	9	8	16	15	18	12	13	140
1875	21	11	6	8	10	13	17	8	11	17	18	13	153
1876	11	18	22	15	7	12	7	12	18	9	16	24	171
1877	25	19	21	16	13	7	14	16	10	14	21	16	192
1878	11	13	8	15	21	14	7	23	8	12	18	12	162
1879	8	19	10	18	19	18	16	18	12	9	6	10	163
1880	6	18	5	13	4	17	20	6	11	17	14	17	148
1881	11	13	13	11	11	10	11	20	14	19	19	13	165
1882	8	9	13	13	9	20	20	13	11	19	20	19	174
1883	17	17	13	6	9	13	18	16	19	14	18	14	174
1884	17	14	7	10	10	7	14	7	13	12	8	17	136
1885	14	18	9	9	17	9	6	8	18	18	15	11	152
1886	22	9	14	13	15	10	13	13	11	21	20	23	184
1887	14	10	12	12	17	2	7	9	16	12	26	18	155
1888	12	14	23	14	8	15	21	18	9	9	20	15	178
1889	7	22	14	20	12	4	20	18	5	24	5	18	169
1890	24	6	19	16	12	20	17	16	7	11	23	7	178
1891	18	0	18	8	18	9	14	21	13	23	18	20	180
1892	14	18	12	10	7	15	13	14	13	20	15	12	163
1893	17	22	5	1	6	9	16	9	15	17	20	11	148
1894	23	16	11	11	14	14	18	17	12	20	18	16	190
1895	24	6	15	12	2	6	14	17	3	14	17	17	147
1396	12	7	20	9	4	8	7	14	24	22	9	22	158
1897	21	17	21	16	11	7	7	15	16	7	13	15	166
Mean	15	13	13	12	11	11	13	14	12	16	16	15	161

TABLE 12.

Instances of Heavy Rains from May 1st, 1872, to Dec. 31st, 1897, wherein the amount exceeded one inch in depth during any twenty-four hours ending at 9 a.m.

Date	Inches	Date	Inches	Date	Inches
1872—May 17	1·24	1881—Feb. 19	1·28	1891—March 9	1·30
" July 30	1·27	" June 5	1·37	" July 26	1·12
" Oct. 30	1·09	" Aug. 12	1·04	" Aug. 20	1·26
1873—July 15	1·51	" 25	1·12	" Oct. 21	1·08
1874—Feb. 26	1·20	" Oct. 22	1·40	1892—Oct. 4	1·45
" Nov. 28	1·06	" Nov. 26	2·04	1893—Sept 28	1·04
1875—July 14	1·38	1882—Sept. 28	1·04	" 29	1·17
" 15	1·30	" Oct. 21	2·03	" Oct. 11	2·03
" Aug 28	1·32	" 27	1·11	1894—Jan. 25	1·32
1876—Aug. 19	1·27	1884—March 3	1·23	" July 10	1·34
1877—Jan. 10	1·02	" Sept. 3	2·06	" 29	1·14
" Aug. 25	1·22	1885—Sept. 16	1·23	" Oct. 26	1·48
" Nov 11	1·24	1886—May 12	1·41	" 30	1·26
1878—April 10	1·33	" Dec. 26	1·83	" Nov. 11	1·72
" May 28	1·25	1887—Aug. 16	1·14	" 14	1·09
" Oct. 25	1·33	" 30	1·02	1895—Dec. 16	1·33
1879—Jan. 1	1·25	" Sept. 3	1·45	1896—June 10	1·58
" April 27	1·03	" Nov. 2	1·12	" Sept. 12	1·20
" May 28	1·52	1888—July 22	1·06	" 24	1·29
" Aug. 19	1·54	" Oct. 29	1·17	1897—July 21	1·02
" Sept. 23	1·20	1889—Aug. 19	1·10		
1880—Sept. 14	1·15	" Oct. 19	1·10		
" Oct. 9	2·67	1890—July 4	1·83		
" 26	1·97	" Aug 26	1·26		

TABLE 13.

The Prevalent Direction of Wind at 9 a.m in each Month and Year—referred to Eight Points of the Compass.

Year.	Jan.	Feb.	March.	April.	May.	June.	July.	Aug.	Sept.	Oct.	Nov.	Dec.	Most Prevalent.
1874.	S.W.	S	S.W.	S.W.	N.E.	N.E.	S.W.	S.W.	S.	S.	N.W.	N W.	S.W.
1875.	S.	N.E.	N.E.	N.E.	S.	S.W.	N.E.	S.	N.E.	N.E.	N.E.	S.W.	N.E.
1876.	S.	S W.	W.	S.	N.E.	S.	S.W.	S.W.	W.	S.	N.	S.	S.
1877.	S.	W	N.	N.	S.W.	S.W.	N.E.	S.W.	N.E.	N.	S.	N W.	S.W.
1878.	S.W.	S.	N.	E.	S.	S.W.	S.W.	S.W.	S.W.	N.E.	N.	N.	S.W.
1879.	N.E.	N.	N.E.	N.	N.	S.	S.W.	S.W.	S.	N.E.	N.	N.	N.
1880.	N.	S.	W.	S.W.	N.E.	S.W.	S.W.	N.E.	W.	N.	N.E.	S.W.	N.E.
1881.	N.	N.E.	S.W.	N.E.	N.E.	S.	S.W.	S.W.	N.	N.	S.W.	S.	S.W.
1882.	S.W.	S.	N E	S.W.	S.W.	W	S.W.	W.	S.W.	W.	W	S W	S.W.
1883.	S.W.	S.	N	N.E.	N.E.	N.E.	S.W.	S.W.	S.W.	W.	S.W.	N.	S.W.
1884.	S.W.	S E	N E	N.E.	N.E.	N.E.	N E	N.E.	N E	N.	N.	S.W.	N.E.
1885.	E.	S	N	N.E.	S.W.	N.E.	S.W.	S.W.	S.W.	S.W.	N.E.	N.	N.
1886.	S.W.	N.E.	N.E.	N.E.	N.E.	N.E.	S.W.	N.E.	N.E.	S.E.	W.	S.W.	N.E.
1887.	S.	N.E.	N.E.	N.E.	S.W.	N.E.	S.W.	W.	S.W.	N.	N.E.	N.E.	N.
1888.	N.E.	N.	N E	N.	S.	N.E.	S.W.	S.W.	N.E.	N	N.	S.	N.E.
1889.	N.E.	N.E.	N.E.	N.E.	N.E.	N.E.	S.W.	S.W.	S.W.	S.W.	W.	N	N.E.
1890.	S.W.	N.E.	N.E.	N.E.	N.	S.W.	S.W.	S.W.	S.W.	S.	S E.	N.E.	S.W.
1891.	W	S W.	N.W.	N.E.	S.W.	N.E.	N.E.	W.	N.E.	N.E.	S.	S.W.	S.W.
1892.	N.W.	S.W.	N.W.	N.E.	N.E.	S.W.	S.W.	S.W.	S.W.	N.E.	N.E.	S.W.	S.W.
1893.	S.W.	S.W.	N.W.	S.W.	N.E.	N.W.	S.W.	S.W.	N.E.	S.W.	S.W.	S.W.	S.W.
1894.	N.E.	N.E.	S.W.	N.E.	N.E.	N.E.	N.E.	N.E.	S.W.	N.E.	N.E.	S.W.	N.E.
1895.	N.W.	N.E.	N W	N.W.	N.E.	S.W.	S.W.	N.E.	S.W.	S.W.	S W	S.W.	S.W.
1896.	N.W.	N.E.	S.W.	N.W.	N.E.	S.W.	S.W.	N.E.	S.W.	S.W.	N.E.	S.W.	N.E.
1897.	N.E.	N W	S W.	N.E.	N.E.	N.E.	N.E.	S.W.	S.W.	S E.	S E.	S.W.	S.W.

TABLE 14.

The Number of Days in each year when the Principal Direction of the Wind was from the following eight points of the compass

	N	N E	E	S E	S	S.W.	W	N W
1874 .	12	65	16	37	41	87	23	84
1875 .	46	65	12	52	32	90	26	42
1876 .	59	36	23	30	76	64	41	37
1877 .	49	30	6	17	52	87	79	45
1878 .	66	33	35	21	52	67	48	43
1879 .	67	51	27	34	52	69	35	30
1880 .	54	84	28	19	38	90	36	17
1881 .	55	69	13	29	52	78	46	23
1882 .	52	43	19	38	45	79	67	22
1883 .	55	62	16	31	40	78	54	29
1884 .	42	75	24	36	38	72	53	26
1885 .	40	98	30	20	46	74	41	16
1886 .	28	102	19	37	32	83	50	14
1887 .	51	128	15	12	27	67	46	19
1888 .	34	95	23	24	40	71	61	18
1889 .	54	88	20	20	44	65	53	21
1890 .	42	68	33	23	28	92	59	20
1891	47	66	25	26	52	91	43	15
1892 .	32	77	20	23	31	97	43	38
1893	31	71	33	19	15	93	45	58
1894	40	65	34	19	19	111	40	37
1895 .	30	79	19	33	27	100	26	51
1896 .	40	81	24	22	17	79	30	73
1897	24	75	21	41	27	103	17	57
Yearly Average }	43	71	22	26	38	82	44	35

TABLE 15.

The Mean Monthly and Yearly Highest Temperature in the Open Air.

	1874.	1875	1876	1877	1878	1879	1880	1881	1882	1883	1884	Mean.
January	46·3	46·1	40·0	46·8	43·9	34·7	38·5	36·1	43·4	44·2	46·6	42·2
February	45·1	39·2	45·0	48·9	46·5	42·7	48·9	42·2	48·0	48·5	47·6	45·7
March	51·4	46·3	48·1	48·6	50·1	49·4	56·3	52·7	56·3	45·9	54·0	50·8
April	59·7	56·6	56·0	54·4	58·5	54·2	58·2	55·8	59·4	59·8	56·5	57·2
May	62·3	65·4	60·2	59·2	65·5	60·8	67·5	66·2	67·2	65·3	67·0	64·2
June	69·7	68·2	69·6	73·6	72·8	67·8	69·1	71·1	69·1	71·2	70·5	70·2
July	77·4	67·8	78·0	72·1	76·3	68·9	74·6	79·5	72·2	72·7	77·5	74·2
August	70·1	73·1	75·8	72·0	73·6	70·8	75·2	71·0	72·1	75·2	81·8	73·7
September	66·8	69·6	65·8	63·2	69·0	66·6	70·7	66·3	66·1	68·7	70·5	67·5
October	58·8	54·8	58·7	58·0	60·0	58·7	55·5	53·7	58·8	58·7	58·1	57·6
November	48·4	46·5	49·2	51·9	44·1	44·0	48·5	52·7	48·8	49·9	46·6	48·2
December	36·7	40·7	46·6	44·7	37·6	38·1	47·4	43·3	44·3	42·9	43·1	42·3
Mean	57·7	56·2	57·8	57·8	58·2	54·7	59·2	57·5	58·8	58·5	59·9	57·8

TABLE 16.

The Mean Monthly and Yearly Highest Temperature in the Shade.

	1874	1875	1876	1877.	1878	1879	1880	1881.	1882.	1883	1884	Mean.
January . . .	44·8	44·8	39·4	46·4	41·9	34·2	36·8	34·3	42·4	43·1	45·4	41·2
February . .	43·2	37·0	42·9	46·5	44·2	40·6	46·6	40·5	45·2	45·9	45·3	43·4
March . . .	48·6	43·2	45·2	45·1	45·8	46·0	51·7	49·0	52·5	42·0	49·4	47·1
April . . .	57·4	52·8	52·0	50·6	54·0	48·9	52·7	51·1	54·5	53·9	50·4	52·5
May . . .	58·7	60·6	54·8	53·9	60·0	54·2	60·1	60·6	61·0	60·3	61·8	58·7
June . . .	66·3	63·5	64·2	68·2	66·6	61·8	63·6	64·2	63·1	66·4	65·5	64·8
July . . .	74·5	63·9	72·2	66·4	69·5	63·1	66·8	73·2	66·1	67·1	70·8	68·5
August . .	67·0	67·7	71·0	66·7	67·5	65·2	69·5	65·2	66·1	69·9	75·3	68·2
September .	64·2	65·3	61·8	58·5	63·9	61·7	66·2	61·5	61·2	63·3	65·6	63·0
October . .	56·5	52·0	56·3	54·5	56·1	55·3	52·7	49·7	55·3	55·2	54·4	54·3
November .	46·9	45·4	47·5	49·8	42·0	40·9	46·3	51·6	46·8	47·9	44·9	46·3
December .	35·4	39·4	45·2	43·4	36·0	36·9	45·9	42·1	43·0	42·0	42·2	41·0
Mean . .	55·3	53·0	54·4	54·2	54·0	50·7	54·9	53·6	54·7	54·7	55·9	54·0

TABLE 17.

Highest Temperature of Solar Radiation in Vacuo in each Month and Year (Bright Bulb).

	1876	1877	1878.	1879.	1880	1881.	1882.	1883.	1884	Extreme
January	63 0	61·4	63 7	51 0	61 6	61·4	55·6	58·2	61 6	63 7
February	64 6	70 0	71 0	64·0	65 0	60·0	66·0	66 0	67 0	71·0
March.	70 2	74 0	71 0	72·6	75·4	71·6	76·4	70 0	77 0	77·0
April	78 4	75·0	77 0	77·1	80·5	76·0	81·4	86 0	77 0	86·0
May	84 2	80 4	85·4	85·0	90·4	87·1	92·0	92 6	94 5	94·5
June	97 6	97 2	98·4	87 0	92 9	92 0	93 5	97 0	97·7	98·4
July	104 0	95 7	97 8	94·1	92 0	106·2	94 5	94 0	98 8	106·2
August	103·0	94 0	89 0	93·0	90 0	90 6	97 2	94·1	106 6	106·6
September . . .	84 6	82 0	88·5	87 1	93 0	86·8	88·0	88·5	92 0	93·0
October . . .	81 7	75 3	81 0	77·8	82 0	76 0	83·6	82 5	77 4	83 6
November . . .	72·0	70 2	59 0	65·3	63 0	70 0	69 2	67 0	67 7	72·0
December . . .	61·0	57 8	56 0	55·4	60 0	56·2	56·0	56 5	56 0	61·0
Absolute	104 0	97 2	98 4	94·1	93 0	106 2	97 2	97 0	106 6	106 6

TABLE 18.

Lowest Temperature of Terrestrial Radiation upon the Surface of Short Grass in each Month and Year.

	1874.	1875.	1876.	1877.	1878.	1879.	1880.	1881.	1882.	1883.	1884.	Extreme
January . . .	25.0	15.4	9.6	20.1	21.2	9.0	14.2	2.0	14.5	17.2	28.2	2.0
February . . .	19.2	25.6	8.2	16.4	19.0	17.6	21.9	14.0	20.0	21.1	23.8	8.2
March . . .	16.2	28.6	17.4	16.0	17.4	17.8	21.0	13.0	19.8	12.8	23.1	12.8
April . . .	27.6	29.4	25.1	32.0	20.2	18.5	27.5	20.8	26.2	23.0	26.0	18.5
May . . .	29.4	36.0	25.0	24.3	31.2	22.4	28.0	20.4	30.5	24.8	28.8	20.4
June . . .	34.0	40.0	33.4	38.1	37.0	35.0	30.4	31.2	31.7	30.8	37.8	30.4
July . . .	43.0	36.2	39.4	42.8	36.1	39.0	37.0	36.5	39.6	39.3	38.8	36.1
August . . .	42.0	39.0	34.0	45.0	41.0	41.0	38.6	34.7	36.6	41.5	39.2	34.0
September .	39.2	41.0	36.2	31.3	32.0	33.8	32.0	33.2	28.5	37.1	37.0	28.5
October . .	32.2	25.2	26.2	23.0	26.5	23.8	19.0	18.8	23.4	29.2	28.8	18.8
November .	29.0	23.1	15.2	24.4	19.2	11.0	11.8	22.2	16.7	25.2	21.8	11.0
December .	18.4	16.8	16.8	21.8	9.8	6.5	12.0	16.0	13.1	21.8	23.6	6.5
Absolute .	16.2	15.4	8.2	16.0	9.8	6.5	11.8	2.0	13.1	12.8	21.8	2.0

TABLE 19.

The Mean Monthly and Yearly Lowest Temperature of Radiation upon Short Grass.

	1874	1875	1876	1877	1878	1879	1880	1881	1882	1883	1884	Mean
January	33.5	36.3	26.9	32.0	30.5	23.0	25.3	20.0	29.5	33.0	34.8	29.5
February	31.8	30.2	30.6	33.5	33.2	29.1	31.1	27.9	30.3	32.6	34.3	31.3
March	33.6	32.8	30.7	28.6	30.6	28.6	33.0	29.4	32.2	25.0	33.6	30.7
April	38.8	36.4	35.9	34.9	34.4	31.9	34.2	32.7	33.6	32.6	34.3	34.5
May	37.9	44.0	35.6	36.6	42.8	33.3	36.4	36.3	37.5	38.0	40.1	38.0
June	45.3	47.3	44.5	47.5	45.8	44.2	44.0	41.7	42.7	44.3	44.8	44.7
July	50.9	50.3	49.8	48.3	48.5	46.5	48.3	48.1	45.8	46.3	49.9	48.4
August	48.3	55.8	48.3	50.1	49.1	50.2	50.3	45.9	44.1	48.2	50.5	49.1
September	48.2	50.6	44.1	40.4	42.8	44.1	44.5	43.9	40.2	46.1	48.0	44.5
October	43.7	42.0	42.7	36.2	40.4	39.5	34.6	34.1	37.9	40.7	37.4	39.0
November	36.0	36.4	34.1	34.3	30.6	28.1	28.8	37.0	31.6	33.4	32.9	33.0
December	27.4	32.5	35.2	29.5	24.6	21.8	30.2	29.8	31.7	32.2	32.9	29.8
Mean	39.6	41.2	38.2	37.7	37.8	35.0	36.7	35.5	36.4	37.7	39.4	37.7

TABLE 20.

Month Mean Temperature of Dew Point at 9 a.m.

	1874.	1875.	1876.	1877.	1878.	1879.	1880.	1881.	1882.	1883.	1884.	Mean.
January .	37·9	40·1	33 6	40 2	35 7	28·8	30·9	26 7	37·0	37·7	39·3	35·2
February .	35·0	31·3	36 6	39·4	37·9	34·9	38·6	34·5	37·6	38·7	38·1	36·6
March . .	37 8	34·1	36·2	35 7	34·2	36·3	38·7	36·7	40·3	30·9	37·9	36·2
April . .	41·8	38·8	41 4	39 5	42·6	38·0	40 2	37 9	42·2	39·1	38·3	39·9
May . .	41·6	46·9	40 9	41 2	49·2	41·2	43 5	45·1	46 9	46 2	46 6	44·4
June . .	47·7	51·5	50·4	51·9	51·7	51·3	51·6	49·2	50 4	51·8	50·1	50·6
July . .	55·6	52·8	55 8	52 9	55·6	52·6	54·8	55·2	53·8	53·1	56·1	54·4
August .	52·4	55·1	53 7	54·1	56·1	54·9	56·9	52·8	52 7	55·9	56·2	54·6
September .	53 3	54·5	51 5	48·7	51·8	52·3	54 7	51·9	50 2	52 9	54·2	52 3
October .	46·9	45·3	48 9	43·2	46·8	47·3	42·5	40·5	48·0	46·9	46 7	45·7
November .	37·7	38·5	39 9	42·6	35·1	30·0	38·7	45·6	38·7	417	38 3	38·8
December .	30·3	34·9	41 2	36 8	30·4	29 6	40 1	36·3	38·0	36 0	36 7	35·5
Mean . .	43·2	43·6	44 2	43·8	43·9	41·4	44·3	42·7	44 6	44·2	44·8	43 7

RECEDING tables, which give results of the two methods of instrumental exposure, would lead us, I think, to infer that it would be desirable to organize the two series of observations for the investigation of local climatology, more particularly in the case of known health resorts, where I apprehend there would not be any great difficulty in obtaining competent observers. I feel assured that in some instances very unexpected and important results would be obtained for the benefit of invalids generally ; and with respect to climatological investigations, as affecting the agriculturist, I cannot suppose any observations would be complete, or even satisfactory, without the records of temperature from fully exposed instruments. It would naturally be expected that the exposed minimum thermometer would give, for the most part, a *much* lower reading than the protected one, in consequence of the early condensation of moisture upon the bulb and its subsequent evaporation from the surface, but I do not find such to be the case generally. The almost constant movement of air upon the Hill prevents this deposition of moisture upon the exposed bulb, and the readings therefore differ very slightly from the protected instrument, while occasionally it reads the higher of the two.

Another point worthy of notice is, that the time of greatest cold during the night does not correspond with that in the valley. I have found upon many occasions that the lowest temperature occurs very generally

E

between the hours of nine and ten in the evening, and subsequently shows a tendency to rise without falling again during the night. It is quite possible that this feature obtains generally upon high ground, but the fact was new to me, and wholly differs from my previous experience on the much lower ground at Uckfield. Hence it follows that it is a somewhat exceptional occurrence to have tender plants injured by frost on Crowborough Hill at any time between the months of March and October.

Referring again to the tables, we find, during the whole series, that great equability of temperature is a marked feature in the annual results, whether we consider the readings from the exposed or protected instruments. The remarkably low temperature of 1879 was conspicuous throughout the whole year. If we omit this year, the average annual temperature will be found to vary only three and a half degrees. It may be as well to state that the monthly mean temperature has been obtained from the summary of the daily maxima and minima, separately considered, and not from the total of the diurnal mean. I think this method gives the best estimate of the monthly mean and avoids the daily loss of certain decimal parts of a degree.

The very equable temperature of the Hill is again confirmed by a reference to Table 7, which gives the mean daily range of temperature as recorded by the protected thermometer. I have selected this table in order that some comparison may be drawn with other instruments under similar conditions of exposure. We here find the greatest annual variation to be only 3° 4 in the course of the 24 years, while during the last ten it has been two and a half degrees. Referring to the mean daily range at well-known inland health resorts, I obtain the following data respecting the few such places mentioned in the "Meteorological Record" for the year 1881, which I here insert by way of comparison with Crowborough —

MEAN DAILY RANGE OF TEMPERATURE.

| Crowborough | ... | 12˚·5 | Cheltenham | ... | 16˚·2 |
| Buxton | ... | ... | 14·1 | Aspley Guise | ... | 14·9 |

In Vol. IV., p. 117, of the "Quarterly Journal of the Meteorological Society," Dr. Tripe has given a comparative table of the mean daily range of temperature at the following places, which probably represent the mildest winter temperature of the British Isles, and even with these the climate of Crowborough in this respect compares very favourably during the months of December, January and February, as the following extract from Dr Tripe's table will render apparent :—

MEAN DAILY RANGE OF TEMPERATURE.

1873-77.	Dec.	Jan.	Feb	Mean.
Scilly Isles	6˚·1	6˚·3	5˚·4	5˚·9
Penzance	5·2	5·4	5·3	5·3
Guernsey	7·6	7 8	7·5	7 6
Ventnor .. .	6 7	7·0	7·7	7·1
Crowborough ..	7 4	8·3	8·3	8 0
Torquay	9·0	8·2	7 6	8 3
Llandudno ...	8 0	10 1	9 2	9·1
Barnstaple	9·1	9·4	9 0	9 1

The period for comparison in the foregoing table refers to the five years 1873-77, both inclusive.

The table has no reference to the actual winter temperature of the above places, all of which have a much higher mean than Crowborough, but merely to the question of equability of temperature, which is a point of the highest importance—hence the following quotation from Celsus "Ex tempestatibus verò optimæ æquales sunt, sive frigidæ, sive calidæ; pessimæ, quæ maximè variant," and hence the practice of sending delicate invalids to the Engadine for a winter residence, notwithstanding the much lower temperature which is found prevalent there than at the favourite British health resorts.

It will probably occasion some surprise that in point of equability of temperature during winter Crowborough should stand next to Ventnor, upon the average of the five years, and that this average of 8° is so nearly that for twenty-four years, viz., 8°·4 !

Crowborough is not so far distant from the sea coast but that it enjoys occasionally the refreshing influence of the sea breezes, which bring with them abundance of ozone and other invigorating products, which are found to be most agreeable during the hot days of summer, as they entirely prevent that oppressive sultriness which pervades less elevated positions

If we omit the results of the cold year 1879 we observe how slight has been the annual variation from the mean of the series, and that the years 1884 and 1893 were the warmest.

CHAPTER III.

THE RAINFALL AT CROWBOROUGH—STORAGE OF WATER—PREVALENT WINDS, &c.

ROWBOROUGH has, upon the average, the heaviest rainfall in the county of Sussex, and this is due in all probability to its elevation above the sea. It must not be inferred, however, from this statement that the number of wet days is proportionate, for as a matter of fact they are less than at Uckfield and the surrounding district ; but the rain, during its continuance, falls more heavily, and the individual drops are frequently of large size from the great condensation of moisture which so frequently occurs on elevated ground. Any amount of rain quickly disappears from the surface, either on account of the gradual slope, on every side, or from its rapid absorption by the porous soil. A knowledge of the actual rainfall is very important to the community of any locality if they should be disposed to avail themselves of the information. In dry seasons, for instance, the amount of deficiency ought to be known, and the indiscriminate and wasteful use of both spring and rain water prevented. Hence the advantage of having the water supply of every district under proper regulation and control. To those who take pleasure in the observance of natural phenomena, a register of the rainfall becomes a source of great interest, and we seldom find that when once commenced it is ever discontinued. Moreover, the longer it can be continued the greater becomes the attached importance and usefulness From a careful examination of the registers at Crowborough, Maresfield* and Uckfield, the annual amount of rain would appear to increase, in fair ratio, as elevation above the level of the sea increases, and maintains a very uniform difference year by year. It is often an extremely interesting study to watch, from this elevated position, the wonderful formation and change in some varieties of composite cloud, the commencement, course and dispersion of showers and thunderstorms, extending over an area of at least three thousand square miles In the case of showers approaching from the southward they appear very often to advance near the South Downs in a somewhat narrow column, especially when near Beachy Head, but upon descending over the Weald they suddenly extend, and, spreading over a large area of country, pass to the eastward of Crowborough. When, however, they appear nearer Brighton the extension assumes a similar character, but the main body of the shower passes to the westward of Crowborough in the direction of Hayward's Heath and Horsham ; so that it frequently happens that showers are passing both to the eastward and westward of Crowborough at the same time The showers which come over the Hill generally approach from a point to the westward of Newhaven, and are generally heavy, but of short continuance. The number of wet days (Table 11) must be understood to mean, in a scientific point of view, whenever a measurable quantity

* Forest Lodge.

(o 1 of an inch) has fallen at any time during the twenty-four hours ending at 9 a.m. It rarely happens that one inch and upwards of rain is registered in this county during any twenty-four hours ; nevertheless, Table 12 gives a list of such instances—and shows that the entire year 1883 passed away without such an occurrence. The average number of wet days will be found to correspond very closely with the average amount of monthly rainfall. October and November have the largest number of wet days, and May and June the least.

During the consecutive months of December, 1876, and January, 1877, upwards of eighteen inches of rain were registered, which represent an unusually heavy fall for the South of England. Generally, the autumnal rains are the heaviest. The spring season is dry, with but few exceptions, and it is also at this time that we notice the usual indications of approaching drought. Table 10 gives the rainfall of the respective seasons, and exhibits the great difference in the amount in some consecutive years Thus for the winter 1876-77 we find the total quantity to have been twenty-one inches, and during the following winter less than eight. These heavy winter rains occasion extensive floods in various parts of Sussex, and some of the low-lying districts are sometimes for several days, and even weeks, under water.

EFORE closing my remarks upon the rainfall of Crowborough I will mention a subject intimately connected therewith—viz., its storage in suitable tanks and reservoirs

Although the consideration of this question is a matter of such great importance in our domestic economy, yet it is quite remarkable how little care is taken by the majority of communities, and private individuals, to ensure a sufficient store of the element which is one of the first essentials of a healthy life; and we know that to the want of a needful supply of pure water, whether the source be from spring or rainfall, are due many of the ailments and no small proportion of the present mortality of the people. The remarkable difference in the fall of rain which has occurred in some consecutive years affords suggestive data for ensuring such a storage of the one as shall supply the deficiency of the other. The rain water which falls from our roofs is in far greater quantity than most persons would credit, and the large surplus of which runs to absolute waste. Many householders are content with a tub, or a small tank, the size of which is wholly out of proportion to the requirements of the family; especially when we take into consideration its rapidly increasing use for domestic purposes. As a rule, it may be taken for granted that if the rain water which falls upon any house or cottage be *all* stored upon a scale, which I shall presently mention, such quantity will be quite sufficient for the use of the inmates; but none must be allowed to run to waste until the requisite amount for storage has been secured.

It has been estimated that the actual quantity of liquid consumed by a man, in active life, is about 180 gallons per annum, and by women and children considerably less; it will probably be a fair estimate to consider the three classes would consume upon the average, per head, 120 gallons per annum. If we have ascertained, by reference to Mr. Symons's Rainfall Report, that the average fall of rain in Sussex for the year 1873 amounted to 28·34 inches, this would indicate that about 166 gallons of water must have fallen upon every square yard of ground in that year, a quantity which would be more than sufficient to supply one person with drinking water, supposing that means were adopted to secure this quantity before any was allowed to run to waste, *in the ordinary way.* I select the year 1873 as being one which had a rainfall so nearly equal to the average of many years.

Assuming then that 166 gallons of water fall upon every square yard of surface, it will not be a very difficult matter to ascertain, from the area of the roof of any house or building, how much water may be collected from it, and from thence to calculate the required size of any reservoir

When estimating the size of a reservoir which will be of sufficient capacity for all purposes, in time of drought, we should take care to have it *large enough ,* and for the supply of a household, consisting of ten persons, storage should be provided at the rate of twelve hundred gallons for every inmate. This amount will probably be found sufficient when *once* obtained, for the incoming of every

shower will tend to restore the daily consumption. A
reservoir, therefore, measuring 30 feet long, 12 wide and
5½ deep, will contain 12,335 gallons. Although a tank
of this size should be twelve feet wide at the top, yet it
should not be more than eleven feet at the bottom, which
will allow such a slope from bottom to top as will prevent
the mischance of frost bursting the side by expansion.
As an illustration of the necessity for this precaution, let
anyone fill an ordinary upright tumbler with water, and
also a V-shaped wine glass, or other vessel, likewise filled
with water, and expose them to the action of severe frost.
It will then be found that the tumbler has been cracked
on one side, and that the other vessel has not been injured
—in fact, it would be impossible to split, by the action
of frost, the V-shaped glass

Another reason for building a reservoir of full size is,
that the greater its capacity, the better will its contents
keep fresh, and the less waste there will be from evaporation. It should be sunk so far in the ground that the *top*
should be two feet below the surface, which protects it
much from frost, and the shelving bank above it should
be at such a distance as will prevent any soil washing
into it during heavy rains The tank need not be arched
or covered over in any way, but kept fully exposed to the
action of sun and weather, and, provided that ordinary
care be taken in preventing the admission of deleterious
substances, the water will remain fresh and good for any
purpose it may be required.

Probably few persons are aware of the vast weight of
rain water which falls annually upon an acre of ground
in this southern county. Referring again to the year
1873, and to the average quantity of 28·34 inches, we

find that its weight per acre will be 2,862 tons, assuming that an inch in depth weighs one hundred and one tons per acre. The number of acres in the county of Sussex is 933,269—then 933,269 × 2,862 = 2,671,015,878 tons of water ! This quantity, then, falls annually in the county, which in gallons would amount to the number of 598,334,000,000. I have previously mentioned that the amount of storage per head of population should be 1,200 gallons; and it is a curious fact that the quantity required for this purpose—viz., 588,606,000 gallons— falls upon the small number of 918 acres, thus leaving an enormous balance to be distributed for the supply of cattle, vegetable, trade and domestic necessities.

In connection with the yearly amount of rainfall and its storage, I will here observe that during the last nine years, taken collectively, there has been a serious deficiency in the annual rainfall and, as a consequence, several severe droughts have occurred. The years 1891 and 1894 were the only instances which gave an excess above the average of twenty-seven years. Although the upland districts of the county have, for the most part, the heaviest rainfall, yet the generally porous nature of the soil rapidly absorbs it, so that in many instances serious inconvenience has occurred I trust, however, that with the prospect, which we have, of a good water supply from a deep spring, situated several hundred feet below the crest of the Hill, this neighbourhood will not be so dependent upon rainfall as hitherto.

The long droughts of 1893, 1895 and 1896 were very general throughout the S.E. of England ; moreover, they happened at a time of year when our average rainfall is so much to be desired.

WIND.

The following tables (13 and 14), respecting the direction of winds, are the results of observations taken daily at nine a.m. Although the S.W. wind has been the most prevalent, as we generally find to be the case in the South of England, yet its direction on the Hill frequently differs from that passing over the lower ground —sometimes, indeed, passing in an exactly opposite direction. I notice occasionally that the interchange of currents is very rapid and fluctuating in the course of twenty-four hours. Of late years the N.E. current has been frequently very persistent, and upon the average of years ranks next in frequency to the S.W.

CHAPTER IV.

ON THE METEOROLOGICAL CHARACTER OF THE SEVERAL MONTHS OF THE YEAR, TOGETHER WITH VARIOUS REMARKS IN REFERENCE THERETO.

JANUARY.

" When all this uniform uncoloured scene
  Shall be dismantled of its fleecy load,
  And flush into variety again,
  From dearth to plenty, and from death to life,
  Is Nature's progress, when she lectures man
  In heavenly truth ; evincing, as she makes
  The grand transition, that there lives and works
  A soul in all things, and that soul is GOD.
  He sets the bright procession on its way,
  And marshals all the order of the year,
  He makes the bounds which winter may not pass,
  And blunts his pointed fury ; in its case,
  Russet and rude, folds up the tender germ,
  Uninjured, with inimitable art,
  And, ere one flowery season fades and dies,
  Designs the blooming wonders of the next "   COWPER

REVIOUS observations stamp this month as the coldest period of the year, and in severe winters, when there has been little or no frost in the previous December, the cold usually commences during the first or second week, accompanied by a keen N.E. wind. Should a change not occur in the course of two or three days, we are nearly certain of having a fall of snow and a continuance of the frost. The mean temperature is 36°·1. In continued frosty weather the temperature falls to 15°, and even lower on a clear night, after a fall of snow. It occasionally happens that these frosts are of short continuance, and are quickly succeeded by a sudden thaw, but such thaws frequently prove but temporary, and the wind soon changes by S E. to E., and N.E., with a return of frost for perhaps a week or ten days longer. On these occasions the trees are beautifully decked with rime, and present a splendid appearance when dazzling in the solar rays of the early morning. In our very uncertain climate we occasionally find that great mildness prevails during the month. This was especially the case in the years 1846, 1851, 1853, 1866, 1877, 1884 and 1890. In 1846 and 1866 the weather was often too warm to bear fires with comfort. Very strong S.W. winds are frequent in such a season, which increase to a hurricane if long continued, and occasion great depression of the barometer. On the other hand, we had very cold weather in the years 1850, 1861, 1867, 1871, 1881, 1891, 1893, 1895 and 1897.

Gisborne, in his " Walks in a Forest," draws the following interesting picture of cattle going to their accustomed pools to drink, and of their attempts to obtain the beverage when it is hard frozen over :

" Sunk in the vale, whose concave depths receive
The waters draining from these shelvy banks,
When the shower beats, yon pool with pallid gleam
Betrays its icy covering. From the glade
Issuing in pensive file, and moving slow,
The cattle all unwitting of the change,
To quench their customary thirst advance.
With wondering stare and fruitless search they trace
The solid margin , now bend low the head
In act to drink , now with fastidious nose
Sniffing the marble floor, and breathing loud,
From the cold touch withdraw. Awhile they stand
In disappointment mute ; with ponderous feet
Then bruise the surface ; to each stroke the woods
Reply ; forth gushes the imprisoned wave."

For several years past the fall of snow in this month
has not attained any considerable depth with the exception of that which accompanied the blizzard of January,
1881 ; but occasional heavy falls of snow have occurred
in the counties of Surrey and Kent from which Sussex
has been almost exempt. On the high ground of Crowborough Hill small quantities of snow lie upon the
ground for several days on account of the dryness of the
air. In very severe weather, such as occurred in 1881,
1891 and 1895, snow *crystals* fall in abundance, which
are well worth attention, with a magnifying glass, and I
do not know a more charming scene than would await us
upon taking a walk among some shrubs, any evening,
after a shower of these crystals had fallen upon them,
and, with lantern in hand, survey the beautiful fairy-like
display of winter's diamonds scattered around ; while the
chromatic refraction from the snow-covered lawn would
present a more marvellous prismatic effect than the sun's
rays produce upon the early morning dew.

'Tis winter's jubilee !
His stores their countless treasures yield.
See how the diamond glances play
In ceaseless blaze from tree and field
A shower of gems is strewed around,
The flowers of winter, rich and rare,
Rubies and sapphires deck the ground,
The topaz, emerald, all are there

The size of these crystals varies from about $\frac{3}{16}$ to $\frac{1}{4}$ of an
inch in diameter. To the observant eye they may readily
be detected when fallen upon our dark clothes Their
circular form, too, renders them distinctly different from
the ordinary snowflake. The following are magnified
representations of some which fell on Crowborough Hill

during the severe frost of January and February, 1895, while some others (less magnified) were observed during the frost of February, 1855. It may at once be noticed that they are of a hexagon form, which, I presume, arises from the fact that crystallization of water occurs at an angle of sixty degrees

Although—

> " Stern Winter's icy breath intensely keen
> Now chills the blood and withers every green,"

yet this season of the year should not even be a dreary one for the Botanist; although Flora does not put on a brilliant appearance, yet there are many objects of interest to be found by the Naturalist

Wild fowl of several kinds remain for the most part throughout the month. Snipes and woodcocks are still to be found, as well as wild ducks and geese in various swampy situations in the county.

Towards the end of the month larks congregate, while the song of the missel thrush, hedge sparrow, thrush and even that of the wren may occasionally be heard Field-fares and redwings are constantly on the wing in search of food in the turnip fields and water meadows In the severe winters of 1838, 1845 and 1855, the crossbill was by no means a rare bird in Sussex. Throughout the winter the house sparrow chirps over his various deeds of wickedness I do not believe he is an insectivorous bird, but rather that he is an arrant thief at the farmers' wheatstacks, where he also finds a place of shelter Many farmers have told me what a cautious bird he is when his self interest is concerned He will never build his nest on a stack built *upon the ground*, but invariably in those which are mounted upon a stone or other framework,

thus rendering it quite evident that he does not wish his friend (?) the rat to find out and empty his nest !

FEBRUARY.

" From sunward rocks the icicle's faint drop
By lonely riverside is heard at times
To break the silence deep, for now the stream
Is mute, or faintly gurgles far below
Its frozen ceiling   Silent stands the mill,
The wheel immovable and shod with ice
The babbling rivulet at each little slope
Flows scantily beneath a lucid veil,
And seems a pearly current liquefied,
While at the shelvy side in thousand shapes
Fantastical the frostwork domes uprear
Their tiny fabrics, gorgeously superb
With ornaments beyond the reach of art.
Here vestibules of State and colonnades,
There gothic castles, grottoes, heather fanes,
Rise in review and quickly disappear,
Or through some airy palace fancy roves,
And studs with ruby lamps the fretted roof,
Or paints with every colour of the bow—
Spotless parterres, all freaked with snow-white flowers—
Flowers that no archetype in nature own,
Or spreads the spiky crystals into fields
Of bearded grain, rustling in Autumn breeze "   GRAHAM.

THIS is the last month of winter, and extremely variable in its character. There is an old proverb—

" February fill dyke, be it black or be it white,
But if it be white it's the better to like,"

but more recent observations tend to set aside the old proverb.   In severe winters, the frosts of the two previous months continue, or return with great intensity,

F

while on several occasions the greatest cold of the year
has occurred in this month. It was a very cold month
in the years 1845, 1847, 1855, 1860, 1886, 1888, and coldest
of all in 1895. Very intense frosts occur occasionally;
thus, at Uckfield, on February 12, 1845, the temperature
fell to 3°, and on February 12, 1847, to 1°! as shown
by thermometers protected from radiation. Snow falls
occasionally, with strong N.E. winds, while at other
times rain falls upon the frozen ground, so that walking
or driving becomes almost an impossibility for a few
hours. A very remarkable instance of this frozen rain
occurred in February, 1855, which I have mentioned in
another publication; but the phenomena which accompanied it was so wonderful, that I will repeat the record.

On the third of that month, about 2 a.m., a little sleet
commenced falling, and an hour afterwards a heavy rain,
which continued for upwards of two hours; while the
temperature of the air for several feet above the earth
remained below the freezing point.

By day light, the pavements, roads, as well as every
tree and shrub, were completely enveloped with a coating
of ice one-sixth of an inch in thickness. All houses on
their S.E. aspect were entirely covered in the same way.
The effect was very extraordinary on the leaves of evergreens; and at 10 a.m., just as a thaw was commencing,
an entire ice-leaf might, with care, be removed from their
upper surface with all the veins and form of the true leaf
delineated thereon with the accuracy of a photograph.
The branches of many of the smaller shrubs were broken
by the weight of the ice. At mid-day most of the trees
had lost their transparent covering, when it was interesting to pick up the various forms of ice-branches which

had fallen from the trees and hedges. It is recorded that a somewhat similar phenomenon happened in the day-time in the month of January, 1771, and again in 1807 ; on the latter occasion rooks, when attempting to fly from the trees, fell to the ground with their wings completely frozen : and for the same reason larks, plovers and other birds were caught in the fields.

This phenomenon is thus described by Phillips in his " Letters from Copenhagen " :—

> " Ere yet the clouds let fall the treasured snow,
> Or winds begun through hazy skies to blow,
> At evening a keen eastern wind arose,
> And the descending rain unsullied froze.
> Soon as the silent shades of night withdrew,
> The ruddy morn disclosed at once to view
> The face of Nature in a rich disguise,
> And heightened every object to my eyes
> For every shrub, and every blade of grass,
> And every painted thorn, seemed wrought in glass ;
> In pearls and rubies rich the hawthorn show,
> While through the ice the crimson berries glow
> The thick sprung reeds the watery marshes yield
> Seem polished lances in a hostile field ;
> The stag in limpid currents, with surprise,
> Sees crystal branches on his forehead rise.
> The spreading oak, the beach, and tow'ring pine,
> Glaz'd over, in the freezing ether shine ,
> The frightened birds the rattling branches shun,
> That wave and glitter in the distant sun
> When, if a sudden gust of wind arise,
> The brittle forest into atoms flies ;
> The crackling wood beneath the tempest bends,
> And in a spangled shower the prospect ends "

In former, more than in recent years, heavy snows have been recorded in this month and many sheep and even human beings have been lost in the deep drifts , hence the following lines by Thomson ·

F 2

68

"Now, Shepherds, to your helpless charge be kind;
Baffle the raging year, and fill their pens
With food at will; lodge them below the storm,
And watch them strict; for, from the bellowing east
In this dire season, oft the whirlwind's wing
Sweeps up the burthen of whole wintry plains
At one wide waft, and o'er the hapless flocks,
Hid in the hollow of two neighbouring hills,
The billowy tempest whelms, till upward urg'd,
The valley to a shining mountain swells,
Tipt with a wreath high curling in the sky."

It was a very mild month in the years 1849, 1856, 1867,
1869, 1883, 1884, 1891 and 1897. In February, 1891, no
rain was registered here, which was an unprecedented
circumstance within living memory. In mild seasons
many of our earliest spring flowers come into bloom on
sheltered borders, and

"If now the sun extends his cheering beam,
And on the landscape casts a golden gleam,
Clear is the sky, and calm and soft the air,
While through thin mist each object looks more fair."

MARCH.

"While yet the Spring is young, while earth unbinds
Her frozen bosom to the western winds,
While mountain snows dissolve against the sun,
And streams, yet new, from precipices run;
E'en in this early dawning of the year,
Produce the plough, and yoke the sturdy steer,
And goad him till he groans beneath his toil,
Till the bright share is buried in the soil.
That crop rewards the greedy peasant's pains,
Which twice the sun and twice the cold sustains,
And bursts the crowded barn with more than promised gains.
But ere we stir the yet unbroken ground
The various course of Seasons must be found;

The weather and the setting of the winds,
The culture suited to the several kinds
Of seeds and plants, and what will thrive and rise,
And what the genius of the soil denies."

" Georgic," 1 , 43

 HE general meteorological features of this month are very irregular, but its main character is that of boisterousness and cold, more particularly during the first fortnight, especially if accompanied by bitterly cold easterly winds. An occasional gale may occur at any time, but it has lately been proved beyond all question of doubt that the time-honoured idea of *equinoctial* gales occurring in this month, with considerable regularity, is no longer tenable (see Quarterly Journal of the Royal Meteorological Society, Vol. xiii., No. 61, Jan., 1887). Sometimes a strong N.E. wind is prevalent, which, when it lasts many days, induces a rapid evaporation from the soil, respecting which we have the following old proverbs —

" March dust is worth a king's ransom.
A dry and cold March never begs its bread
March in Janiveer, Janiveer in March I fear
March hack ham , comes in like a lion, goes out like a lamb.
March grass never did good
A windy March and a showery April make a beautiful May
A March wisher is never a good fisher.
So many fogs in March, so many frosts in May.
March birds are best "

Should the N.E. winds not set in till April, March is often a wet month, with the wind frequently veering between N W. and S W March, however, is occasionally cold nearly throughout This was particularly the case in the years 1845, 1855, 1865, 1883 and 1892. The first-mentioned instance was the coldest of which we have any satisfactory record, when its mean temperature was several degrees lower than the average for January. Snowstorms occur occasionally which give a very wintry appearance to the landscape, but, as the sun begins at this time to have more power, the snow seldom remains long upon the ground.

> " When Februeer is come and gone
> The snow lays upon a hot stone "

It was a mild month in the years 1848, 1854, 1859, 1871, 1882, 1884, 1893 and 1896. Hence it is frequently mild. In some years considerable warm has been observed during the latter part of the month and temperature in the shade will rise to 70° and upwards. Upon the whole, however, vegetation makes but little progress, as any premature warmth is quickly followed by cold nights and chilling winds, to the great injury of advancing foliage.

Of our bird friends, the throstle makes himself conspicuous, upon which Grahame devotes the following lines :—

> " Varied as his plumes, and as his plumes
> Blend beauteous, each with each, so run his notes
> Smoothly, with many a happy rise and fall.
> How prettily, upon his parded breast,
> The vividly contrasted tints unite
> To please the admiring eye ! So loud and soft,
> And high and low, all in his notes combine,
> In alternation sweet, to charm the ear.
> Full earlier than the blackbird he begins
> His vernal strain Regardless of the frown
> Which winter casts upon the vernal day,
> Though snowy flakes melt in the primrose cup,
> He, warbling on, awaits the sunny beam
> That mild gleams down, and spreads o'er all the grove."

APRIL.

"A thousand bills are busy now, the skies
Are winnowed by a thousand fluttering wings,
While all the feathered race their annual rites
Ardent begin, and choose where best to build,
With more than human skill, some cautious seek
Sequestered spots, while some, more confident,
Scarce ask a covert. Wiser, these elude
The foes that prey upon their several kinds,
Those to the hedge repair, with velvet down
Of budding sallows beautifully white
The cavern loving wren sequestered seeks
The verdant shelter of the hollow stump,
And with congenial moss, harmless deceit,
Constructs a safe abode   On topmost boughs
The glossy raven, and the hoarse voiced crow,
Rocked by the storm, erect their airy nests,
The ousel, lone frequenter of the grove
Of fragrant pines, in solemn depth of shade
Finds rest, or 'mid the holly's shining leaves,
A simple bush the piping thrush contents,
Though in the woodland concert he aloft
Trills from his spotted throat a powerful strain,
And scorns the humbler quire   The lark too asks
A lowly dwelling, hid beneath a turf,
Or hollow, trodden by the sinking hoof;
Songster of Heaven ! who to the sun such lays
Pours forth, as Earth ne'er owns.   Within the hedge
The sparrow lays her sky stained eggs   The barn,
With eaves o'erpendent, holds the chattering tribe,
Secret the linnet seeks the tangled copse
The white owl seeks some antique ruined wall,
Fearless of rapine ; or in hollow trees,
Which age has caverned, safely courts repose;
The thievish pie, in two-fold colours clad,
Roofs o'er her curious nest with firm wreathed twigs,
And sidelong forms her cautious door; she dreads
The taloned kite, or pouncing hawk, savage
Herself, with craft suspicion ever dwells "

BIDLAKE.

LTHOUGH this is our Mid-Spring month, when we may reasonably expect some warm and genial weather, yet there is, perhaps, no other month in which we are exposed to such great and sudden changes of temperature. The increasing power of the sun's rays, and drying easterly winds, cause excessive evaporation. Some days may be warm and genial, while on the other hand days of wintry rigour are experienced with heavy showers of hail or snow. In April, 1849, a heavy fall of snow was followed by such a severe frost as to destroy all the garden fruits.

It was a very cold month in the years 1847, 1849, 1860, 1879, 1881, 1884, 1888 and 1891, and it was very mild in the years 1844, 1854, 1865, 1874, 1882, 1893 and 1894. In April, 1865, the sudden warmth, after the cold of the previous month, was very remarkable. Very wet weather seldom occurs, but the quantity of rain was above the average in the years 1848, 1856, 1871, 1882, 1889 and 1890. '

The atmosphere is occasionally very clear in showery weather and from the hill top upwards of one hundred parish churches may be seen very distinctly with a three-inch telescope. In this month, too, we may often see those beautiful masses of cumulostratus cloud from which genial showers descend

As the summit of Crowborough Hill commands a view of country extending over several thousand square miles it is of no little interest, in the Spring and Summer seasons, to watch the course of thunderstorms and, occasionally, even their commencement and final dispersion.

During the third week, at the latest, we are accustomed to the appearance of the following birds among many others, as the wryneck, cuckoo, nightingale, swallow, redstart, willow wren and other migratory birds, the marten and swift come later The earlier varieties of butterflies also appear, besides the sulphur species (Goneptyrix Rhamni), which generally appears in March and occasionally so early as February. During warm evenings the common bat (Vespertilio) may be seen flitting around the house Its appearance is always welcome and usually indicates fine weather for two or three days Our flowers, of course, increase in tenfold number and give assurance of the treat we may expect in the following month.

M A Y.

" By zephyrs led comes genial May,
  With brighter green she decks the cheerful mead ;
  Breathes either bland to wake the genial seed,
  Bids the swoll'n buds their crimson folds disclose,
  And with her own warm blushes tints the rose
  Now the plumed tenants of the copse and grove
  Disport on circling wing, and chaunt of love,
  Swelling the melody of waking birds !
  The woodman's song, and low of distant herds !
  Where silv'ry riv'lets play through flow'ry meads
  And woodbines give their sweets, and limes their shades
  Bathed in soft dew and fanned by western winds
  Each field its bosom to the gale unbinds !
  The blade dares boldly rise, new suns beneath,
  The tender vine puts forth her flexile wreath,
  And freed from chilling blasts and northern shower
  Spreads without fear, each shoot, and leaf, and flower."

ORE generally this month is characterised by a great increase of warmth and sunshine, while the still increasing power of the sun's rays manifests itself by the rapid advance of vegetation. The leafing season is now general, and is completed, for the most part, by the close of the month with the exception of the mulberry, whose foliage is seldom much advanced before the first week in June. The beauty of natural scenery becomes most attractive, and is much enhanced by the splendid varieties of cloud which adorn the sky.

As in April, so in this month, our climate is subject to great vicissitudes of temperature. It was a cold month in the years 1845, 1855, 1877, 1879, 1885, 1891 and 1894. In the instance of 1879 vegetation was very generally injured, more especially the fruit, cereal and hop crops. It was a warm month in the years 1847, 1857, 1862, 1868, 1878, 1882, 1889, 1893 and 1895. It was a wet month in the years 1843, 1856, 1860 and 1878. It was very dry in 1844, 1851, 1866, 1874, 1880, 1884, 1893, 1895 and 1896. The most prevalent winds are the N.E. and S.W. The easterly winds at this season seriously affect the young and tender foliage, which suffers also from the accompanying dewless nights. This month sometimes alternates with September. Notwithstanding these drawbacks the last month of Spring is for the most part fine and pleasant for outdoor exercise and amusements.

Our migratory birds have very generally arrived and the chief of them may be heard in full song. Many butterflies are on the wing. Bees, too, are of course very active and have thrown off their early swarms.

"A swarm of bees in May
Is worth a load of hay,
But a swarm in July
Is never worth a fly"   OLD PROVERB.

" Roused by the gleamy warmth from long repose,
Th' awakened hive with cheerful murmur glows;
To hail returning Spring the myriads run,
Poise the light wing and sparkle in the sun.
Yet half afraid to trust th' uncertain sky,
At first in short and eddying rings they fly,
Till bolder grown, through fields of air they roam,
And bear, with fearless hum, their burthens home "

I must here introduce some beautiful lines, by Coleridge,
upon the nightingale —

" But never elsewhere in one place I knew
So many nightingales , and far and near
They answer and provoke each other's songs—
With warmest and capricious passagings,
And numerous musical and swift jug jug,
And one low piping sound more sweet than all—
Stirring the air with such a harmony,
That, should you close your eyes, you must almost
Forget it was not day."

Old John Skelton, who lived at the beginning of the
fifteenth century, devoted these lines to the nightingale:

Sterre of the morowe graye,
The blossome on the spraye,
The fresheste flowre of May,
Maydenly demure,
Of woman hede the lure,
Wherefore I make you sure,
It were an hevenly helthe,
It were an endlesse welthe,
A life for God hymselfe,
To here this nyghtyngale
Among the byrdes smale,
Warbelynge in the vale
Dug, Dug, ing, ing,
Good yere and good lucke
With chucke, chucke, chucke, chucke.

JUNE.

" A thousand beauties lost to vulgar eyes
Now to the scrutinising search are spread ;
The grasses elegant, though not proud robed ;
The mallow purpling o'er the pleasant sides
Of pathways green, mixed with the helpless vetch
That climbs for aid Deceitful nightshade dressed
In hues inviting Every splashy vale,
Each dry, entangled copse, enpurpled glows
With orchis blooms ; while in the moistened plain
The meadow-sweet its luscious fragrance yields
And then what odours from the hedgerow breathe
When the soft shower calls forth the hidden sweets !
The clover richly feeds the stealthful gale ,
The strawberry, blushing, hides its modest face
Beneath the mantling leaves "   BIDLAKE

HE first of our three Summer months is usually characterised from its commencement by a considerable increase of temperature. In rare instances only do we find summer attained before this date. The N E. wind of the Spring months now retires before that from the westward. Vegetation proceeds most rapidly towards perfection, and, by many, the general appearance of the landscape is considered to be the most beautiful of any period of the year The dews are frequently very heavy, and compensate for the extra evaporation from the soil.

It was rather a cold month in the years 1852, 1855, 1860, 1869, 1871, 1882 and 1890. During many years past there has not been any frost during this month, on Crowborough Hill, which is much more than can be said of the lower ground surrounding it. The temperature was very high in the years 1846, 1857, 1858, 1866 and 1877. A marked feature in the temperature is that in a series of years it departs very little from the average.

The month was very wet in the years 1852, 1860, 1871, 1872 and 1879; and very dry in the years 1844, 1858, 1870, 1877 and 1889. In 1844 the severe drought which commenced in April and May continued, with the exception of a few trifling showers, throughout the month of June. Accounts from all parts of the country represented the pasturage as being very seriously affected, and presenting a most sterile appearance. The wheat crop, as in almost every instance of drought in the Spring months, alone maintained a healthy condition. The old proverb which says that " Drought never bred dearth in England" is generally correct. The driest June on record was that in the year 1858, but the drought was confined to that particular month. In June, 1852, after a considerable drought in the spring, rain fell more or less on 23 days, and the total amount was upwards of seven inches, while in the neighbourhood of Lewes it was nearly eight inches. This was the largest rainfall which had occurred in June during the present century. It has been observed that from Midsummer day to the end of the first week in July we have rather showery weather, with occasional thunderstorms; facts which should be taken into consideration by the farmer.

Few birds continue their song after the end of this month. The yellow hammer, goldfinch and golden-crested wren may chirp sometimes. The cuckoo's note also ceases Innumerable insects are called into life by the heat of this month, and afford an endless amuse-ment to the admirer of Nature's works. Many of these minute creatures are discovered only by the aid of the

microscope, and are alluded to by Cowper in the
following beautiful lines :—

> " How sweet to muse upon His skill displayed
> (Infinite skill !) in all that He has made ;
> To trace in Nature's most minute design
> The signature and stamp of Power Divine ,
> Contrivance exquisite, expressed with ease,
> Where unassisted sight no beauty sees,
> The shapely limb and lubricated joint
> Within the small dimensions of a point ;
> Muscle and nerve miraculously spun,   _
> His mighty work, who speaks, and it is done ;
> Th' invisible in things scarce seen revealed ,
> To whom an atom is an ample field ! "

The grasshopper now makes his appearance, called by
the ancients " sweet prophet of the summer," and held
in great esteem by them.   They were regarded by all as
the happiest and most innocent of creatures—not, we
will suppose, for the reasons given by Xenarchus when
he says ·—

> " Happy the Cicadas' lives,
> Since they all have voiceless wives."

Towards the end of this, and during the whole of the
two subsequent months, myriads of nocturnal creatures
may be found moving about, at their vocations, if by
chance we seek them by the aid of a lantern—creatures
which are never seen during the light of day.

Some will be found preying upon others—some feeding
upon their favourite plants—some committing depreda-
tions upon our choice flowers, while all, or nearly all of
them, hurry away at our approach.   A tithe of the
insects which carry on their active pursuits during the
deep silence of the night would be too numerous to
mention here—nevertheless, we may observe that the
most conspicuous insect, the female glow-worm, which

somewhat resembles a caterpillar, possesses the wonderful faculty of being able to extinguish its signal
light on the approach of a nocturnal bird, and can also,
at will, trim its lamp with great brilliancy. The male,
on the contrary, is a winged creature, rarely met with.
It also emits a dim light, on flying, from four luminous
spots, and the head is surrounded with a horny plate
which impedes lateral and upward vision.

JULY.

" Calls forth the labouring hinds, in standing rows,
With slow approaching step and levelled stroke,
The early mower bending o'er his scythe,
Lays low the slender grass , emblem of man,
Falling beneath the ruthless hand of Time
Then follows blithe, equipped with fork and rake,
In light array the train of nymphs and swains ;
Wide o'er the field, their labour seeming sport,
They toss the withering herbage   Light it flies
The grateful sweetness of the new mown hay,
Breathing refreshment, fans the toiling swain,
And soon the jocund dale and echoing hill
Resound with merriment.   The simple jest,
The village tale of scandal, and the taunts
Of rude, unpolished wit, raise sudden bursts
Of laughter from beneath the spreading oak,
Where thrown at ease, and sheltered from the sun,
The plain repast and wholesome beverage cheer
Their spirits."   OLD POEM.

F all the months of the year July is the warmest.
The winds are generally from the westward,
but in very hot seasons an easterly current
will sometimes prevail for a few days, which
opposes the upper current of air from the
westward, and eventually causes severe

thunderstorms. Should the storm be violent, and extend over a large area, the weather becomes cooler for a fortnight or more; and when it happens towards the end of July, so great a change occurs that we have no return of really hot weather   Some of the most beautiful forms of cloud may be seen during this month, especially the cirrus, cirro-cumulus, and cumulo-stratus, which reminds us of the following lines by Bloomfield :—

> "There views the white-robed clouds in clusters driven,
> And all the glorious pageantry of Heaven,
> Low on the utmost bound'ry of the sight,
> The rising vapours catch the silver light ·
> Thence Fancy measures, as they parting fly,
> Which first will throw its shadows on the eye,
> Passing the source of light, and *thence* away,
> Succeeded quick by brighter still than they;
> For yet above these wafted clouds are seen
> (In a remoter sky, still more serene)
> Others detached in ranges through the air,
> Spotless as snow, and countless as they're fair ;
> Scattered immensely wide from east to west,
> The beauteous semblance of a Flock at rest
> These, to the raptured mind, aloud proclaim
> Their mighty Shepherd's everlasting Name."

The excessive evaporation from the soil causes enormous masses of condensed vapour to be formed at no great distance from the earth   These constitute the latter variety of cloud, which is always present during heavy showers, and when congregated, generally discharge themselves in actual thunderstorms.

It was a very hot month in the years 1847, 1852, 1859, 1870, 1876, 1878, 1881 and 1887.   In the last instance the temperature was supposed to have been higher than was ever recorded in England.   Such, however, was not the case, as the temperature in the shade was *higher* over

the South of England in July, 1847, when for three consecutive days it was considerably above 90°—viz , 13th,
95° , 14th, 98°; and 15th, 93° !

The month was gloomy and cold in the years 1845, 1860,
1862, 1867, 1875, 1879, 1882 and 1888, to the great injury
of the cereal crops. On the other hand the month was
remarkably dry in the years 1847, 1852, 1863, 1864, 1869
and 1876. In 1869 the drought was very unusual, and
only two slight showers fell during the entire month. In
1842, however, this month was rainless

In early seasons the harvest has commenced about the
15th, but it commences more usually about the end of
this month or in the first week in August. The weather
is often showery during the first ten days, and therefore
unfavourable for the completion of hay harvests in
those seasons when much rain has fallen just after Midsummer Day Should a storm be unusually severe, and
the clouds at a considerable elevation, large hail, or
flattened pieces of ice, will fall and commit great havoc
among the crops of corn, hops, hot-houses, &c. This
precipitation differs materially from that which occurs
in the ordinary cold showers of March and April.

Notwithstanding this is the warmest month of the year,
most of the feathered tribe have nearly discontinued
their notes. Fresh flowers, in their natural order of succession, come into bloom as the season advances , while
those which adorned the fields in May and June hasten
to ripen their seed.

The common snake may frequently be seen crossing
the dusty road in sultry weather. This reptile having
no fang is perfectly harmless ; nevertheless, every opportunity is generally taken of killing it. It feeds on

G

insects, field mice, harvest mice, and many pests of the
field, and should, therefore, be considered rather as a
friend than a foe. The common bat is now very busy in
warm weather, and destroys an enormous number of
annoying insects, many tribes of which are now in full
vigour.

ON A SUMMER'S MORNING.

" But when mild Morn, in saffron stole,
First issues from her eastern goal,
Let not my dew feet fail to climb
Some breezy summit's brow sublime,
Whence Nature's universal face
Illumined smiles with new-born grace ;
The misty streams that wind below,
With silver sparkling lustre glow ;
The groves and castled cliffs appear
Invested all in radiance clear ,
O ! every village charm beneath !
The smoke that mounts in azure wreath ,
O beauteous rural interchange !
The simple spire and elmy grange ;
Content, indulging blissful hours,
Whistles o'er the fragrant flowers ,
And cattle, roused to pastures new,
Shake jocund from their sides the dew."

AUGUST.

" Here the furze,
Enriched among its spines, with golden flowers
Scents the keen air ; while all its thorny groups,
Wide scattered o'er the waste, are full of life ,
For 'midst its yellow bloom, the assembled chats
Wave high the tremulous wing, and with shrill notes,
But clear and pleasant, cheer the extensive heath
Linnets in numerous flocks frequent it, too,
And bashful, hiding in these scenes, remote
From his congeners, they make the woods
And the thick copses echo to their song

The stonechat makes his domicile , and while
His patient mate with downy bosom warms
Their future young , the winchant his lay sings
Loud to the shaggy wild.   The erica here,
That o'er the Caledonian hills sublime
Spreads its dark mantle, where the bees delight
To seek their purest honey, flourishes;
Sometimes with bells like amethysts, and then
Paler, and shaded like the maiden's cheek
With gradual blushes, other while as white
As rime that hangs upon the frozen spray "   SMITH.

 N this, the last month of summer, we find its mean temperature, upon the average, to be less than that of July, yet in some years the greatest heat is not attained till this month. The high temperature *at night* constitutes a peculiar feature of this period. By the middle of the month the soil becomes so much heated by the continuance of summer heat that after a fall of rain a rapid evaporation occurs from the surface, and the atmosphere, thus loaded with moisture, becomes exceedingly oppressive   The maximum temperature in the shade is generally very uniform, and differs but slightly from that of the previous month.   Westerly winds are the most prevalent, with but little variation   With respect to thunderstorms, the action of the wind is much the same as last month, and severe storms occasionally occur in different parts of the country.   The beautiful scenery displayed among the ever-changing clouds is equal to that of the other summer months, and enhances the prospect in the now matured landscape.   It was a very hot month in the years 1842, 1846, 1856, 1857, 1871, 1880, 1884, 1887 and 1893.   In 1842 the heat was excessive, and on several days the temperature in the shade

was 90° and upwards. There had not been any rain in July, and the surface of the ground had become so hard and dry, that reflected solar heat influenced that in the shade. During the first four days of August, 1856, the daily highest temperature ranged from 90° to 92° in the shade This month was also very hot in the year 1857, and was supposed to have been the hottest August (1842 excepted) since the year 1780

It was a cool month in the years 1845, 1848, 1860, 1864 and 1888. On the 10th in 1848 a frost occurred, after some showers of rain and snow had fallen during the day, and on the following morning the corn was found frozen in the sheaves, an unprecedented recorded occurrence in the South of England The rainfall, upon the average, exceeds that for July, which is partly to be attributed to the large quantity which falls in thunder showers. It was, however, a particularly wet month in the years 1852, 1860, 1878, 1879, 1881 and 1891, and very dry in the years 1849, 1855, 1880, 1883, 1885 and 1895. Harvest now becomes general, and in forward seasons hop-picking commences during the last week.

About the middle of the month the swift takes its departure to more southerly regions. Various birds, as the finches, linnets, lapwings, &c., congregate, and the note of the redbreast is heard again

The number of plants in flower is much lessened, but the waste lands are now brilliant with the varieties of heath which grow in great profusion and luxuriance, viz., Erica tetralix, E. cinerea and Calluna Vulgaris. Of these kinds many shades of colour may be detected, and I have found occasionally the white variety of E. tetralix

and E cinerea. In some of the bogs may be found
Hypericum elodes, Malaxis paludosa, Scutellaria minor,
Drosera rotumdifolia, &c., while on the heath and other
plants may be observed the beautiful parasite Cuscuta
Europœa

In former years, and in company with the late Mr.
Wm Borrer, of Henfield, I found the rare Isnardia
palustris in the adjoining parish of Buxted, and, on the
bank of Maresfield mill pond, the Elatine hexandra.

The common glow-worm, " the little planet of the rural
scene," may be noticed in some abundance ; and I will
here remark that it is not only the glow-worm which
loses its lustre by the light of day. There is a centipede,
which infests our greenhouses, whose presence may be
detected by its bright phosphorescence at night. There
is also a peculiarly reddish-looking worm which is not
only luminous in itself, but leaves a trail of phosphorescent light in damp weather.

The delightfully calm and warm evenings which are
usual in this season of the year have been admirably
described by an American poet

" All, all was still—
As if the earth now slept to wake no more ·
In such a scene the soul oft walks abroad,
For SILENCE is the energy of GOD !
Not in the blackest tempest's midnight scowl,
The earthquake's rocking or the whirlwind's howl,
Not from the crashing, thunder rifted cloud
Does His immortal mandate speak so loud,
As when the *silent night* around her throws
Her star bespangled mantle of repose ,
And as all nature sleeps in tranquil smiles,
What sweet yet lofty thought her soul beguiles !
There's not an object 'neath the moon's bright beam,
There's not a shadow darkening on the stream,

There's not a star that jewels yonder skies,
Whose bright reflection on the water lies,
That does not in the lifted mind awake
Thoughts that of love and heaven alike partake."

The poet Valdarno alludes to the charm of a summer's evening in the following lines :—

" Now at the close of this soft summer's day,
    Inclined upon the river's flowery side,
I pause to see the sportive fishes play,
    And cut with finny oars the sparkling tide
Silent and still is all creation round ,
    The rural music of the warblers cease ,
A mantling vapour broods across the ground,
    And all the elements are hushed to peace
The setting rays, with various tints o'erspread,
    Upon the placid mirror glow confest,
And not a bullrush moves her velvet head ;
    For not a breeze sighs o'er her glittering breast
Happy are those whose conscious bosoms are
    Like a declining evening, calm and fair."

The harvest time is thus described by Thomson ·—

" The harvest treasures all
Now gathered in, beyond the range of storms,
Sure to the swain ; the circling fence shut up ,
And instant Winter's utmost rage defied,
While, loose to the festive joy, the country round
Laughs with the loud sincerity of mirth,
Shook to the winds their cares   The toil-worn youth,
By the quick sense of music taught alone,
Leaps wildly graceful in the lively dance.
Her every charm abroad, the village toast,
Young, buxom, warm in native beauty rich,
Darts not unmeaning looks , and where her eye
Points an approving smile, with double force
The cudgel rattles, and the wrestler twines."

The following lines are by Bloomfield in reference to harvest home :—

" Here once a year, distinction lowers her crest ,
The master, servant, and the merry guest,
Are equal all ; and round the happy ring
The reaper's eyes exulting glances flung,

And warmed with gratitude he quits his place,
With sunburnt hands and ale enlivened face,
Refills the jug, his honoured host to tend,
To serve at once the master and the friend;
Proud thus to meet his smiles, to share his tale,
His nuts, his conversation and his ale."

SEPTEMBER.

" When is the aspect which Nature wears
    The loveliest and dearest ?   Say, is it in Spring ?
When its blossoms the apple tree beauteously bears
    And birds on each spray are beginning to sing ?
Or is it in Summer's fervid pride ?
When the foliage is leafy on every side,
And tempts us at noon in the green-wood to bide,
    And list to the wild bird's warbling ?

" Lovely is Nature in seasons like these ,
    But lovelier when *Autumn's* tints are spread
On the landscape round ; and the wind-swept trees
    Their shady honours reluctantly shed ;
When the bright sun sheds a watery beam
On the changing leaves and the glistening stream ;
Like smiles on a sorrowing cheek, that gleam
    When its woes and cares for a moment are fled."

E. BARTON.

EPTEMBER, the first of the autumnal months,
is very variable in its character. In some
years it has been like one of the spring
months, while in others it has proved the
hottest month of the year, with brilliant skies
and great drought. The mean temperature
is materially affected by the reduction in the length
of day; nevertheless, in warm autumns, after a rather
cool season, its general character is that of true
summer. When the month is fine there is not a more

delightful period of the year on account of that peculiar
softness and serenity of atmosphere, which is seldom
experienced in any other month. It was a very warm
month in the years 1843, 1846, 1857, 1858, 1865, 1875,
1880, 1884 and 1895. September, 1843, was an extraordinary instance of late summer-like heat. On the
first day the temperature rose to 90° in the shade; on
the 2nd, 87°; and on ten other days the highest daily
temperature ranged from 80° to 85·5°. I believe there is
no other instance on record of such continued heat at
this period of the year The heat of September, 1846,
was a continuance of the great heat of the two previous
months, and it was not till the morning of the 29th that
there was any warning of autumn's approach. The
daily temperature during the first three weeks ranged
from 70° to 82·5°, and at night it very rarely fell below
50° till the 29th. No rain fell during the first three
weeks.

Another remarkable instance of splendid weather in
September occurred in the year 1865. With the exception of a very slight shower on the 21st no rain fell
during the month, while on fifteen days the sky was
absolutely cloudless It was a somewhat cold month in
the years 1845, 1847, 1860, 1863, 1877, 1887 and 1896,
hence, it is oftener warm than otherwise. A crisis
generally occurs about the time of the equinox, and
wherever the wind happens to be at that time, from it
we may frequently determine the character of the weather
during the ensuing quarter. Westerly winds are by far
the most frequent, but they occasionally yielded to those
from the N.E. In the course of a long series of years
the rainfall is found to be heavier during the autumn

than at any other season of the year, but September is the driest of the three months.

Very few of our indigenous plants come into bloom this month. Towards its close the swallow takes its departure from us.

> " Amusive birds ! say where your hid retreat,[*]
> When the frost rages and the tempests beat ,
> Whence you return, by such nice instinct led,
> When Spring, sweet season, lifts her bloomy head ?
> Such baffled searches mock man's prying pride,
> The God of Nature is your secret guide "
>
> GILBERT WHITE.

Some birds at this season resume their song after a temporary silence.

> "The Thrush, the Blackbird, and the Woodlark now,
> Cheerer of night, their pleasing song resume ,
> The Stone Curlew his chattering note repeats ,
> And the Woodlark continual breaks the depth
> Of sylvan darkness with discordant moans."

The phenomena attendant upon sunrise and sunset, at this season of the year, are well worthy our attention, for it is certain that we nowhere meet with a more pleasing show of Nature than at this time. The richest decoration that human fancy can imagine must sink into insignificance when compared with a spectacle in which radiance and beauty are so pre-eminent.

OCTOBER

> " And when the fields with scattered grain supply
> No more the restless tenants of the sty,
> From oak to oak they run with eager haste,
> And, wrangling, share the first delicious taste
> Of fallen acorns , yet but thinly found
> Till the strong gale has shook them to the ground

* Bell's Edition, Vol. I , p. 71.

It comes, and roaring woods obedient wave.
Their home, well pleased, the joint adventurers leave ;
The trudging sow leads forth her numerous young,
Playful, and white and clean, the briers among,
Till briers and thorns increasing, fence them round,
Where last year's mould'ring leaves bestrew the ground,
And o'er their heads, loud lashed by furious squalls,
Bright from their cups the rattling treasure falls ;
Hot, thirsty food, whence doubly sweet and cool,
The welcome margin of some rush-grown pool."

BLOOMFIELD.

 CTOBER is frequently stormy and wet. The decrease of temperature is considerable, being more than six degrees less than September ; nevertheless, the month is often warm, considering the shortness of the days, thus compensating for the cold of the longer days in April and May. After heavy rains the sky is particularly blue, and in warm seasons is dotted with the beautiful cirrocumulus cloud. The gossamer web decks the hedges and stubble of the cornfields, indicating thereby a further continuation of fine weather. On some of the finest evenings we still have some beautiful sunsets, and a deep rosy tint extends far along the horizon. The first frosty mornings now occur, which are often the precursors of rain. Thunderstorms rarely happen, unless the first half of the month has been warmer than usual.

During the latter half of the month gales of wind are frequent from S.W., which cause considerable depressions of the barometer, and a low mean daily reading. The cause of this depression is supposed to originate from the great change of temperature which usually takes place towards the end of the month.

Hence there is a loss of balance in the amount of vapour contained in the equatorial and polar currents. When the latter gains any amount of vapour, which the former loses, the exchange will perhaps account for the great rainfalls and the frequent gales of wind with which we are visited at this season of the year. Instances of unusual warmth occurred in the years 1847, 1851, 1856, 1857, 1861, 1874, 1876, 1878, 1886, 1891, 1893 and 1897. On October 12th, 1847, the highest temperature in the shade was as much as 71°. This month continued very warm throughout, with a great prevalence of westerly wind, and a moderate rainfall. October, 1856, was a warm and pleasant month, when the average highest daily temperature was upwards of 62°, and it frequently ranged between 65° and 68° during the second and third weeks. In October, 1857, the heat was unusually great, and on three days the maximum temperature in the shade ranged between 70° and 74°, while it was 72° so late as the 16th. The warmest October, however, was that in the year 1861, when the mean temperature was 4·5° above the average. On four days the temperature in the shade was 70° and upwards. N E. winds were prevalent, and the rainfall was below the average. Cold weather prevailed in the years 1842, 1844, 1850, 1867, 1881, 1885 and 1892. In 1842 severe frosts occurred on eleven nights, and on the mornings of 21st and 22nd the temperature fell 12 degrees below the freezing point, while frosty afflorescence on the windows reminded us of midwinter. In some parts of England the cold was even more severe than in Sussex. The mean temperature of October, 1844, was more than four degrees below the average.

October, 1850, was also very cold, and the mean temperature was nearly six degrees below the average. October, 1867, was almost as cold as the previous instance, and unusually severe frosts were recorded during the first fortnight. On the morning of the 6th the temperature of radiation was fifteen degrees below the freezing point.

The chief meteorological feature in the month of October is the great rainfall, which exceeds that of any other month. On rare occasions snow falls to a considerable depth Each season furnishes its own enjoyments, if we can but realise them, and there are accompaniments to that of autumn which are singularly impressive It is, however, the woodlands which now exhibit the most strongly-marked character. Many of the mossy and fungoid tribes are in their full luxuriance and beauty, so that even the fallen stem of an old oak becomes a landscape, and, as an old poet says—

> " Oft the small plant layeth
> Its fairy gem beside the giant tree."

The curious forms of lichen are now well worth observing, as they present an endless variety of appearance. About the middle of the month the common marten disappears, also the sand-marten. The common swallow and wagtail finally take their departure.

For the most part this month is devoid of floral attractions, but fruits and seeds claim our attention.

The hedges are bright with the cheerful colours of the holly and privet, which tend to compensate for the departing foliage

NOVEMBER

" Come, bleak November, in thy wildness come ,
 Thy mornings clothed in rime, thy evenings chill ;
E'en these have power to tempt me from my home,
 E'en these have beauty to delight me still
Though Nature lingers in her mourning weeds,
 And wails the dying year in gusty blast,
Still added beauty to the last proceeds,
 And wildness triumphs when her bloom is past
Though long grass all the day is drenched in dew,
 And splashy pathways lead me o'er the greens ,
Though naked fields hang loosely on the view,
 Long lost to harvest and its busy scenes ,
Yet in the distance shines the painted bough,
 Leaves changed to ev'ry colour ere they die,
And through the valley rivers widen now,
 Once little brooks which Summer dribbled dry
Those yellow leaves that litter on the grass,
 'Mong dry brown stalks that lately blossomed, there,
Instil a mournful pleasure as they pass ,
 For melancholy has its joys to spare,
A joy that dwells in Autumn's lonely walks,
 And whispers, like a vision, what shall be,
How flowers shall blossom on those withered stalks,
 And green leaves clothe each nearly naked tree "   CLARE.

NOVEMBER is generally thought to be a very dreary month, and, with a few exceptions, the atmosphere is for the most part unsettled, gloomy and damp The S.W. wind is prevalent, and most of the heaviest gales of wind on record have occurred in this month. A sudden decrease of temperature may at any time be expected, with sharp frosts and slight falls of snow , but very severe frosts seldom commence till the last week, and are not usually of long continuance Although the month is characterised by a general cloudiness of sky

and a considerable number of wet days, yet great variation is observed in the actual amount of rainfall. In
a series of years the mean quantity exceeds that for
September, but is less than that for October. Instances
of unusual warmth in November occurred in the years
1846, 1847, 1852, 1857, 1881, 1894 and 1895. During the
first week in November, 1846, the temperature was at or
above 60° on three days, and up to summer heat in the
full rays of the sun. In November, 1847, the temperature of the two first days was remarkably high—higher,
indeed, both in the shade and in the sun than on several
days in the months of May and June. This high
temperature, accompanied by genial winds, continued
both day and night to the 17th, when the first sensible
diminution of warmth was observed in consequence of
the wind blowing suddenly, and with some violence,
from the northward. November, 1852, was remarkable
for high temperature, slight thunderstorms, gales of
wind, heavy rain and floods November, 1857, was also
very warm. The mean temperature was nearly three
and a half degrees above the average.

Very cold weather seldom prevails in the southern
counties during November, but a remarkable instance
occurred in the year 1851, when the cold was greater
than had been experienced in this month since the year
1786. Cold weather was experienced in this month in
the years 1861, 1867, 1871, 1879, 1890, 1893 and 1896.
Our forest trees generally lose their leaves by the first
week, and should a sudden frost occur, after a wet day,
the foliage falls to the ground very suddenly ; nevertheless the woodlands, here and there, exhibit a beautiful
variety of rich mingling hues.

Nearly all our summer and autumnal flowers are gone save a very few in some sheltered spots, but in their absence the bright green of the ivy, holly and mosses stand forth in all the vividness and freshness of a new vegetation.

The various kinds of fungi are now very abundant, and there is much to admire in their elegance of form and varying tints

Great quantities of winter birds now hasten to our comparatively warmer region. The woodpigeon, the latest of the winter birds, arrives The various tribes of insects seek their winter quarters The more tender burrow in the earth, beneath the reach of frost, and as the cold increases their animal functions appear to cease, so that they require neither food nor air. It is very pleasing to consider with what extraordinary instinct all these insects are provided for the purpose of their self-preservation during an inclement season, so that when plants cease to grow, and flowers to blossom, they require neither the protection of the one, nor the juices of the other.

DECEMBER.

" Where waves the leaf,
Or rings with harmony the merry vale ?
Day's harbinger no song performs, no song
Or solo anthem deigns sweet Philomel
The golden woodpecker laughs loud no more.
The pye no longer prates, no longer scolds
The saucy jay Who sees the goldfinch now
The feathered groundsel pluck, or hears him sing
In bower of apple blossoms perched ? Who sees
The chimney-haunting swallow skim the pool,
And quaintly dip, or hear his early song
Twittered to dawning day ? All, all are hushed

The very bee her merry toil foregoes,
Nor seeks her nectar to be sought in vain.
Only the solitary robin sings,
And, perched aloft, with melancholy note,
Chaunts out the dirge of autumn."   OLD POEM.

HEN we examine the mean temperature of December we find a considerable variation in different years; thus in 1890 it was 28·4°, and in 1876, 42·3°; moreover, it is only 1·2° colder than January upon the average of twenty-four years.

Generally, this month may be said to be mild and rather stormy, for the real severity of winter seldom commences before the last week, while the month and year expire either in gloomy, damp weather, or in a state of frost and snow, according to the prevailing character of the season during the few previous weeks. If the month should prove mild a considerable quantity of rain frequently falls, but if cold it is almost invariably dry.

The direction of the wind varies as much or more than in any other month. Should the S.W. prevail the atmosphere is very much disturbed by severe storms of wind, heavy rain, and even lightning and thunder; but if north, settled frost accompanied by heavy snow may occur, even at the beginning of the month. The gales from the westward are now and then very heavy, accompanied by a great depression of the barometer. It was a very mild month in the years 1843, 1852, 1857, 1868, 1876, 1880 and 1897.

On the morning of Christmas Day, 1868, the thrush and lark were singing as in early Spring, and swarms of gnats were observed in sheltered situations.

On the other hand December was a very cold month in the years 1844, 1846, 1855, 1878, 1879 and 1890

In 1844 the cold was more severe than had been known in December since the year 1788, when the mean was eight degrees below the average.

As a rule the month of December is very dreary and unpleasant; "but every medal has its reverse."

Whatever may be experienced from the cold, dreary days and long nights of winter, all is compensated for by the cheerful sunlight of Spring and the lively associations connected with it. Some birds and quadrupeds have retired to their winter conditions and concealment, from which not even the calls of hunger appear to force them. Even the hedgehog, to which Mrs. C. Smith alludes in the following lines, is in a torpid condition.

> " Wherefore should man or thoughtless boy
> Thy quiet harmless life destroy,
>   Innoxious urchin ?—for thy food
> Is but the beetle and the fly,
> And all thy harmless luxury
>   The swarming insects of the wood

> " Should man, to whom his God has given
> Reason, the brightest ray of heaven,
>   Delight to hurt, in senseless mirth,
> Inferior animals ?—and dare
> To use his power in waging war
>   Against his brethren of the earth ?

> " Poor creature ! to the woods resort,
> Lest, lingering here, inhuman sport
>   Should render vain thy thorny case ;
> And whelming water, deep and cold,
> Make thee thy spiny ball unfold,
>   And show thy simple negro face ! "

The whole race of insects which filled our pathways with life and motion are now either buried in sleep or actually no longer exist, except in the unformed rudiments of a future progeny. Winter, however, has its charms and usefulness; in fact, the reduction of temperature and its accompaniments are absolutely necessary for our English constitutions. Let the consideration, then, of the unspeakable advantages which we enjoy in our island home not only banish every repining thought that we are not placed in still milder regions and serener skies, but teach us to regard the Divine Being with ever increasing love and unceasing adoration.

> "NATURE never did betray
> The heart that loved her, 'tis her privilege
> Through all the years of this our life, to lead
> From joy to joy, for she can so inform
> The mind that is within us, so impress
> With quietness and beauty, and so feed
> With lofty thoughts, that neither evil tongues,
> Rash judgments, nor the sneers of selfish men,
> Nor greetings where no kindness is, nor all
> The dreary intercourse of daily life,
> Shall e'er prevail against us, or disturb
> Our cheerful faith, that all which we behold
> Is full of blessings "   WORDSWORTH.

VIEW OF UCKFIELD FROM THE SOUTH. 1871.

CHAPTER V.

A RECORD OF VARIOUS NATURAL PHENOMENA, &C., FROM JANUARY 1ST, 1871, TO DECEMBER 31ST, 1897.

Y giving the following monthly records of each year respectively, many meteorological details are supplied which will be found useful when referring to any of the previous meteorological tables, and, in this collective form, they give the chief points of interest which I have previously embodied in my annual Reports.

From January 1st, 1871, to May, 1872, these monthly observations were recorded at Uckfield, but from the latter date, to December, 1897, at my Observatory on Crowborough Hill.

1871.

JANUARY.

E V E R E weather prevailed throughout this month and its mean temperature was as much as five degrees below the average of the previous 28 years. On the morning of the 5th the temperature fell to 10°·4, and on the 14th to 14°·8. The highest temperature was 46°·4 on the 16th. Frost occurred on every night but five. The rainfall was slightly below the average A beautiful double solar halo, with very distinct prismastic colours, was visible about one o'clock on the 10th.

FEBRUARY.

After the severe weather of the preceding month, a period of warmer temperature set in, and continued, for the most part, throughout this month. The readings of the barometer were high, and the rainfall below the average. Some fine prismatic haloes were visible on the 2nd, 4th and 11th. The 22nd was a remarkably fine day for the season, and the temperature in the sun's rays reached nearly 70°. A great variety of cloud was observable during the last week.

MARCH.

With the exception of an occasional frosty night, the weather was fine, dry and mild for the season. The mean temperature was above the average by nearly three degrees, and the rainfall less than usual. The weather during the last week was very trying for many invalids, as the temperature in the sun's rays was high, but very low in the shade in consequence of continuous cold easterly winds Some rather heavy rain, accompanied by snow, fell on the 15th, followed by a slight frost at night. On nine days during the month the sky was cloudless.

APRIL.

The mean temperature of this month was above the average, and fine weather prevailed during the first ten days without any rain whatever, and the sky was frequently cloudless. From the 10th a considerable amount of rain fell, and the total quantity for the month was rather more than two inches above the average. Upon the whole it was the wettest April since the year 1856. A solar halo was visible on the 14th, and a slight thunderstorm passed over on the 30th. The nightingale was first heard on the 10th, and the cuckoo on the following day.

MAY.

This was a very cold, dry and unseasonable month until the last week. Its mean temperature was four degrees below the average, so that it was the coldest May since 1845. North-easterly winds were very prevalent, with cloudless skies on many days, causing a very rapid evaporation from the soil and low temperature at night, so that vegetation advanced slowly and imperfectly. A thunderstorm occurred on the 8th, with a slight shower. I particularly noticed that the holly trees were remarkably full of blossom—both the standard trees and those in hedge-rows.

JUNE.

The month came in with a very low temperature and a great prevalence of N.E. wind. Many persons had recourse to fires on the 2nd, 3rd and 4th, the temperature having been very low both day and night, and the monthly mean three degrees below the average. The rainfall was nearly two inches above the average. Thunderstorms occurred in this district on the 20th and 21st, but on Midsummer Day the temperature was lower than it was on April 14th.

JULY

Was also a rather cool summer month, and the mean temperature was nearly one degree below the average. The only warm days were the 17th and 18th, when the highest temperature in the shade was $83^{c} \cdot 6$ and $80^{\circ} \cdot 6$ respectively. South-westerly wind was the most prevalent, and the rainfall slightly above the average. I observed swarms of winged ants on the 7th.

AUGUST.

It must be recorded of this month that it was one of the finest, warmest and most brilliant summer months of which we have any satisfactory record. The sky was absolutely cloudless on eighteen days and twenty-one nights. The mean temperature was about four degrees above the average. For eight consecutive days the maximum in the shade varied from $81^{\circ} 8$ to $89^{\circ} \cdot 4$. On the 12th a bright bulb thermometer, in the full rays of the sun, but suspended in free air, registered a temperature of $102^{\circ} 1$. The rainfall was about equal to half the average, and the greater part fell during the night of the 17th. A bright parhelion was visible at 6 p m. on the 22nd

SEPTEMBER

Was, upon the whole, a fine month, although the rainfall slightly exceeded the average A marked feature was the great prevalence of N E wind, with scarcely any variation, from the 10th to the 21st inclusive The weather was very stormy on the 27th. Swallows commenced congregating on the 22nd.

OCTOBER.

This was a somewhat dry month for the time of year and rather cold. The mean temperature was two degrees below the average, but frost occurred on one night only. The weather was very fine during the second week, with some warm breezes from the S.E The wind was very fluctuating between S.E. and N W. The rainfall was an inch and a half below the average It should be recorded that on the morning of the 1st 0·54 of an inch fell in about five minutes !

NOVEMBER

This was a very cold month, with a great prevalence of N.E wind. The temperature was more than five degrees below the average, and proved to be the coldest November for many years past ; nevertheless, there were a few fine autumnal days, which are always appreciated at this season of the year The rainfall was not equal to a fourth of the average amount. Brilliant Auroræ were visible on the 9th and 10th, and to a less extent on the 11th. From the 8th to the 16th Encke's Comet was an interesting object on account of its peculiar fan-shaped appearance.

DECEMBER.

The weather during the first half of this month was extremely cold and dry, and the mean temperature was nearly three degrees below the average. The frost on several nights was severe, particularly on the 7th and 8th. The wind during this period was chiefly northerly and north-westerly, but during the latter part of the month westerly, with stormy weather on the 20th. The rainfall was much below the average, and the greater part fell during the third week. Jupiter's fourth satellite was quite dark during its transit on the night of the 30th.

1872

JANUARY.

THIS was a very mild, stormy, wet month throughout. Lightning and thunder occurred on the 6th and 23rd. The barometer fell to 28·765 inches (reduced) on the 24th. The mean temperature was more than two degrees, and the rainfall two and a half inches, above the average

FEBRUARY

Was also a very mild month, but with less than the average quantity of rain. The mean temperature was four degrees above the average, while many days were warm and pleasant for the season of the year. During the evening of the 4th there was a remarkable display of the Aurora Borealis, which almost equalled the grand appearance of October, 1870. Fine solar haloes were formed on the 9th and 19th, and lunar haloes on the 19th and 23rd. At the end of the month peach trees and the willow were in bloom, as well as many spring flowers A friend* informed me that he certainly heard the nightingale in January, and a person living in Barcombe parish asserts that he heard the bird at the latter part of this month. I believe these to be the only instances on record of the nightingale having been heard at this season of the year if we except the instance of Cowper when he says in his letter to Johnson: " You talk of primroses which you pulled on Christmas Day, but what think you of me who heard a nightingale on New Year's Day ? Perhaps I am the only man in England who can boast of such good fortune."†

MARCH

Must be considered to have been another mild month, the mean temperature having been nearly three degrees above the average ; nevertheless, there were frequent slight frosts at night, which proved a salutary check to the prematurely advancing foliage. Many small meteors were seen during the evening and night of the 31st.

APRIL.

The mean temperature of this month was about equal to the average, and there were only two slight frosts at night From the 20th to 24th, both inclusive, was a somewhat stormy period, and thunder showers occurred

* The late Mr. Coventry Patmore.　　　† Quoted by Mr. Patmore

on the 17th and 25th. On the latter day some remarkable masses of highly electric clouds appeared over the
Channel during the evening. The cuckoo and nightingale were both heard on the 13th, and I saw a swallow
on the 19th.

MAY.

This month was, upon the whole, somewhat cool and
showery, with an excess of more than an inch in the
amount of rainfall. This excess, however, was due to
the heavy rain on the 17th. The mean temperature was
nearly two degrees below the average. Unusually severe
frosts occurred during the nights of the 12th and 18th,
which in many places were very injurious to the young
foliage.

JUNE.

With the exception of three hot days about the middle
of the month the weather was cool and showery. The
mean temperature was two degrees below the average,
but the rainfall was nearly two inches in excess, distributed over fifteen days. Very stormy weather prevailed
from the 7th to 11th, both inclusive, with occasional
showers of hail. A remarkable hailstorm passed over
the Observatory about 6 p.m on the 24th. The hailstones were of large size, and the circumference of most
of them equalled that of a halfpenny. They were
irregularly-pointed pieces of ice, having several nuclei.
The ground was quite covered with them for some time
after the passage of the storm. This storm was very
much more severe at Heron's Ghyll,* an estate situated
about three miles to the south of the Observatory. It

* In the adjoining parish of Buxted.

was thus described to me by Coventry Patmore, Esq. :—
The "hailstorm was quite unlike anything I have ever
before or since seen or heard of The afternoon was fine
and quiet, when I saw a dense grey veil, apparently a
furlong or so in breadth, approaching the house from the
south. It was about a mile off when I first noticed it, as
I knew by its obscuring in its course certain objects
which lay at that distance. Sunshine was on either side
of it. In a few minutes it reached the house. There
was one clap of thunder, whether at the time of its
arrival or a little while before I do not recollect. For
somewhat less than two minutes the hail came down,
with a sudden but not very violent blast of wind, in such
quantities that nothing could be seen thirty yards from
our windows. In those two minutes my rain-gauge
measured nearly one inch and a quarter—that is to say,
about as much as falls in an ordinary heavy downpour of
twenty-four hours' duration The forms of the hailstones and their way of falling were not less remarkable
than their quantity About half of them were ordinary
hailstones as to spherical shape and construction, in
concentric layers, only they were about the size of
ordinary marbles. The other moiety were clear discs of
ice of about the diameter of a penny piece and twice as
thick, perfectly well formed, and in numberless cases
having small projections on one or both sides, which
made them look like the covers of small stewpans with
their handles Here and there was a mass of clear ice
of a different form The largest I picked up was about
the size of a bantam's egg, hollow, and formed with
spiral ridges. I did not weigh any of these hailstones,
but a neighbour told me that he had picked up eight

which weighed an average of two ounces each. I do not think that I saw any of more than half that weight. But what surprised me more than their size was their way of coming down. In my eagerness to examine the stones I hastened out of the window from which I was looking without my hat on. I felt the blows of the ice-balls almost as little as if they had been snowflakes. No glass was broken, no trees or shrubs injured ; and a friend who was driving two high-spirited horses through the thickest of it told me that they took no notice of it whatever, though he should have been sorry to have been driving them through an ordinary hailstorm. The only way I can see of accounting for this extraordinary fact is the supposition that these masses of ice were formed and sustained in a funnel of wind, of which the extreme point or nose did not reach the earth, although it passed close above it ; so that when the weight of the stones overcame the sustaining force of the hurricane they had only a hundred or two feet to fall through." After the passage of this storm the temperature decreased con-siderably, as the highest temperature of the 25th was 13 degrees lower than that of the 24th. The month closed with fine, bright weather.

JULY.

This month was characterized by greater heat, both day and night, than had occurred in July since the year 1859. The mean temperature was nearly three degrees above the average. On twelve days the highest tempera-ture in the shade ranged from 80° to 88°·2. The rainfall was below the average. During the evening of the 11th two storms came off the sea, one of which passed from

Cuckmere to the westward, and the other from Beachy Head to the eastward. On several days the atmosphere was very diaphanous for the time of year, and very distant objects were unusually distinct.

AUGUST

The first part of this month was cool, with almost daily rain to the 11th, but the total amount for the month was considerably below the average The mean temperature was low, and as much as 1°·5 below the average. The wind was variable Thunderstorms occurred on the 7th and 8th, after which came a heavy gale from the S E. The weather was very stormy and unsettled both on the 9th, 10th and 11th. On 30th an Aurora was visible to the northward at 9 p m

SEPTEMBER.

This was a fine and agreeable month, although its mean temperature was more than a degree below the average. The rainfall was one inch below the average. The wind was chiefly westerly, and blew with the force of a hurricane on the 27th. On the morning of the 23rd a frost occurred on the lower ground, which did much injury to dahlias and other tender plants.

OCTOBER.

This month was cold, stormy and very wet. The mean temperature was more than 4° below the average, and the rainfall one inch in excess. A strong gale prevailed from S.W. on the 29th and 30th, with heavy rain. Very vivid but distant lightning was visible on the 4th, 11th and 26th.

NOVEMBER.

The mean temperature was slightly below the average, and the rainfall more than double the usual quantity. There was a strong gale from the south on the 1st, and from the S.W. on the 26th Thunderstorms occurred on the 2nd, 20th, and 30th, with hail showers. A bright Aurora was visible on the 12th, notwithstanding the moonlight.

DECEMBER.

This was a month of heavy rain also, and the total fall was three inches and a quarter above the average. In consequence of the great rains during the last three months the soil was completely saturated, which seriously delayed agricultural work. A terrific gale burst over this district on the 8th. The mean temperature was above the average, and there were only three frosty nights throughout the month. Lightning was seen on the 9th.

1873.

JANUARY.

THE heavy rain, and stormy, unsettled weather, which commenced on October 15th, 1872, continued, with but little interruption, to the 23rd of this month. The rainfall during this period, of rather more than three months, amounted to 22·78 inches. The mean temperature was considerably above the average. On the 19th, at 11 p.m., the actual reading of my barometer was as low as 27·670 inches, which, corrected to sea level, was 28·541 inches. The depression was still greater during the night, accompanied by a great decrease of temperature   An Aurora was visible during the evening of the 7th.

FEBRUARY.

This month was very cold and frosty throughout, and the mean temperature was considerably below the average ; while for several days together the mean daily temperature was below the freezing point, as shown by a thermometer protected from radiation.   Snow fell to a considerable depth on 2nd, 9th, 22nd, 23rd and 24th. On the 2nd a peculiar frosty efflorescence on the windows rendered every object in the landscape of a beautiful violet colour.   I am inclined to believe that this phenomenon was due to the prismatic effect of certain saline particles deposited during the gales of the preceding month.   On 21st every tree and shrub was beautifully decked with rime.   The maximum temperature of the twenty-four hours was only $27°·8$.

MARCH.

The mean temperature was considerably above the average, more particularly during the last ten days, notwithstanding the prevalence of easterly winds.   The rainfall slightly exceeded the average   Showers of hail and snow were frequent, more particularly on the 10th and 11th.   From 6 to 8 p m. on 30th frequent thunder was heard to the westward of the Observatory, and vivid lightning was visible over the English Channel.   ¸

APRIL.

The mean temperature was rather below the average, for although the middle of the month was fine and warm for the season, yet very cold weather prevailed during the last week. The rainfall was less than half the average, although it fell more or less on thirteen days At 6 45 a.m. on the 3rd a mock sun was visible, and the sun was surrounded by a halo of 35° in diameter. At 6.50 they disappeared, and almost immediately afterwards the entire halo became beautifully prismatic. The 6th was remarkable for much electrical disturbance, particularly during the afternoon At 3.45 p m a shower of snowballs fell, each being equal in size to that of an ordinary marble. On 15th and 16th frequent lightning was visible, also on the latter day a very violent squall of wind came on from E.N.E., about 10 a m, and having continued for about ten minutes subsided as suddenly as it had commenced. At this time a thunderstorm was passing from S.E to E. over the Channel. On 25th, bright Aurora, 7 p.m

MAY.

The mean temperature was about two degrees below the average, with entire freedom from the frosts which occurred, on several nights, in localities situated 400 or 500 feet below the level of the Observatory. The rainfall was less than half the average The morning of 26th was not favourable for observing the progress of the solar eclipse, which was visible by glimpses only. There were many irregularities observable upon the moon's limb, and, as usual, the moon's disc appeared much darker than the nuclei of the solar spots.

JUNE.

The mean temperature was about the average. The two warmest days were the 4th and 19th, when the maximum temperature in the shade was 76° and 79°·6 respectively. Although the rainfall considerably exceeded the average, yet the month could not be considered to have been of a wet character. The sky was more overcast than is usual at this season of the year, a circumstance which acted very prejudicially upon all the cereal crops, which were in a very backward condition.

JULY.

The mean temperature was rather more than one degree above the average, and fine summer weather prevailed during the month, with the exception of a period from 13th to 18th, both inclusive. The hottest days were the 21st, 22nd and 23rd. The rainfall was above the average, but the excess was entirely due to the very heavy rain on 13th. This was the heaviest rain which I have ever recorded in July, unaccompanied by lightning and thunder. So far as I have been able to ascertain, the largest quantity which fell in Sussex was registered at this Observatory, viz, 1·51 inches.

AUGUST.

The mean temperature was very nearly the average, and, during the first fortnight, the weather was very fine and hot. Scarcely any rain fell till the night of the 10th. The 8th was the hottest day which has been experienced in Sussex since July, 1868. The rainfall was considerably above the average, in consequence of the heavy rains which fell very unfortunately during the latter part of the month, and seriously impeded the progress of corn harvest. Thunderstorms occurred in this district on 19th, 24th and 25th. The storm of the 24th was one

I

of unusual violence. The morning had been fine, but sultry, and about 1 p.m. some very heavy masses of electric cloud appeared over the English Channel, to the S.W., which, during the afternoon, gradually approached, opposed by a brisk easterly current. It reached this Hill about 4 45 and precipitated a heavy shower. During the whole of the evening the storm was more or less violent, the lightning very vivid, and for above two hours almost incessant. Showers fell at intervals. About eleven o'clock the storm passed away to the N.E. During the height of the storm I observed some very remarkable lightning, which emanated more particularly from a mass of cloud which came across the Weald, from the direction of Beachy Head, and passed to the westward of the Observatory, towards the Surrey Hills

SEPTEMBER.

The mean temperature was somewhat below the average. The heavy rains which fell during the latter part of the previous month continued with but little intermission to the 15th, from which time no more rain fell to the close of the month. The last fortnight was fine, dry and pleasant, which allowed the latter part of corn harvest and hop-picking to be completed without interruption.

OCTOBER.

The mean temperature was equal to the average and the rainfall nearly half an inch in excess. The finest weather occurred during the first and last week. On the morning of the 8th lightning and thunder were noticed in the S.W. The 10th, 11th and 12th were very stormy and wet. During the evening of the 17th a number of small meteors were observed. On the 23rd and 24th distant lightning and thunder.

NOVEMBER.

The mean temperature was somewhat above the average. From 10th to 21st the weather was particularly dry, fine and very favourable for all agricultural operations. The wind during this period was easterly, but not cold, and evaporation from the soil was very rapid for the season of the year. Vivid lightning was visible over the English Channel on the evening of the 7th and morning of 27th. One large meteor and many small ones were observed on the evening of 23rd.

DECEMBER.

This month was remarkably fine and dry. The mean temperature was above the average. A brilliant meteor was visible to the eastward at 7 p.m. on 3rd. No rain fell till the evening of 15th. On 27th showers of hail and snow were frequent. On the 28th, during the greater part of the day, the whole of the Weald was enveloped in fog, but the Observatory, and about 100 feet of the hill below it, was entirely free. This horizontal layer of fog, with the sun shining brightly on its upper surface, presented a scene similar to that which has been obtained from a balloon after it has ascended above a large expanse of cloud.

1874.

JANUARY.

THE mean temperature was about four degrees above the average. On many days the temperature of the sun's rays more nearly resembled that of March than January. Contrary to what has been usual in many previous instances of unusual mildness at this season, the rainfall was below, instead of above, the average. About 10 a.m. of 6th two beautiful parhelia were visible; on the 7th, a prismatic solar halo. The 18th was very stormy with much rain. In consequence of the great mildness, the following flowers were in bloom during the greater part of the month: Several kinds of roses, African marigolds, mignonette, fuchsias, primroses, dandelion, polyanthus, wallflower, hepatica, pyrus japonica, vinca minor, &c. The leaves of the crocus, snowdrop and daffodil appeared above ground in sheltered places.

FEBRUARY.

The mean temperature of February was rather more than one degree above the average, and the rainfall, in consequence of the very heavy rain on the 26th, was also slightly above the average. From 12th to 17th was a very stormy period, with frequent showers. During the afternoon of 25th a very cold S.E. current of wind set in, which increased to the force of a gale at night, and continued more or less till about 5 a.m. of 27th, with very heavy rain during the greater part of the time. The wind then veered to S., and some lightning and thunder were noticed over the sea to the S.E. The various flowers which were in bloom last month were observable also in this. Near the beginning of the month the lark, thrush and blackbird were in full song. Bees appeared during the last few days, and also a few sulphur butterflies and small moths. The common bat came out on several occasions after the gnats, which had rather prematurely appeared. Abundance of toad spawn was observable during the last week. During the evening of the 4th there was a grand display of the Aurora

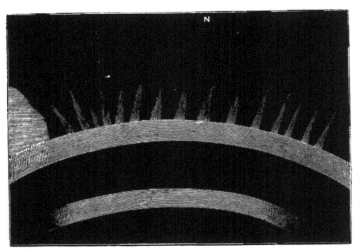

VIEW OF AURORA BOREALIS AS SEEN FROM THE OBSERVATORY, FEB. 4.
The Star placed among the streamers is Alpha Cygni.

Borealis, of which the preceding engraving is a representation as it appeared from the Observatory at intervals between 8.10 and 8.40. A second arch is very rarely seen in the south of England. Further particulars of this Aurora may be found in " Symons's Meteorological Magazine" for this month.

MARCH.

The mean temperature was about two degrees above the average, but from 9th to 12th, both inclusive, it was very low for the season, and nearly three degrees below the freezing point. The rainfall was very deficient, not amounting to half the average During the evening and night of the 28th a strong S.W. gale prevailed. The 31st was a very stormy day, with driving rain. Westerly winds were the most frequent.

APRIL.

The mean temperature was nearly three degrees, and the rainfall half an inch above the average. Temperature generally was very equable for the season. From 17th to 30th the weather was particularly fine, dry and pleasant, several days and nights being cloudless. Very stormy weather was experienced in this locality during the first four days from points between S.W. and S E. On the 4th frequent lightning was seen and also on 21st and 22nd. A splendid rainbow appeared on the 6th. In consequence of steady fine and warm weather during the latter part of the month, vegetation advanced very rapidly. The cuckoo and nightingale arrived during the third week, as well as some swallows, but the latter were *very few in number*. There were scarcely any martens.

MAY.

The mean temperature was considerably below the average—chiefly in consequence of the low temperature at night during the first three weeks. In many parts of the Weald these severe frosts seriously injured the young and tender foliage of the oak, ash, chestnut, hazel, sycamore and even the bramble. In some gardens the potato haulm was cut down to the ground, as well as the bine of the hop plant. At Crowborough the temperature of the air was never one degree below the freezing point, but at Uckfield and Buxted five degrees of frost and upwards were registered on several mornings. The rainfall was very deficient, and but slightly exceeded one-fourth of the average. Vivid lightning and thunder were prevalent throughout this district on the 8th and 25th.

JUNE.

The mean temperature was slightly below the average, in consequence of the great prevalence of easterly winds during the first three weeks The rainfall was very nearly the average and the greater part of which fell during the last week. There was electrical disturbance on the 11th and 28th.

JULY.

This was a fine summer month and the temperature very high during the second and third weeks, both in the shade and in the sun The maximum temperature in the shade occurred on the 9th, but that in the sun on the 11th, when a solar radiation thermometer (in vacuo) registered 149°. The rainfall was only one-fourth the average amount. Between Uckfield and Lewes the quantity was still less and scarcity of water for cattle became a serious inconvenience. There was much electrical disturbance during the month. A fine view of the comet was obtained from the Observatory during the first fortnight.

AUGUST.

The mean temperature was below the average. With the exception of the third week the weather was cool and showery. The rainfall was about half an inch below the average, the greater part of which fell during the first fortnight. The month was almost entirely free from electrical disturbance, but unusually strong winds prevailed from 9th to 15th. On the 19th large swarms of ladybirds appeared in this district.

SEPTEMBER.

The mean temperature was two degrees above the average and the weather was remarkable for its great variability. The rainfall was somewhat above the average and the greater part fell during the second and fourth weeks. Wind from due south was the most frequent, which was remarkable as being the only instance of the equatorial current having been in excess of all others in any month during the last thirty years and upwards. There was much electrical disturbance on the 9th, 10th, 23rd, 27th and 30th. Soon after 10 p m. on the latter day a quarter of an inch of rain fell in the course of five minutes; and after midnight there was some vivid lightning with thunder and hail showers. A beautiful pink Aurora was visible after midnight of the 10th and a bright Aurora in N.N.W. at 9 p.m. on the 16th.

OCTOBER.

The mean temperature was also above the average. There was an entire absence of frost on the Hill. It was the wettest month of the year and therefore maintained its usual character. Southerly winds were again very frequent and blew with considerable velocity on the 6th and 25th. The most severe thunderstorm of this year passed over this county during the evening of the 15th. Between 5 and 6 p.m. a highly-charged electric mass of cloud extended across the county from south to north in a nearly straight line of forty miles, the electrical display from which for upwards of an hour was very grand. During the height of the storm the lightning was of a peculiar copper colour, but became subsequently of a beautiful violet tint. An Aurora Borealis was visible during the evenings of 7th and 13th.

NOVEMBER.

The mean temperature was somewhat above the average, as the weather was unusually warm during the first ten days. On the evening of the 10th the wind veered rather suddenly to the northward and a slight frost occurred on the following morning. From this time to the close of the month the night temperature remained rather low for the season with an occasional slight frost. The rainfall was rather less than the average. During the severe gale of 28th and 29th the barometer fell to 28·684 inches at sea level. A slight Aurora was visible during the evenings of 9th and 13th. About 4 a.m. of the 21st I noticed the very unusual phenomenon of a RED MOON-SET. The carmine colour was so bright that it attracted my notice through the window blind. The colour was formed upon the upper portions of distant fog, which was lying nearly horizontally with the setting moon. There was a slight frost, which was followed by a clear and brilliant day.

DECEMBER.

This was not only the coldest month of the year, but also the coldest December since 1844 in the South of England. The mean temperature was seven degrees below the average and frost occurred on twenty-six nights, so that the mean night temperature was as much as five degrees below the freezing point. The fall of snow on the 16th and 17th amounted to about thirteen inches on the level, which was the deepest fall for upwards of twenty years. There had not been so much snow in *December* since the year 1836. The amount of rain and melted snow considerably exceeded the average. Some beautiful snow crystals fell on 16th and 28th. Lightning was visible during the evenings of 7th, 11th and 16th. The N.W. was the most prevalent wind The month and year ended with hard frost.

1875.

JANUARY.

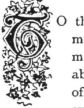 O the severe weather of December, 1874, this month presented a striking contrast Its mean temperature was more than five degrees above the average and it was probably one of the warmest Januaries which have been experienced in this county during the present century. Rain fell, more or less, on twenty-one days and the total fall was one inch above the average. The frost of the previous month gave way on the first day of

the new year, when we had the finest example of a silver thaw which has been experienced in Sussex since Feb 3, 1855. After the second morning there were only two frosts during the remainder of the month, while from the 12th to 20th, both inclusive, the night temperature exceeded the average of that for May! The prevalent winds were those between S.E. and S.W. At the end of the month crocus, snowdrop and hepatica might be seen in bloom in sheltered situations.

FEBRUARY.

Winter returned upon us during the greater part of this month, and was more remarkable for its steady continuance than for any intense severity. The mean temperature was more than four degrees below the average, and so low a temperature had not been observed in February since 1855. Frost occurred, more, or less, on twenty nights, and the lowest temperature, 20°·2, was registered on the 23rd. Northerly winds were prevalent, and a high atmospheric pressure, particularly on the 5th and 15th. The rainfall was more than half an inch below the average. An Aurora Borealis was visible at 7 p m. on the 26th.

MARCH.

The mean temperature was below the average, but the weather was for the most part seasonable and dry ; the latter condition being always favourable to the grain crops The rainfall was considerably below the average. Snow showers fell occasionally. A lunar halo was visible on the 15th.

APRIL

Was a fine month, but somewhat cold and dry, with frequent slight frosts. The wind was chiefly northerly, with a clear sky. The rainfall was considerably below the average. To the 17th vegetation generally was more backward than had been observed since the year 1837. Not a leaf was to be seen except upon the larch, honeysuckle and bramble. A very remarkable decrease of temperature occurred on the 21st during the afternoon, and at 9 p.m. the temperature had fallen no less than 35° below the highest for the day. The highest temperature in the shade on the 21st was 74°, but on the 22nd only 41°!!

MAY.

The mean temperature was above the average ; a fine spring month and entirely free from frost. The rainfall was again below the average. Slight thunderstorms occurred in this district, and on the 19th, in an adjoining parish, hailstones fell at noon about the size of ordinary marbles. During the evening of the 12th the cockchafer *(Melolontha vulgaris)* appeared in immense numbers.

JUNE.

The mean temperature of this month was more than a degree below the average, and the month was, for the most part, gloomy, with frequent and somewhat heavy rains, particularly in the third and fourth weeks. Slight thunderstorms were frequent in the county. The wind was chiefly westerly, and on several days moved with great velocity, particularly on 13th, 14th and 15th.

JULY.

This month, with the exception of the last week, was gloomy, cold and wet. The mean temperature was considerably below, and the rainfall above, the average. A large quantity of rain fell during the third week. The hay harvest was late and very little of it was secured in good condition. Thunderstorms occurred on several days, but were of short continuance.

AUGUST.

This was the warmest and most pleasant of the summer months. Rain fell on seven days only, which, including that of the 28th, was more than an inch below the average. Slight thunderstorms occurred at intervals.

SEPTEMBER.

During the first three weeks the weather was very fine and pleasant, but during the last nine days rain fell, more or less, on every day but one. There was frequent electrical disturbance, more particularly on the 8th, 9th, 16th, 19th, 24th and 27th. The mean temperature was three degrees above the average, and the rainfall deficiency was one inch.

OCTOBER.

The mean temperature of this month was about four degrees below the average, and the rainfall considerably above the average. Some electrical disturbance was observed on the 11th, 21st and 22nd. Both a solar and lunar halo were visible on the 13th, and a parhelion on the 21st. The wind blew very generally from the eastward, and frequently with some force, particularly on the 26th.

NOVEMBER.

This month was also rather cold and wet, the mean temperature being below, and the rainfall above, the average. It was very heavy on the 7th and 10th, causing a high flood over the low grounds in this district. On the 20th there was a great reduction of temperature, and during the last few days both frost and snow. Solar and lunar haloes were frequent

DECEMBER.

Severe frost was prevalent during the first ten days of the month, and although the subsequent weather was much milder yet the mean for the whole month was about three degrees below the average. The rainfall was less than half the average amount Christmas Day was remarkably fine and pleasant, and its mean temperature was 41°·6 ! Heavy gales occurred on 21st and 22nd A solar halo visible at noon on 21st.

———

1876

JANUARY.

T HE mean temperature of January was rather more than one degree below the average. During the night of the 4th a very sudden and considerable decrease of temperature occurred, from which time to the evening of the 16th was a period of continuous hard frost, with occasional snow showers. The mean temperature of each of these days was below the freezing point. On the 8th the maximum was only 23°·4 ! The lowest temperature for the month was recorded on the 9th, viz., 14°·7, and on grass 9°·6. From the 16th to the close of the month the temperature both day and night was about equal to the average for this season, and frost occurred on one night only.

FEBRUARY.

The first two days of this month were particularly fine and mild for the season. The coldest morning was the 12th, when the temperature fell to 23°·6. From the 14th to the end of the month the weather was comparatively fine and mild, with scarcely any frost. Upon the whole, the mean temperature for the entire month was about equal to the average. The rainfall was more than double the average, the chief part of which fell during the third and fourth weeks, accompanied at intervals by very stormy weather.

MARCH.

This month was cold and wet ; rain fell more or less on twenty-one days, but the daily quantity was not large. Cold weather with slight falls of snow occurred during the third week. The mean temperature was below the average. A severe gale occurred on the night of the 8th, with a low reading of the barometer. On the morning of the 12th a violent gale commenced, and at intervals, during the forenoon, blew quite a hurricane. Very stormy weather prevailed also on the 14th and 15th. The rainfall was nearly double the average.

APRIL.

This month was cold for the season, particularly during the first fortnight ; and there were frequent falls of snow during the second week. The precipitation for the entire month was fully a third more than the average. On the 12th some lightning and thunder, with a shower of snowballs, about 2 p.m.; this was followed on the 13th by a violent hurricane and a heavy shower of hail and snow.

MAY

Was very cold and dry during the three first weeks, with an unusual prevalence of N. and N.E. winds. The weather was more genial during the last week, which was enhanced by some refreshing showers. A solar halo visible on the 23rd. The total rainfall was not equal to half the average, and fell on seven days only.

JUNE.

Upon the whole, this was a fine summer month; nevertheless, the mean temperature was considerably below the average, as was also the rainfall. The wind proved very variable. Solar haloes visible on the 7th and 8th, and some distant lightning on the 21st.

JULY

Was a very fine, hot and dry summer month, and the weather was most favourable for all agricultural work. The mean temperature was much above the average; but the rainfall was scarcely a fifth of the usual quantity. A sudden reduction of temperature occurred on the evening of the 17th; the maximum for the day had been 85°, but by 6 p.m. it had fallen to 58°!

AUGUST.

This was another brilliant summer month, but the actual mean temperature was not equal to that for July.

The rainfall was much above the average in consequence of the heavy thunderstorm on the 19th and the stormy wet weather of the last two days. No rain fell between 4th and 17th. The air was remarkably dry on the 13th, and at 4 p.m. the temperature of the Dew Point was 31°·4 below that of the air.

SEPTEMBER

Was a wet and rather cold month, the mean temperature having been two degrees below, and the rainfall double the average. The rain was very heavy on the last day, accompanied by a cold easterly wind and a low barometer. Lightning and thunder occurred on the 6th, 7th, 16th, 18th and 24th. On the 7th a rainbow was seen to the northward, respecting which Seneca has said—" A meridie ortus magnam vim aquarum vehit."

OCTOBER.

The mean temperature of October was about equal to the average of many years; but the rainfall was deficient and not much more than a fourth part of the usual amount. Stormy weather prevailed on the 9th, 10th and 11th; but from the 14th to the end of the month only one shower was recorded Southerly winds were by far the most prevalent.

NOVEMBER.

The weather during this month was very showery, but the total quantity of rain recorded was not much above the average. The mean temperature, too, was also above the usual mean. Westerly winds were the most prevalent. A lunar halo was visible at 9 p.m. on the 28th.

K

DECEMBER.

The atmospheric disturbance which prevailed over Western Europe, and the British Isles in particular, during the month of December, was of a violent and unusual character, and must have been due, in a great measure, to the contact of large masses of air of very unequal temperatures. In the south of England, southerly, and in higher latitudes, northerly and easterly, winds were very prevalent The results of these atmospheric conditions were evinced by such violent gales of wind, excessive falls of rain, hail, snow and inundations along this coast, as are not often experienced in the month of December. Temperature was high for the season and nearly four degrees above the average. Slight frosts occurred on four nights only and to a very inconsiderable amount, as the lowest temperature in the shade was 29°·4 on the morning of the 26th. The fluctuations of the barometer were frequent and large. The lowest recorded readings (reduced) at this Observatory were 28·497 inches at 9 a.m. of the 4th, 28·667 at 1.30 p.m. of the 5th and 28·721 at 9 p.m. of the 20th.

1877.

JANUARY.

THE mean temperature was more than three degrees above the average and the rainfall was the largest which I have recorded for January to this date. The heavy rains, which were so persistent during December, continued throughout this month, so that the total for the two months amounted to eighteen inches and a quarter! Soon after midnight of the 4th a severe hailstorm passed over, which aroused the whole neighbourhood. Solar haloes were seen on 23rd and 31st and a lunar halo on 24th.

FEBRUARY

Was a mild month, with frequent rains, which, however, were not so heavy as those of the two preceding months and the total fall was not very much above the average. The mean temperature was three degrees above the average. The weather was often stormy, more particularly on the 3rd, 12th, 20th and 26th. The wind blew very constantly from the westward. Solar haloes occurred on the 3rd and 15th. Lunar haloes on 24th, 25th and 28th.

MARCH.

This was a somewhat cold and showery month; the mean temperature having been one degree below and the rainfall rather more than one inch above the average. Frost occurred more or less on fifteen nights, which gave a very decided check to the prematurely advancing foliage. The 20th was a very cold day, with drifting snow, and the highest temperature was only 35°! The wind was very fluctuating, between N. and S.W. A solar halo was seen on 23rd and a lunar halo on 25th.

APRIL

Was also a cold month. The mean temperature was nearly three degrees below the average. The rainfall was above the average and fell more or less on sixteen days. Thunderstorms occurred in this district on the 4th, 9th, 11th and 22nd. In the last instance the lightning was at first of a blue and subsequently of a copper colour.

A lunar halo was seen on the 20th. The wind was generally from the northward. During the few warm days of the fourth week vegetation advanced rapidly.

MAY.

The weather during this month was very variable and the temperature nearly four degrees below the average During the first week frosts of unusual severity occurred on the low grounds to the great injury of the fruit blossom and tender vegetables. Gales passed over on 17th, 27th, 28th and 31st of greater force than usual at this season of the year. The rainfall was rather above the average

JUNE.

On the 1st we had a heavy gale, with some lightning, thunder and hail showers. At intervals the wind was at the force of a hurricane. The 2nd was also somewhat stormy at first, but on the 3rd there was a great rise of temperature. The mean temperature was about two degrees above the average. The rainfall was less than half the usual amount and the greater part fell during the storm of the 11th. Thunderstorms were reported on the 4th and 11th, particularly on the latter day.

JULY.

This was the coldest month of the summer, and the coldest July during the past ten years. The wind blew constantly from the westward, and the atmosphere was very calm The rainfall was a third more than the average of many years. The largest quantity fell on the 14th. Thunder showers were prevalent in this district on the 3rd, 6th and 7th.

AUGUST.

This was the warmest month of the summer; nevertheless, the mean temperature was below the average. The weather was very showery, particularly during the last week, and stormy on 8th, 9th, 19th and 20th. On the 25th the rainfall amounted to nearly an inch, and the total fall for the month was nearly an inch above the average. The wind was chiefly from the southward. A severe thunderstorm passed to the westward on the 25th, when the lightning was very vivid. The wind was chiefly from the S.W.

SEPTEMBER.

This month was, for the most part, cold and dry, with a very great prevalence of northerly wind The mean temperature was much below the average, as was also the rainfall. On the 2nd the atmosphere was remarkably clear, and a large number of vessels were visible in the Channel. Lightning and thunder occurred during the night. The weather was stormy on the 14th and 15th

OCTOBER.

This month had also a low mean temperature, but the weather was, upon the whole, very fine and dry during the first three weeks. Much rain fell during the last week, and the total fall for the month was slightly below the average of years. Very stormy weather prevailed on the 14th, 15th, 23rd and 30th. The month passed away without any frost.

NOVEMBER.

This was a very mild month, and exceedingly wet. The mean temperature was two degrees above the average, and the rainfall more than double the usual quantity. It was the wettest November during the period of my register. Gales occurred on the 6th, 7th, 9th, 11th, 12th, and frequently during the last week. The wind was for the most part southerly.

DECEMBER.

The mean temperature of this month was about equal to, and the rainfall a little below, the average. Some days were very bright and pleasant for the time of year, and the month passed away without any particular gale from any quarter. There were several frosty nights, but the cold was not severe. Westerly winds were the most prevalent. A solar halo was visible on the 28th. The last day of the month and year was very bright, with a gentle breeze from the N.W.

1878.

JANUARY.

THE mean temperature of this month was rather below the average, without an instance of any severity of frost. The 26th was the coldest morning, when the recorded temperature was less than six degrees below the freezing point.

The rainfall was below the average, and the greater part fell on the 27th and 28th. The wind was chiefly westerly. During the second and third weeks the weather was very fine and pleasant for the season of the year, and the barometer continued very high. The only stormy day was the 21st. As a further instance of the mildness of the season, I may mention that the following flowers were in bloom on the 11th : African marigold, polyanthus, primroses, nemophila insignis and discoidalis, yellow jasmine, &c.

FEBRUARY

Was a milder month, with a temperature slightly above the average. Although frosts were frequent at night during the first fortnight, yet they were not severe, and the greatest degree of cold was 27° 5 on the 8th. The rainfall was slightly above the average, and the wind was very frequently southerly. The sky was much overcast throughout the month.

MARCH.

This month was cold and dry, with a high barometer. The mean temperature was nearly two degrees below the average. During the last nine days the weather was unusually cold for the end of March, frost occurred on every night, and there was a considerable fall of snow on the 28th, which, with the rainfall on the 31st, rendered the total amount for the month equal to the average

APRIL

In consequence of the great prevalence of easterly wind, the mean temperature of this month was more than a degree below the average. On the 5th there were frequent showers, with lightning and thunder The rainfall was considerably above the average of 1·80 inches. On the night of the 10th the rainfall was continuous, and did not cease until 3 p.m. of the 11th. A solar halo was visible on the 13th and a lunar on the 15th.

MAY.

The mean temperature was about equal to the average, and there was a great prevalence of southerly wind. The month was chiefly remarkable for the great rainfall, which was nearly double the average. The weather was very stormy for the season from 15th to 20th. On the 28th a severe thunderstorm occurred, during which a house was struck and a pony killed near the Observatory. The barometer was again rather low.

JUNE.

During this month the weather was showery until after the 21st, when a great increase of temperature prevailed to the end of the month, which, after the cool, wet weather of the previous month, was most acceptable to the advancing cereal crops. Several thunderstorms visited this district during this last week of hot weather, particularly on the 23rd, 26th and 30th The rainfall slightly exceeded the average and fell more or less on fourteen days

JULY.

Upon the whole this was a fine summer month, with a considerable amount of sunshine and small rainfall The mean temperature was about equal to the average, with a very generally high temperature at night. Thunderstorms visited this district on 3rd, 8th, 21st, 22nd and 23rd.

AUGUST.

This was a very unfavourable time for all harvest operations in this county. The mean temperature was below the average, and there were only seven days throughout the month without more or less of rain, so that the total quantity far exceeded the average. This district was visited by thunderstorms on the 3rd, 6th, 16th, 24th, 29th and 30th. The storm on the 29th was very severe at Brighton and East Grinstead. At the latter place three valuable horses were killed by lightning.

SEPTEMBER.

The first half of this month was fine and dry, but the mean temperature was rather below the average. A thunderstorm occurred on the 8th, which, however, was more severe to the southward. The weather was stormy on the 18th, after the heavy rain on the previous night. The rainfall was considerably below the average. The weather was very favourable for the completion of harvest and hop-picking.

OCTOBER.

The month may be considered to have been seasonable, but stormy at intervals, more particularly on the 7th, 9th, 10th, 22nd and 24th. The gale during the early morning of the 22nd was very severe, but subsided at last very suddenly.˙ Very heavy rain fell during the night of the 25th, otherwise the rainfall for the month would have been much below the average. A slight frost occurred during the night of the 29th.

NOVEMBER.

This was a very gloomy, cold and wet month. The mean temperature was lower than it had been since the year 1851, although there were but few frosts at night. The most remarkable feature was the low temperature during the day, which was doubtless owing to the great prevalence of northerly wind. Lightning was visible to the S.E. on the 1st and 11th.

DECEMBER

Was a very cold month throughout, with continued prevalence of northerly wind. The mean temperature was six degrees below the average. Frost was recorded on 24 nights and was very severe. On many days the temperature remained below the freezing point, at its maximum. The rainfall was about equal to the average, but was rather heavy during the last week. The last day was stormy, with rain, and from 4 to 6 p.m. the wind blew with the force of a hurricane, and increasing temperature.

____

1879.

I T will be apparent, from our subsequent remarks, that this year was in some respects the most remarkable of the current century, and its meteorological history deserves especial record. The small amount of sunshine, the generally humid state of atmosphere, the heavy rains in those particular months when the reverse is so much to be desired, all tended to render this year one of the most disastrous to the agriculturist on record. It is probable that so unkind a year had not been experienced in England since 1816.

Although some months of the year were extremely wet, yet the amount of rainfall for the whole year did not very much exceed the average.

JANUARY.

Although the concluding days of the last month and the commencement of the new year enjoyed a warmer temperature, yet the frost returned with some severity on the 4th of this month and continued uninterruptedly to the end—the mean temperature was below the freezing point and as much as seven and a half degrees below the average of many years. It was the coldest January since 1838. The rainfall exceeded the average, but the greater part (2·05 inches) fell on the 1st and 2nd. On the 11th hard frost had prevailed throughout the day and snow crystals had fallen occasionally. From the 19th to the 31st the temperature was only twice above the freezing point.

FEBRUARY.

The frost continued during the first four days, after which there was a considerable rise in temperature for more than a fortnight. The weather became colder during the last week, with some sharp frosts at night. The mean temperature was more than two degrees below the average. The rainfall was more than double the average, so that by the end of the month the soil was in a very cold and saturated condition. The 10th was a very stormy day, with heavy rain. Snow showers were frequent on 20th and 21st.

It will be seen, therefore, that the winter of 1878-9 was unusually protracted and severe. During the autumn of 1878 indications were not wanting that the ensuing winter would be, as to its general character, much colder than had been experienced for several years. Of these indications the following were more particularly observed· (1) In Ireland, wildfowl of various kinds appeared early, and in quantities far exceeding anything of the kind either on record or in tradition. (2) On the south coast of England, some geese, wild ducks, fieldfares and other winter birds appeared somewhat early. (3) The early disappearance of the swallow and other migratory birds. (4) The squirrel was very actively employed in collecting its winter food. (5) Wasps, although few in number during the summer, became languid at an early period of the autumn and sought the protection of buildings. (6) Many of the more common varieties of small birds congregated in large flocks, in the fields and hedgerows, during the month of November. (7) The fall of the leaf was later than usual, notwithstanding the early frosts. (8) The long continuance of northerly winds during November exceeded every instance of the kind on record.

The winter may be said to have commenced during the last three days of October, when the first decided decrease of temperature was recorded. On the 30th a few flakes of snow were observed to fall and the temperature of the air fell below the freezing point, viz., to 28° and terrestrial radiation to 26°·5.

This period of cold weather was more remarkable for its persistence than its intensity, as the temperature recorded by a thermometer, fully exposed at four feet above the soil, was never lower than 17° 5.

The temperature recorded at Crowborough contrasted very favourably with that reported from places situated at a less elevation above the sea level, and I consider it probable that the frost, on cold nights, was less intense on the heights of Crowborough (796 feet above the level of the sea) than at any other locality in Sussex. This supposition would confirm the now generally acknowledged fact that places situated on the summit of high ground, in the South of England, are less subject to extremes, whether of heat or cold, than those situated several hundred feet lower.

MARCH.

The mean temperature was also below the average, and had there been more sunshine the weather would have been more conformable to the spring season. Frost occurred at intervals; but from the 22nd to 27th, both inclusive, some severity was experienced with frequent snow showers. The rainfall was below the average; in fact, it was the driest month since July, 1876—less than an inch having fallen. The only sunshine, of any continuance, occurred during the first few days, the remainder of the month being very gloomy and cold.

APRIL.

With respect to this month it was, if possible, more ungenial than several of its predecessors. The mean temperature was upwards of five degrees below the average, and as to the rainfall, it was nearly double the usual quantity for this month. On the 12th snow fell to the depth of six and a half inches, which was a larger quantity than had fallen at any time during the past winter. Northerly winds were the most prevalent, so that, by the end of the month, vegetation generally was unusually backward.

MAY.

The mean temperature of this month did not exhibit any improvement, and the record showed a deficiency of nearly seven degrees, and also the fact that it was the coldest May on record. The temperature of the air was below the freezing point on several nights, while on fifteen nights the temperature of radiation indicated unusual severity for the time of year. Cold showers, and occasionally snow, fell very frequently, but not to any great amount until the 28th, when upwards of an inch and a half was registered.

Thus at the close of spring vegetation generally, and more particularly garden and cereal crops, were at least a month or six weeks later than usual, and even at that date* the foliage of the oak, ash and poplar was not fully expanded. The fruit blossom was rendered more safe by the lateness of the season, and promised an abundant crop

JUNE.

The hope entertained that with the first month of summer a period of warmer temperature and more sunshine would ensue met with a grievous disappointment. The mean temperature was about five degrees below the average, and the rainfall considerably in excess. Until the last week there were not three consecutive days without rain, while in too many parts of the country there was not even this temporary cessation. The sky was never free from cloud for a single day, and the weather, altogether, was of a most dreary character.

JULY.

During the first three weeks of this month rain fell more or less upon every day but one. It was a remarkable month even for an English summer. As the mean temperature was six degrees below the average, we can only record that it was a dull, cold, sunless month, inducing most disastrous effects upon every kind of

* June 4th.

THE OLD BRIDGE AT UCKFIELD. TAKEN DOWN, FEBRUARY, 1859.

agricultural and garden produce. The rainfall was again above the average, but there was a cessation of the precipitation from the 22nd to 30th, both inclusive—an interval which had not occurred since March. At the close of the month haymaking in this district had scarcely become general. The cereal crops were in a very unpromising condition.

AUGUST

Was yet another month of low, ungenial temperature and excessive rainfall, and, as regards the latter, it was by far the wettest of the three summer months. The only dry period was from the 9th to the 15th, both inclusive, but this interval was succeeded by thirteen consecutive days of heavy and almost continuous rain. Severe thunderstorms visited this district on the 21st, and to a less extent on the 2nd. The mean temperature did not depart so much from the average as in the two preceding months, but the rainfall exceeded it by more than two inches.

With respect to the general character of the summer I will observe that the mean temperature of June, July and August was as much as five degrees below the average temperature of our summers, and was a cold and most ungenial summer. The nearest approach to it was the summer of 1860. During the ten days ending with August 28th no less a quantity than 5·43 inches of rain fell at Crowborough, and 3·65 inches at Uckfield. This immense fall of rain, in so short a space of time, produced higher floods between Uckfield and Lewes than had ever been remembered at this season of the year.

The following table will show the various conditions of temperature recorded here during the summer :—

1879	June	July	August	During the Summer
Highest temperature in the Shade	68 0	77 0	75 3	77 0
Lowest	40·4	45 0	45·0	40·4
Mean highest	61 8	63 1	65 2	63 3
Mean lowest	48 0	49 5	52 3	49 9
Mean of highest and lowest .	54·9	56 3	58·7	56 6
Mean daily range	13 8	13 6	12 9	13 4
Mean dew point at 9 a m	51·3	52 6	54 9	52·9
Mean highest Solar radiation in vacuo	78 2	78 4	80·2	78·9
Mean lowest upon the surface of grass	44 2	46 5	50 2	46 9
Prevalent winds	S.	S.W.	S W.	S.W.

I will mention that butterflies, as might be expected, were very scarce during the spring and summer months, with the exception of the Clouded Yellow *(Colias Edusa)*, which appeared in great numbers. It has been stated that this variety only puts in a septennial appearance, but I have never been able to confirm this statement. Swallows and especially swifts were fewer, but house martins more numerous than usual.

SEPTEMBER.

During the first week the weather somewhat improved. A more genial temperature obtained, and no rain fell; more than three inches, however, were registered between the 8th and 24th. Very fine weather, and almost cloudless skies, prevailed during the 25th, 26th and 27th. The mean temperature was two degrees and a half below the average The amount of cloud was less than in any other month of this cloudy year.

OCTOBER.

Although the temperature of this month was still below the average, yet there was a great diminution in the amount of rainfall; the month was much drier than usual; in fact, it was the only instance during the previous thirty-six years wherein the total rainfall for October had been less than one inch in depth. The really fine weather during the first fortnight was most enjoyable, but it came too late to be of any essential service in mitigating agricultural distress. Very little frost occurred, notwithstanding that northerly wind was so prevalent.

NOVEMBER.

This was a very cold month and the mean temperature as much as six degrees below the average. Northerly wind was very continuous, with frequent hard frost and some heavy snow, particularly on the 20th, 21st, 25th and 26th. The rainfall was considerably below the average The snow on the 21st had the peculiar character of clinging very closely to evergreen shrubs, whereby many branches were broken or injured. On the 26th some snow crystals were observed.

DECEMBER.

The last month of this remarkable year was characterised by severe frost, and, consequently, by a low mean temperature, which was of the same value as in

L

the corresponding month of 1878. On several nights the temperature fell below 20°, and the mean was seven degrees below the average. The quantity of rain and melted snow did not amount to half the average. During the severe weather on the 1st some beautiful snow crystals fell, but their diameter was less than usual. On the 4th a brilliant solar halo, with two parhelia, was visible soon after noon. The hoar frost on the windows imparted a prismatic appearance to the landscape. The frost was very severe on the morning of the 17th, when the temperature fell to 15°·4.

1880.

JANUARY.

HIS month was very cold, but there was a considerable amount of brilliant sunshine, and very little rain or snow. It was the driest January since 1861. The mean temperature was several degrees below the average, but the frost was not remarkable for any intensity. The coldest morning was the 26th, when the temperature fell to 19°·6, and frost was recorded on every night but five On the 8th a dense fog and rain prevailed throughout the day, and, as the temperature remained below the freezing point, the moisture accumulated to such an extent upon the evergreen shrubs that many branches were in danger of being broken by the mere weight of ice.

FEBRUARY.

The comparatively mild weather of this month was quite a relief from the severity of its predecessor. The mean temperature was two degrees above the average, and very little frost was registered. The greatest cold occurred on the morning of the 2nd, but the temperature only fell to 30° o The 8th was quite a mild day, and distant thunder was heard to the N.W. The weather was very stormy on the 7th, 9th, 19th and 20th The rainfall was more than an inch above the average. The wind was southerly.

MARCH.

This was a remarkably genial month for the season of the year, notwithstanding the great prevalence of N E. wind, and had it not been for the somewhat heavy rains on the 2nd and 31st it would have been one of the driest on record. Not a drop of rain fell between the 7th and 31st A brilliant and highly prismatic meteor was observed towards the N.W about 8 p.m. on the 29th.

APRIL

The weather was, as usual, extremely variable during this month. Showers were frequent during the first fortnight, but the third week was very fine and dry for the most part. During this month, also, the N.E. wind was very prevalent. In reference to shade temperature, there was no frost. The cuckoo was first heard on the 14th, and the nightingale on the 17th The rainfall was as nearly as possible the average quantity.

MAY

This was a remarkably dry month. As usual in these dry seasons there was a great prevalence of N.E. wind, in consequence of which the mean temperature was somewhat below the average. No frost occurred upon the Hill, but we heard of frequent frosts upon the valley, which was very injurious to the fruit blossom. On the 20th dense haze was spread over the landscape and thunder heard at intervals. From the 25th to the close of the month there was a considerable rise of temperature.

JUNE.

The mean temperature was below the average, and the weather generally was rather cool and unseasonable; it improved, however, during the last week. Rain fell more or less on 17 days, but the total for the month did not equal the average. Thunder was heard in this district on the 18th, 24th and 26th.

JULY.

This month was chiefly remarkable for frequent rains, thunderstorms and an unusual prevalence of S.W. wind. The mean temperature was below the average. Thunderstorms (but not of a violent character) occurred on the 10th, 13th, 15th, 17th, 24th and 30th. The storm on the 15th was the most severe; a house was struck at Uckfield and a cow at Warbleton. The rainfall was very heavy during the night of the 25th.

AUGUST.

The sky was, for the most part, much overcast, which, together with an unusual prevalence of N.E. wind, rendered this month very unfavourable for the completion of harvest. The mean temperature was about equal to the average. The highest temperature in the shade was only 76°·2 on the 10th.

SEPTEMBER.

The weather was, for the most part, fine and dry during the first and last ten days, but some heavy rains fell between these periods. More than an inch of rain fell during the night of the 14th, and nearly one inch on the 18th, so that the total considerably exceeded the average.

OCTOBER

Was a very cold and wet month. The mean temperature was more than four degrees below, and the rainfall nearly three inches above, the average. The first two days were comparatively warm, but during the night of the 2nd there was a remarkable decrease of temperature , the difference in the minimum being 18°, as compared with the previous night. On the 9th, after several wet days, a great rainfall occurred in this county, and at Crowborough I recorded the largest daily amount, which, from 9 a.m. of the 8th to 9 a.m. of the 9th, was 2·67 inches ! Had the quantity been recorded from midnight of the 8th to midnight of the 9th it would have exceeded three inches ! Soon after midnight of the 19th a heavy rain commenced, which was followed by a deep snow till near noon of the 20th and its average depth was eight inches. The foliage being still upon the oak trees, large boughs were broken off by the mere weight of snow. Another heavy rain fell on the 26th, when upwards of an inch was recorded. The frost was not severe after the snow on the 21st , the lowest temperature was 27°·6 in the shade and 26°·6 in the open. There was a great prevalence of N.E. wind.

NOVEMBER.

The weather at the commencement of this month was fine and bright, but the north wind was still prevalent. The mean temperature was about equal to the average. A considerable quantity of rain fell during the second week and on the 16th, during a heavy gale from the S.W., the barometer fell, at sea level, to 28·926 inches at 9 a.m. and to 28·807 by 1 p.m. On the 18th there was a great decrease of temperature, followed by heavy rain and snow. During the remainder of the month the weather was extremely variable.

DECEMBER.

The mean temperature was above the average and the weather generally was mild and dry to the 12th, but from that date to the close of the month there were only three days without rain, the total quantity being an inch above the average. Some slight frosts occurred during the latter part of the month.

1881.

JANUARY.

THIS was a very wintry month, the mean temperature was about six degrees below the average, and a greater intensity of frost was recorded than for several years past On the morning of the 22nd the lowest temperature of the air was just nine degrees, or 23° of frost! while the temperature of radiation from short grass was two degrees!

A prominent feature of the severe frost which prevailed
from the 12th to 25th, both inclusive, was the great
difference between the lowest temperature of the air, at
four feet from the ground, and that of terrestrial radiation,
which, during these thirteen days, amounted, upon the
average, to 7°·5. A heavy gale and snowstorm prevailed
during the night of the 17th and following day. The
snow was very fine and penetrated in a remarkable
manner into the roofs of buildings and casements, which
being unsuspected by many persons no precautions were
taken to remove it, so that when the thaw came the
ceilings of upper rooms were much injured thereby. The
average depth of snow was about eight inches, but in
exposed situations it had drifted to the depth of several
feet. Snow crystals fell in considerable quantities on
the 22nd A prismatic solar halo was visible about
1 p.m on the 17th On the 31st there was a brilliant
display of the Aurora Borealis.

FEBRUARY

Was a rather cold, but, upon the whole, a seasonable
month, there were frequent frosts. The last morning
was the coldest, when the temperature fell to 26°·2. The
mean temperature was slightly below the average and
there was a great prevalence of northerly wind. A very
heavy rain fell on the 19th, the quantity registered was
1·28 inches.

MARCH.

The mean temperature was equal to the average,
although, at intervals, there were some sharp frosts at
night. A large quantity of rain fell during the first
week, so that the total for the month exceeded the

average. The weather was fine and pleasant during the third week. Some snow showers fell on the 21st and 22nd, and the latter day was the coldest during the month.

APRIL.

The month was cold and dry, with a continuance of frosty nights and bleak N.E. wind. The mean temperature was nearly four degrees below the average, and the rainfall less than an inch, the average being 1·82 inch. A little snow fell on the 20th, and on the 26th frequent thunder showers with hail. A large solar halo was visible on the 7th, and a lunar on the 12th.

MAY.

The mean temperature was below the average. There were some slight frosts during the first night, on the grass, but the temperature of the air was not below the freezing point at any time. The chief part of the rain fell during the third week, and, upon the whole, the month was dry, with the N E. wind very prevalent. On the 11th a brilliant solar halo was visible from 11 a.m. to 3 p.m.

JUNE

Was a somewhat cold month, and would have been a very dry one but for the heavy rain which fell on the 5th. The mean temperature was more than three degrees below the average, and the night temperature during the second week was very low for the season. On the morning of the 9th, the temperature on the grass fell just below the freezing point, but fortunately without any apparent injury to the potato haulm and other tender vegetables. The weather was more genial during the last fortnight, which very much compensated for the previous cold Some lightning was seen during the night of 17th.

JULY

Was a fine summer month, with a high mean temperature and small rainfall. To the 22nd, rain fell on two days only, and to a very trifling amount; the greater part fell during the last six days. On the 5th the weather was very hot, and during the evening frequent and vivid lightning of a bluish colour was visible to the southward. From the 6th to the 11th there was a decrease of temperature, after which warm weather returned, and continued to the end of the month. The highest temperature in the shade was $91°\cdot5$, on the 15th.

AUGUST.

This was a most unfavourable month for the harvest. The mean temperature was several degrees below the average, and from the 7th to the close of the month there were only four days without rain, which exceeded one inch in depth both on the 12th and 26th. Westerly winds were the most prevalent.

SEPTEMBER.

A considerable amount of rain fell also in this month, and it was very heavy on the 5th and 24th. The mean temperature was below the average; nevertheless, the night temperature was peculiarly high for the season. Northerly winds were frequent, with much haze on several days, particularly on the 16th. Lightning was visible on the 6th and 18th. A parhelion was visible on the 21st.

OCTOBER.

This was a cold month, with occasional frosts at night. The mean temperature was fully six degrees below the average, and there was again a great prevalence of northerly wind. The rainfall was considerably less than usual, but was heavy on the 22nd, when as much as 1·40 inches fell. Heavy gale on the 14th, but very little rain fell.

NOVEMBER

Was warmer than the previous month, and about four degrees above the average. A considerable quantity of rain fell, particularly on the 26th. In addition to the gale on the 16th very severe gales occurred on the 22nd, 26th and 27th. At 2 a.m of the latter date a terrific squall occurred, with torrents of rain and hail, which continued, with varying force, all that day and night.

DECEMBER.

The mean temperature was about equal to the average. Nevertheless, there was much cold weather at intervals, with frequent, but not severe, frosts The rainfall exceeded the average. A considerable amount of snow fell on the 9th and 10th, which attached itself in large masses to the evergreen shrubs. The weather was stormy on the 17th and 20th On several days, both at sunrise and sunset, the brilliant tints upon the neighbouring clouds were very remarkable. From the 20th to the close of the month the atmosphere was very gloomy, but dry.

1882.

JANUARY.

HE temperature of this month was mild, and the mean above the average. The wind was very equally distributed. The rainfall was much below the average, and the month may be considered to have been very dry, as it rained only once from the 10th to the end of the month. The heaviest rain was on the 8th, which had been preceded by a bright parhelion in the morning, and on the next day I noticed many primroses in bloom. The latter part of the month was dry and pleasant The marked feature of the month was the very high readings of the barometer, which for the four consecutive days, viz., January 16th to 19th, inclusive, were the highest of which we have any reliable record. The following·are readings taken by me at 9 a.m. on each of these days :—

1882.	Height of Barometer.
January 16 ⋯ . ⋯ ⋯ .	30·838 inches.
,, 17 ⋯ ⋯ ⋯	30 943 ,,
,, 18 ⋯ ⋯ ⋯	30·967 ,,
,, 19 . ⋯ ⋯	30·926 ,,

During the second week the following spring flowers were in bloom—such as the polyanthus, auricula, Devonshire cowslip, daisy, heartsease, &c. Thrushes were in full song on the 11th.

FEBRUARY.

This month was also mild, and the mean temperature nearly three degrees above the average, while the rainfall was rather less, the greater part of which fell during the last five days. The wind was for the most part southerly. The second week was particularly mild and pleasant, when I observed the following plants in bloom, viz.: Primrose, snowdrop, crocus, wallflower, nettle, mezereon, wild strawberry, water ranunculus (var. contortus), anemone, dandelion, celandine, ivy-leaved speedwell, hazel, dog's mercury; and on the 28th the cuckoo flower and greater stitchwort. The honey bee was busy on the 12th. Toad spawn was seen on the 14th, when sparrows' and starlings' nests were commenced

The following butterflies also appeared: Gonepteryx Rhamni and Pontia Brassicæ on the 16th; Venessa Io and Vanessa Urticæ on the 20th.

MARCH.

Instead of this month being unseasonably cold, after the mild winter, its general character was that of continued mildness, a high mean temperature and a small rainfall. The only heavy rain fell during the night of the 25th. Snow showers occurred on the 21st and 22nd. A prismatic solar halo was visible for some time on the 20th.

As an instance of the mildness of the season I will mention that I saw a gooseberry tree in full leaf on the 13th, and on the 17th several varieties of butterflies. The wind was chiefly westerly.

APRIL.

The mean temperature was about equal to the average, while during the first half of the month the weather was fine and pleasant, notwithstanding an easterly wind The rainfall was above the average, in consequence of the heavy rain on the 13th and showery weather during the last ten days. On the evening of the 28th I noticed some large masses of composite cloud, to the eastward, at sunset, tinted a peculiar rose colour, indicative of the approaching gale, which was very severe during the afternoon of the 29th. There was scarcely a trace of frost throughout the month, and vegetation advanced rapidly.

MAY.

The mean temperature was also about the average of many years, and the month generally was warm and pleasant, with very little rain, and the total quantity for the month was scarcely equal to half the average A lunar halo was visible on the 3rd and some electrical disturbance was noticed in this district on the 22nd. The weather was rather stormy and wet on the 25th, after which it became finer to the end of the month.

JUNE.

It was a dripping month, and rain fell more or less on 19 days, but we should remember that —

> "A dripping June
> Keeps all things in tune,"

and finally the total amount was not quite equal to the average The mean temperature was about three degrees below the average, and upon the whole the weather was rather cold at night. At 10 p.m. on the 1st a large lunar halo was visible, exhibiting a mock moon with prismatic colours on the western side—a rare phenomenon! On the 7th a sharp hail storm, while thunder showers were passing to the north of the Observatory. The month closed with gloomy, sultry weather, and much haze over the landscape.

JULY.

This month was cold, gloomy and wet. The mean temperature was upwards of three degrees below the average, while the rainfall was more than double the usual amount, and fell more or less on 20 days, 14 of which were consecutive. The S.W. wind was very constant. The 5th and 6th were stormy, with heavy rain, and just one inch was recorded for the two days. During the evenings of the 13th and 15th some very peculiar salmon-coloured clouds surrounded the sun They had a very brilliant appearance, while some rosy tints lit up a large bank of clouds, extending horizontally to the eastward. After sunset there was a peculiar pink glow upon some clouds over the Channel.

AUGUST.

During the first fortnight the weather was very fine, dry and pleasant, notwithstanding a considerable prevalence of northerly wind. The latter half of the month was more cool and showery, with a great prevalence of westerly wind and a low barometer. The mean temperature was nearly three degrees below, and the rainfall not equal to, the average. It was an unfavourable time for the completion of harvest and the commencement of hop-picking.

SEPTEMBER.

With the exception of the 1st, 5th and 11th, when some heavy showers fell, the weather was tolerably fine to the 18th, when some heavy rain came during the night. The mean temperature was below the average, but the rainfall was somewhat in excess. A sudden decrease of temperature occurred on the 14th, and thunderstorms were visible in the distance. On the 21st, at noon, a very low rainbow appeared in the north, its upper concavity appeared to be almost lying upon the ground. On the 28th a heavy rain fell during the night

OCTOBER.

The mean temperature of this month was about equal to the average. The chief feature was the very heavy rainfall. A parhelion was visible during the afternoon of the 23rd, and a bright rainbow to the eastward A heavy gale occurred on the 24th, and about 10.15 a.m. it blew a hurricane for a few minutes. On the 26th a rainbow at noon. The last day was very fine and pleasant for the season.

On the second evening of the month there was such a very brilliant display of the Aurora Borealis as can seldom be witnessed in our latitude. The following are some details of its appearance, and that its magnitude and the area over which it was seen was very unusual is proved by the fact that it was seen, not only over the United Kingdom and Southern Europe, but also over the continent of Australia. On the evening of Oct 2, as I was walking home, about 6h. 45m., my attention was drawn to a pink auroral glow extending from the western horizon upwards between Arcturus and Ursa Major. A somewhat interrupted auroral arch was visible from the north-eastern horizon, a little to the east of Capella, to past Arcturus on the west. At this time there was an extraordinary appearance to the south of my position. It consisted of detached patches or clouds of magnetic (phosphorescent-looking) light, nearly equi-distant, and stretching across the entire sky from the S.W. horizon to a point a little north of east (probably E.N.E.). The five principal clouds were in the constellations Hercules, Aquila, Pegasus, Aries and Taurus, but there appeared to be others stretching away upon the horizon, on either side, as far as the eye could reach. The general appearance resembled the repeated images of a chandelier in a room with opposite pier glasses. These magnetic clouds did *not* shift their position, but gradually faded away, the one nearest to my meridian disappearing first. Turning again to the northwards, there were some tall streamers extending from the N.W. horizon nearly to the zenith. At 8h. 45m. the auroral arch in N.N.W. horizon was very clearly defined. It had its greatest convexity immediately beneath Ursa Major, and extended along the horizon, as measured by a theodolite, exactly 90°. Small streamers for some time afterwards very frequently arose from the arch towards Ursa Major, and particularly in the direction of the "pointers." At 9h. 15m. brilliant streamers appeared along the entire length of the arch, and there were also some patches of auroral light here and there, which were continually shifting one after another, but always to the westward. At 9h. 17m. a cumuloid cloud passed very nearly along the line of greatest brilliancy, and presented a striking contrast, every undulation of the cloud being distinctly visible. By this time the arch had extended about 10° further to the westward. At 9h. 20m. streamers increased in brilliancy, numbers and length, and presented a very grand and imposing scene contrasted with the dark sky. At 9h. 25m. the moon was rising, and the eastern termination of the arch had become much less bright, but the brightness increased to the westward. At 9h. 30m. the hitherto well-defined arch was very much broken up, and a few minutes afterwards there was only a diffused light to the westward. At 9h. 45m. the phenomenon had almost disappeared.

NOVEMBER.

This was another wet month, but with a mean temperature about equal to the average; nevertheless there were some rather sharp frosts during the third week, with some snow, or sleet, at intervals. The rainfall was nearly an inch above the average, and the mean reading of the barometer was low. The weather was very stormy, amounting to a gale, on the 2nd. Rain fell more or less on twenty days, and the amount which was registered from Oct. 19th to Nov. 7th, both inclusive, was 8·10 inches ! Another display of the Aurora Borealis occurred on the 17th.

DECEMBER.

The first part of this month was cold, with sharp frosts every night during the first fortnight. Some snow fell on the 6th and 7th and rather heavily on the latter day. The rainfall was somewhat above the average. Several nights were very clear and the atmosphere in a most favourable condition for astronomical observations. The last day of the month and year was exceedingly damp,

M

dark and gloomy, but unusually mild for the season
Showers fell at intervals and were more decidedly continuous after 10 p.m.

1883.

JANUARY

AS mild, with frequent fluctuations of temperature and sudden variations in the direction of the wind. Rain fell more or less on
17 days, but on no occasion was the amount
large. Some snow fell on the 9th and again
on the 24th, during a gale from the S.E.
A strong gale was also prevalent on the 28th and 29th,
which continued almost uninterruptedly on the latter day.

FEBRUARY

Was very mild also and scarcely any frost occurred. The
morning of the 17th was the coldest, but even then the
lowest temperature was not more than two degrees below
the freezing point. A great quantity of rain fell during
the first three weeks, so that the total for the month considerably exceeded the average. The wind varied very
much between S.E. and W. Gales were rather frequent,
especially on the 1st, 9th and 10th

MARCH

Was the coldest month of the year, as often happens
when the two or three winter months have been milder
than usual. The mean temperature was nearly six
degrees below the average and therefore the coldest since

March, 1865 The frost was severe during the second week, accompanied by keen northerly winds and frequent slight falls of snow. The rainfall was very much below the average.

APRIL.

The mean temperature was a little above the average, but the usual fluctuations peculiar to this month were not wanting There were, however, only four frosty nights and the greatest cold was 28°·8 on the morning of the 24th It was a remarkably dry month and the first seventeen days passed away without a shower. A rather heavy fall of snow occurred on the 23rd, which, however, soon melted under the increasing heat of the sun's rays. This snow lay very heavily upon evergreen shrubs, some of which received injury from its weight.

MAY.

Although there were some frosty nights during the first week, yet the mean temperature of the month was about equal to the average. After the 12th the night temperature was much warmer, and vegetation advanced very rapidly. There was, however, a frequent prevalence of northerly wind. The rainfall was rather above the average, and very heavy on the 11th during the passage of some thunder showers. During the latter part of the month there was brilliant sunshine on several days.

JUNE.

The temperature of this month was slightly above the average of the last few years, but there was very little real summer weather throughout the month. During the first fortnight there was a great prevalence of N E wind, and (with the exception of the rain during a thunderstorm on the 9th) an entire absence of rain. This storm was very heavy to the N.W. of this Hill, where many hop gardens and general foliage received serious damage from the fall of very large hailstones.

JULY.

This was a very dull and showery month, rain falling more or less on eighteen days, nevertheless, the total fall did not equal the average amount The mean height of the barometer was the lowest for the year. Westerly winds were the most prevalent.

AUGUST.

This was the hottest month of the year, and the mean temperature was above the average of the other summer months. Many days were characterized by cloudless skies and brilliant sunshine. The harvest progressed very satisfactorily. The atmospheric pressure was, upon the whole, very equable, and the mean was above the average. The first half of the month was showery, but the total rainfall was much below the average.

SEPTEMBER.

The mean temperature of this month was also somewhat above the average. There were a few fine days, but the month was, upon the whole, dull and showery. The total rainfall was considerably above the average. A rather severe gale occurred on the 2nd, with a considerable fall of the barometer, which was the only occasion throughout the year when the reduced reading at 9 a.m. was below 29·000 inches; viz., 28·907.

OCTOBER

The mean temperature was about equal to, and the rainfall considerably less than, the average, although the wind was, for the most part, westerly. The month passed without any frost or any particular gale.

NOVEMBER

The mean temperature was about equal to the average, but the rainfall was considerably in excess. The reading of the barometer was low on the 6th and 25th. On the latter occasion the weather was stormy with much lightning and thunder at midnight, accompanied by heavy rain and hail. The westerly winds were again very prevalent, but variable. Slight frosts occurred during the second week.

DECEMBER

With the exception of some rather sharp frosts near the beginning of this month, the weather was very mild throughout, accompanied by great atmospheric pressure, particularly during the last week. A somewhat heavy snowstorm occurred on the 6th, which was almost the only snow shower during the winter of 1883-4. A very dense fog prevailed both day and night during the last week, which appears to have been general over the S. and S.E of England. The rainfall was much below the average, which is somewhat unusual when the month is characterized by mild weather

THE PHENOMENAL SUNSETS, &c.

1883.

The beautiful phenomena which were observed during the last few months of 1883 over the greater part of the world, in connection with sunrise and sunset, may be regarded, I think, as almost unique so far as our records extend, and more particularly in their long continuance. Readers of our various scientific periodicals must have become acquainted with several theories which have been advanced respecting their origin. The primary idea appears to have been that they were the result of the great volcanic eruption at Krakatao, on which occasion an enormous amount of volcanic dust was forced up, retained in, and floated about, the higher strata of the atmosphere. I could never entirely accept this theory; but at the same time I do not hold the great eruption at Krakatao and other places by any means unconnected with these phenomena, especially if it should be conceded that these dust particles constituted a nucleus around which frozen aqueous vapour was collected. From the vast amount of terrestrial displacement occurrent, and the equally vast amount of sea water which rushed into the chasm, an inconceivable quantity of steam, charged with the various saline ingredients of which sea water is composed, was forced up to an extraordinary height, where, on account of a low temperature, it became suddenly crystallised. These saline particles would naturally crystallise into their respective normal forms, and exhibit the various colours due to the refractive indices of their components. The colours assumed by the layers of cloud nearest the earth would doubtless originate from the refraction of those coloured ice particles situated in the upper atmosphere, which latter would, of course, not be visible to any one observer, unless, at his station, the emergent refracted ray reached his eye. Hence the time would be accounted for which elapsed between what would be considered an unusually fine sunset and the after-glow.

From my exceptionally good position for observing the various phases of these very interesting phenomena, I watched, with care and attention, their frequent appearance and disappearance upon the occasions of the more brilliant displays in the months of November, December and January.

I usually noticed that at the approach of these phenomena an extremely faint violet-tinted semi-circle, or bow, of four or five degrees in diameter, appeared above, and on either side of the sun, which tint would last, as a rule, not more than two or three minutes, when there was a change to a greenish hue, which continued about the same time ; this was succeeded by an orange tint. Subsequently, and at an uncertain interval, the lower portion of this orange-tinted stratum assumed a red tint which was much more persistent, and finally this red stratum, together with the remaining portion or the orange, became of a very deep red, and sometimes even of a scarlet colour, producing that splendid glow along the horizon which extended many degrees both to the east and west of the point of sunset. On one occasion it extended just 90° on either side ; I allude particularly to the evening of December 23rd.

The question arises why these phenomena were not *constantly* visible ? I should consider that their visibility much depended upon the incident and reflected rays not being interrupted to any one observer, and as the angles between these would be very considerable, the phenomena would be seen at a very considerable height above the surface of the earth, or not at all. Extensive areas of cloud, so common during the winter season, would, of course, be a frequent cause of interruption. The hypothesis that the crystallization of saline particles is an important factor in the production of these phenomena is supported, I think, by the record of the displays having been at their greatest brilliancy in cold weather, as exemplified, in a remarkable manner, during the first week of December.

For several weeks past I have frequently noticed that the upper layer of a composite cloud has been tinged of a very light salmon, or copper colour, irrespective of any particular cloud formation, and I have noticed, further, that when there has been no well-defined cloud in the neighbourhood of the sun, the latter has been surrounded by a haze of aqueous vapour, of a similar tint, which has extended three or four degrees from the limb. One of the grandest sunsets occurred here on the evening of January 16th, 1884. On the morning of that day a dense fog rested on Crowborough Hill, but shortly before noon the fog sank somewhat, from its summit, but still enveloped the surrounding country, the Observatory alone being above it. Just upon sunset the usual violet tint became visible near the sun, and a pinkish haze above, which extended nearly to the zenith—a sure commencement of a brilliant display. Upon the horizon, and for about three degrees above it, the sky soon assumed a decidedly green colour which very shortly changed to a brilliant scarlet band, which extended from the S.E. to the W.N.W. points on the horizon. The whole district of the country below me was thus enveloped in fog, the upper surface of which was heaped up into irregular and undulating masses. By degrees, this surface situated to the S.W. of my position became lit up with a beautiful pink colour, by reflection from the intensely red glow upon the horizon, which being interrupted here and there by the fog undulations, these latter had the appearance of huge rocks arising from a blood-stained sea—the scene was magnificent.

In conclusion I will mention that on the morning of August 27th, near sunrise, I noticed a precisely similar phenomenon as regards the various tints, and their relative positions, as I did on so many mornings during the winter months, which strengthens my belief in the supposition that aqueous vapour, under exceptional conditions, was chiefly concerned in the production of these wonderful phenomena.

1884.

JANUARY

THE winter of 1883-84 was very mild and its mean temperature was 2° 2 above the average of the previous eleven years. During the whole of this month frost was recorded only four times and on one occasion only to the amount of four degrees. The rainfall was above the average and the greater part fell during the last week. On the evening of the 25th frequent lightning was visible here and this was followed by a strong gale and heavy rain throughout the night. There was a slight sprinkling of snow on the morning of the 27th and one degree of frost.

FEBRUARY

Was also a mild winter month. The temperature was nearly two degrees above the average. Frost was registered on five nights only and the lowest reading was on the last morning. The rainfall was less than the average. Southerly winds were the most frequent. Very stormy weather prevailed on the 11th, accompanied by thunder and heavy hail. About 2 p.m. on this day the darkness was very unusual for a short time.

MARCH.

This was a very pleasant spring month, although northerly winds were somewhat prevalent. The temperature was two and a half degrees above the average and the total rainfall slightly in excess, owing to a very heavy rain during the night of the third, which amounted to nearly one inch and a quarter. Several days were almost cloudless, with a very genial warmth. On the 18th the temperature in the rays of the sun was 77°. On the 25th some sleet and hail showers fell in the neighbourhood and a slight frost occurred at night.

APRIL.

This was a comparatively cold month and the temperature more than a degree below the average. N E. winds were very prevalent and on several nights during the fourth week there were some sharp frosts. Rain fell more or less on fourteen days, but in small quantities, and the total for the month was half-an-inch less than the average

MAY.

This was a very fine and pleasant month. The mean temperature was considerably above the average and there was an entire absence of frost. The rainfall was not an eighth part of the average, although it fell more or less on seven days. None whatever fell between the 17th and the 3rd of June. The amount of cloud was much less than the average. Some vivid lightning was visible in the S.E. during the evening of the 12th

JUNE

Was another fine and pleasant month, although the mean temperature scarcely equalled the average. Rain fell more or less on ten days and in consequence of some heavy showers during the first week the total for the month slightly exceeded the average. The wind was again chiefly from the northward, but very slight in force. Thunder was heard on the 7th and 29th.

JULY.

This was a very fine summer month, without any excessive heat or oppressive condition of the atmosphere either in the sun or in the shade. The mean temperature was two degrees above the average. The highest temperature in the shade was 80° 2, which is relatively low for the time of year Rain fell on 15 days, but the several amounts were trifling with the exception of that on the 24th, which was nearly half-an-inch. Lightning was seen on the 4th and 24th and on 25th a thunderstorm was visible to the southward Winds were for the most part westerly.

AUGUST.

This was the warmest and most agreeable summer month which has been experienced in the South of England for several years. The number of almost cloudless days was very remarkable. The average amount of cloud at 9 a m. was only 3 6 (0·10) and the mean temperature was nearly five degrees above the average of the previous eleven years. The highest temperature in the shade was 88°·9 on the 11th and in the open air 95°·2 on the 8th. Solar radiation in vacuo reached 106°·6 on the same day, while a thermometer with a black bulb contrivance rose to 148°·5. The total fall for the month would have been very small but for some heavy showers which fell on the 27th. The 25th was a very remarkable day. The morning had been warm and even sultry and the temperature in the shade reached 78°·7. About 2 p.m. the sky became suddenly densely overcast and at 3 p.m. the darkness was so great that ordinary print could only be read close to a window. The wind was blowing strongly from the N.W. The reduction of temperature was very great: thus, at 2 p.m. on the 24th it was 87° and at the same hour on this day only 53°.

SEPTEMBER.

This was also a warm and pleasant month. The mean temperature was between three and four degrees above the average. On several days the heat was registered 70° and upwards in the shade, and 80° and upwards in the open air. The 17th was the hottest day. The rainfall was nearly an inch above the average of many years, a very welcome quantity after so long a drought. I believe it was the South of England only which came in for this rain, and that the drought continued in the North for some time longer. At Crowborough no less than 3 35 inches fell during the four days, 2 06 inches of which fell on the 3rd Throughout the month the night temperature was remarkably high for the season. Barnard's comet was visible here on the evening of the 23rd.

OCTOBER.

The mean temperature of this month was very close upon the average. So late as the 16th the temperature in the shade rose to 63°, and to 77° in the sun's rays. Although the night temperature was below the average, yet there was an almost entire absence of frost. The prevalent winds were from N W. to N.E. The rainfall was about a quarter of the average of many years, although it fell more or less on fourteen days. The 10th was the coldest day, and some slight snow showers fell between three and four o'clock in the afternoon. I saw Wolfe's comet for the first time during the eclipse of the moon on the 4th. It was not by any means a conspicuous object, even in a telescope of seven inches aperture, and was of course never visible to the naked eye.

NOVEMBER.

The mean temperature was rather more than one degree below the average, and some rather sharp frosts occurred during the fourth week, with some snow on 21st and 30th. The drought, which may be said to have recurred from the second week in September, continued to the last day of this month. The total fall of rain and melted snow was two-thirds less than the average, and fell on six days only. The most prevalent winds were from N. and E. A brilliant solar halo with parhelion was observed during the morning of the 30th, followed by some heavy showers of snow and sleet during the evening and night.

DECEMBER.

With the last day of November the long drought, which had prevailed in England since March 10th, may be considered to have ended with the continuous rains which fell during the first three weeks of this month. In the South of England the underground springs began now to rise, and water was no longer a scarcity. The mean temperature was rather more than one degree above the average. The winds were for the most part westerly, and gales moderate. The rainfall was an inch and a half above the average. Vivid lightning was visible throughout the night of the 18th, and distant thunder was heard occasionally.

1885.

JANUARY.

THIS was the coldest January during the previous four years, and the mean temperature was nearly three degrees below the average of eleven years. Although frost occurred on twenty-five nights, yet it was never very severe. The coldest morning was the 21st, when the temperature of the air fell to 21°, and on the grass to 16°·2, which proved to be the lowest temperature during the entire winter. Some snow fell during the third week, but a much larger quantity fell to the eastward of the Hill and remained a long time. The total quantity of rain and snow did not amount to the average. The barometer was frequently low for the time of year, more particularly on the 11th. Lightning was seen at intervals during the evening of the 31st.

FEBRUARY.

This was a very mild month ; the temperature higher than in any February since 1877, and nearly two and a half degrees above the average of twelve years. The only cold weather occurred during the third week, when the temperature fell to 24° on the morning of the 21st. The rainfall was nearly two inches above the average of fifteen years The wind was, for the most part, southerly, and frequently stormy, more particularly on the 2nd, 6th, 15th and 16th. Some lightning and thunder in this district on the morning of the 2nd, during the gale. Beautifully tinted clouds were frequently observed near the western horizon after sunset on several occasions.

MARCH.

The temperature of this month was nearly one degree below the average, as well as altogether colder than the preceding month. The unusually long prevalence of north-easterly winds, which commenced on the 6th of this month, was a marked feature throughout the year. Slight frosts occurred on twenty nights, but the lowest temperature was only 26°·9 on the morning of the 10th. A considerable quantity of snow fell during the night of the 21st. The amount of rain and melted snow was rather below the average, and the several showers fell on nine days only.

APRIL

Although the mean temperature of this month was somewhat above the average of the last fifteen years, yet it was not by any means a genial spring month. The north-easterly winds were almost as prevalent as they were in March, and they were accompanied by frequent frosts at night during the first half of the month. The warmest period was during the third week, which was dry and pleasant. The rainfall was one inch below the average, and, as in the preceding month, fell on nine days only. On the morning of the 20th the air was remarkably dry, the temperature of the dew point being 22°·2 below it—viz., dry bulb 63°, wet bulb 51°. After the shower on the 28th, vegetation advanced more rapidly.

MAY.

The mean temperature of this month was nearly three degrees below the average, although the north-easterly winds had given way to those from the westward. During the first three weeks the night temperature was cold and ungenial to the advancing vegetation, while occasionally a slight frost occurred. Upon the whole, the spring was a *late one*, and the daily highest temperature was scarcely equal to the average until the last nine days. The rainfall was above the average, and fell more or less on seventeen days. On the evening of the 27th a bright lunar halo was visible.

JUNE.

The mean temperature was more than one degree above the average of twelve years, nevertheless there was again an unusual prevalence of north-easterly winds during one half of the month. The long summer drought now commenced, and on many days the dryness of the air was remarkable, particularly on the 13th and 24th The amount of rainfall was only one-third of the average of fifteen years, and fell on nine days in small amounts Some lightning and thunder occurred on the 6th, during the night.

JULY.

This was a brilliant summer month without any extreme heat or oppressive sultriness of the atmosphere, any tendency to which was subdued by the general prevalence of north-easterly winds and frequent cloudless skies, the amount of cloud for the month having been 4 9 (o 10). On one day only did the exposed self-registering thermometer indicate a temperature of 90°, while the highest in the shade was 84°·1. The lowest temperature occurred on the morning of the 1st, 43°·2. The rainfall was even more deficient than in the preceding month, and amounted to less than a sixth of the average, so that near the close of the month vegetation had suffered considerably, while the supply of water for general purposes had become very scanty.

AUGUST.

This, the third summer month, was also remarkable for the drought which commenced and had continued, with scarcely any interruption, since the end of May. The mean temperature was nearly two degrees less than July, and, like that month, was not remarkable for intensity Throughout the entire month the temperature in the shade exceeded 76° on two days only, while the highest registered by the exposed thermometer was

N

86° on the 17th. The rainfall was not a sixth of the average. As might be expected, the air throughout the month was very dry, and the average daily temperature of the dew point was ten degrees below it. A remarkable instance of this dryness of the air occurred about 1 30 p.m. on the 17th, when the dry bulb reading was 76° and the wet bulb 60°! The temperature of the dew point would, therefore, be 27°·4 below that of the surrounding air, in the shade.

SEPTEMBER.

Although the mean temperature of this month was below the average, yet its general character was that of a continuance of summer, notwithstanding the frequent days of rainfall. On thirteen days the temperature of the air was upwards of seventy degrees, while the night temperature was high for the season. The long summer drought came to an end on the second day and, with three exceptions, rain fell more or less on the fifteen succeeding days—the large amount of nearly one inch and a quarter on the 16th—and the total quantity for the month exceeded the average by one inch and a half. On the second, soon after sunset, some very curious beams of a reddish colour, about three degrees wide, ascended several degrees above the horizon near the point of sunset, while the interspaces were of a bright green colour.

OCTOBER.

This month was both cold and wet, although there was scarcely any absolute frost. The mean temperature was three degrees below and the rainfall somewhat above the average. A somewhat heavy gale occurred on the evening of the 2nd and the weather was stormy on the 4th and 6th   A very peculiar haze was present during the afternoon of the 18th, so that at 3 p.m. the sun did not shine more brightly than the moon at full. An exceedingly dense haze was again prevalent during the afternoon of the 29th.

NOVEMBER

The mean temperature of this month was somewhat above the average. Slight frosts occurred during the third week, otherwise the weather was, upon the whole, mild, seasonable and dry, until the last week, when a large amount of rain fell; nevertheless, the total amount did not equal the average of the last fifteen years. The sky was much covered by cloud and the winds were very fairly distributed, the N.E. having been the most prevalent   The month was tolerably free from any stormy weather until the last three days. A heavy gale occurred on the morning of the 28th for several hours.

DECEMBER.

The mean temperature was slightly above the average and tolerably uniform throughout. The only cold weather occurred during the second week, and on the morning of the 11th the greatest cold during the year was registered, viz., $19°\cdot5$ in the open air and $21°\cdot8$ in the shade   The winds were again very equally distributed, with an almost entire absence of stormy weather. Some snow fell on the 9th and 29th. The rainfall was two inches below the average, although it fell more or less on eleven days. Parhelia visible at 9 a.m. on 29th   The year ended with dark, gloomy weather.

N 2

1886.

JANUARY.

HE long frost commenced here on the 6th, on which day the highest temperature in the shade was only 32°, and heavy snow had fallen during the previous night to the depth of seven inches. This particular fall of snow clung very tenaciously to the evergreen shrubs and trees, to the great injury of many of them.

The sharp frost on the night of the 11th, after some rainfall during the day, rendered the roads on the 12th more coated with firm ice than I had observed for many years past, so that throughout the day walking or driving was almost impossible, except upon quite level ground. On the 20th severe hoar frost coated evergreen shrubs with unusually long spicules of rime. On the 21st snow fell here to the depth of about two inches and was succeeded by sharp frost at night. From this date there was a steady continuance of frost to the last day of the month, when the weather became stormy and wet. Although the frost during this month was so continuous, yet it was never remarkable for that intensity which we have recorded in some previous cold winters.

FEBRUARY.

Its mean temperature had not been so low and the frost so persistent since the year 1855, which was one of the coldest Februaries on record. It was the coldest month of the winter and frost was recorded for every night but three. During the latter half of the month the wind prevailed steadily from the N.E., without changing its direction for a single day. With respect to the lowest actual temperature, the Hill maintained its usual moderate condition. The coldest night was the 8th, when the temperature fell to 23°·2, or rather less than nine degrees of frost. The highest day temperature was 46°·2 on the 2nd.

The amount of rainfall and melted snow was very small in this district, although it fell more or less on nine days.

MARCH.

After the termination of our appointed winter months, however, the frost rather increased than abated, while its persistence and unseasonable severity, during the first eighteen days, were very remarkable and certainly unprecedented for many years. On two occasions during these eighteen days the cold was greater than in February, especially during the nights of the 6th and 15th.

The change to milder temperature, with some rainfall, came rather suddenly on the 19th and the frost was at an end.

During the last twelve days the weather became very mild and a considerable quantity of rain fell. The 30th was a very stormy day and the wind increased to a gale during the afternoon and evening. The mean temperature of the entire month was three degrees below the average.

APRIL.

An agreeable change of temperature occurred during this month, although the mean did not exceed the average. The 10th was the only day which could be considered cold for the season, and this was followed by a fall of snow on the 11th. The remainder of the month was fine, with very little rain.

MAY.

During the first ten days the weather was fine, without any rain, and on five days the sky was almost cloudless. This fine weather terminated with the very heavy rainfall on the 12th, and the remainder of the month was rather gloomy, with frequent heavy rain, particularly from the 20th to 27th, both inclusive. The total fall was double the average, but this was in great measure due to the large quantity which fell on the 12th. The mean temperature was rather above the average.

JUNE.

Although the mean temperature was so nearly the average, yet it was by no means a pleasant summer month, the weather being often gloomy and cold. It was, however, a very dry month, the rainfall being less than half the average of a long series of years. The N.E. wind was the most prevalent.

JULY

The mean temperature was below the average and, with the exception of the first week, the weather was upon the whole cool and ungenial for the time of year. The rainfall was above the average and the greater part fell during the second and fourth weeks A heavy thunderstorm visited this district on the last day, when the lightning struck a house at Mayfield, inflicting a considerable amount of damage. A brilliant prismatic solar halo was seen in this neighbourhood on the 20th.

AUGUST

The mean temperature was somewhat below the average and the rainfall also, although it fell more or less on thirteen days. The readings of the barometer were very steady, with but little fluctuation, and their mean somewhat above the average. The warmest weather occurred during the last week, when the night temperature was particularly high for the time of year. Some lightning was visible during the evening of the 23rd.

SEPTEMBER.

The first few days were very warm and summerlike, the highest temperature in the shade on the 1st was as high as 83°, and even on the 14th it was upwards of 80°. Upon the whole the weather was very agreeable throughout the month, and the atmosphere very calm until the 27th, when we had a moderate gale from the S W. Considerable electrical disturbance occurred here on the 3rd and 4th. The N E. wind was the most frequent, particularly at the period of the equinox. The mean temperature was two degrees above the average and as to the rainfall it was less than half the average quantity.

OCTOBER.

The mean temperature was upwards of three degrees above the average   The high daily temperature during the first week was very remarkable and exceeded the average for June. It was the warmest October which has been experienced in the South of England since the year 1865   The highest temperature in the shade was 73° 7 on the 4th, and on the 1st and 5th it was upwards of 70°. The temperature of the sun's rays (ther. in vacuo) during the first six days varied between 80°·2 and 89°·1. The night temperature was also high and the entire month passed away without the slightest trace of frost upon this Hill. Northerly winds were almost absent and the most prevalent were from the S.E. The rainfall was below the average, although rain fell more or less on 21 days. S.W. gales occurred on the 12th and 15th. Frequent lightning was visible to the westward on 19th and 20th.

NOVEMBER

Was also a mild month and the mean temperature a little above the average. Slight frosts occurred on the 8th and 19th, but upon the whole the temperature was very uniform and seasonable. A large quantity of rain fell during the first 16 days and the total for the month exceeded the average. Westerly winds were the most prevalent.

DECEMBER.

The mean temperature was rather more than two degrees below the average and the month, altogether, was very cold and rainy. Frost occurred on every night but six and rain fell more or less on 23 days, so that the total quantity for the month was nearly double the average. On the 5th a very fine prismatic solar halo (A B C) was visible here at 10.20 a.m. for about twenty minutes. The mock suns at D and E, as well as the inverted segment of a secondary halo, were brilliantly prismatic. The most remarkable portion of the phenomenon was the small diameter (six degrees) of the segment H I K, while the diameter of the primary was exactly 45°. A gale from S.W. occurred during the evening and night of the 6th and again during the night of the 7th and early morning of the 8th. At 9 p.m. on the latter day the reading of my barometer was lower than I had ever previously observed, viz., 28·400 inches at sea level.

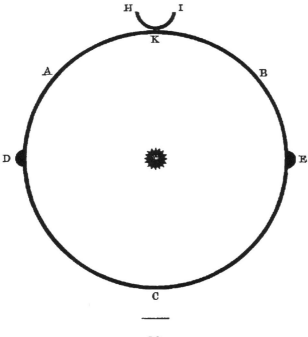

1887.

JANUARY.

ITH the exception of the first two days of the New Year the weather was very cold and gloomy, and the temperature of the entire month was 2°·5 below the average of many years. After a fall of snow on the 17th the wind veered suddenly to the southward, which induced a considerable rise of temperature, and this continued for the most part during the remainder of the month. The rainfall was slightly below the average, but the chief part of the precipitation consisted of the snow which fell during the first fortnight. Gales occurred on the 3rd and 11th from the S.E. A fine prismatic corona surrounded the moon on the night of the 8th, and a solar halo was visible during the afternoon of the 14th.

FEBRUARY.

The mean temperature of this month was very slightly below the average. Many days were warm and pleasant, more particularly during the last week, but there were some rather sharp frosts during the second and third weeks, which considerably reduced the mean monthly temperature. The month was very dry and the total rainfall less than half the average. A gale was prevalent on the 3rd, during which the barometer continued rising, and on the morning of the 4th its reading was as high as 30 387 inches. A fine lunar halo was visible at 9 p.m. of the 5th.

MARCH.

This month was cold and wintry with a great prevalence of N. and N E. winds. Its mean temperature was rather more than two degrees below the average, and on several nights the frosts were severe for the time of year. Rain or snow fell on twelve days, but the total fall was below the average. The latter part of the month was somewhat finer and warmer, with variable winds, but some snow fell during the night of the 31st.

APRIL.

With the exception of the year 1879 the weather had not been so cold in the month of April since 1860, which was about the coldest April on record. The mean temperature was upwards of four degrees below the average. The rainfall was also below the average and scarcely any rain fell before the 21st. On the mornings of the 18th and 19th the dryness of the air was very remarkable and caused the temperature of the Dew Point to be as much as 20° below it. A series of gales from the N.E. were almost continuous on the 5th, 6th and 7th, with occasional showers of sleet or snow in small quantities.

MAY.

The mean temperature of this month was below the average to the extent of nearly two degrees. This low temperature, accompanied as it was by a too frequently overcast sky and an extraordinary prevalence of N.E winds, had a most depressing influence upon animal and vegetable life. The rainfall was below the average, although showers were frequent, especially during the third week. The morning of the 21st was comparatively mild, but at 3 p.m. some showers of sleet and hail fell, and at 4 p.m. the wind shifted from S. to N.W , with heavy showers of hail, sleet and snow, so that by 5 p.m. grass fields, roofs of houses and all good radiating surfaces became covered with snow and presented quite a wintry appearance, while the temperature fell suddenly from 47° to 32°·5, which proved injurious to some fruit blossoms, which had already been injured by the gale on the 19th. During the last week vegetation slowly advanced, notwithstanding the cold and ungenial winds. The wheat crop looked well. Apple trees just showing blossom.

JUNE.

This month, probably, will long be remembered for its brilliancy, genial warmth and great drought after the third day, notwithstanding which its actual mean temperature but slightly exceeded the average of many years. The rainfall was less than half the average, all of which fell on the 2nd and 3rd. The first day was warm and pleasant, but the 2nd and 3rd were much colder, with ·78 of an inch of rain on the former and ·31 on the latter day. From this date throughout the entire month we had uninterrupted summer weather, notwithstanding the prevalence of N.E. wind. The heat was not *excessive* at any time, and the maximum temperature in the shade reached 81° on one day only, while a fully exposed thermometer registered 87°, and another, in vacuo, 99°·5. On the afternoon of the 9th the sky was ornamented in all directions by varied and beautiful specimens of the Cirrus cloud, which, however, all disappeared before sunset.

JULY.

The fine summer weather which prevailed in June was continuous throughout this month. With the exception of one day, the 4th, the heat was never oppressive. The highest temperature registered in the shade was 86°·8. The mean was three degrees above the average, and although the mean daily range amounted to 21°·3 yet the lowest night temperature fell on four occasions only below 50°. The rainfall amounted to only one-fourth of the average. After the great heat of the 4th the moon assumed a peculiar golden hue at her rising, and I noticed the same appearance on the succeeding evening. A thunderstorm was seen to the northward during the evening of the 16th. On many occasions a very dense haze pervaded the landscape, so that objects comparatively near were rendered very indistinct

AUGUST.

The fine summer weather which commenced on June 4th continued without any important interruption to the morning of the 17th of this month, when a thunderstorm came up from S.W., with heavy rain, which terminated the long summer drought. The mean temperature was two degrees above the average. The 7th and 8th were the two warmest days, when the temperature in the shade exceeded 84° On the former day a bright bulb thermometer in vacuo registered 104°·6. Upon the whole the temperature was very pleasant to the 17th, without any excessive heat. The air on several occasions was remarkably dry, particularly on the 6th, 7th and 8th. Thus at 1 p.m. on the 6th the temperature of the Dew Point below that of the air was 32°·2 ; on the 7th, 26°·5 ; and on the 8th, 30°·3 ! The rainfall, chiefly on account of the heavy rains on the 17th and 30th, was rather above the average. On the 22nd numerous small meteors emanated from the constellation Aquila. The harvest was very early in this county, and a considerable quantity of corn was secured in excellent condition and of good quality.

SEPTEMBER

The commencement of this month was stormy and wet. A severe gale occurred during the night of the 1st, and continued, with more or less violence, all day of the 2nd, which wrought such considerable damage to the hop gardens that several, in exposed situations, were scarcely worth the picking. The mean temperature of the month was very low; indeed, it had not been so low since September, 1863. It was as much as five degrees below the average. The total rainfall was nearly half-an-inch more than usual. A slight thunderstorm occurred on the 6th, and very vivid lightning was observed to the S.E. on the morning of the 29th. The fruit crop was very partial this autumn, and had been seriously injured by the gales on August 31st and September 2nd. Apples and pears did not keep well, when gathered, which may perhaps be accounted for by their having received too suddenly a large quantity of moisture after the long drought.

OCTOBER.

This month was also very cold, and an early fall of snow occurred on the 11th. The mid-day temperature was frequently low for the time of year, and sharp frost was recorded rather frequently during the latter half of the month; consequently, the mean temperature was five degrees below the average of many years. The readings of the barometer were somewhat high until the last few days. The rainfall was two inches and a half below the average.

NOVEMBER

Was a cold, gloomy, wet month, and the mean temperature one degree and a quarter below the average. After the first week the mid-day temperature was low, while at night several severe frosts were experienced. The N.E. wind was again extremely prevalent. The rainfall was one inch and a half above the average, and was very heavy on the 2nd, 7th and 28th. On and after the 16th I noticed some very fine glows upon the aqueous vapour near the horizon both before sunrise and after sunset, which reminded me very forcibly of the splendid displays which I observed during the winter of 1883-84.

DECEMBER.

The mean temperature was two degrees and a half below the average, the sky much covered by cloud, and showers of rain and snow were frequent. From the 18th to 31st a somewhat severe frost continued with a very cold northerly wind. The 8th was a very boisterous day ; a gale was recorded from the S E. on the 12th and from the S.W. on the 14th and 16th. On the 14th heavy rain fell after the subsidence of the gale. The month's rainfall was very slightly above the average. On various occasions both before sunrise and after sunset the aqueous vapour near the horizon, and for several degrees above it, exhibited even more brilliant hues than I had observed in November. Upon every cloudless morning during the months of November and December the planet VENUS appeared a lovely and conspicuous object above the S.E. horizon while pursuing her path at first toward, and subsequently from, the point of her extreme western elongation. The late dark winter mornings gave the lady planet a great opportunity of displaying her beautiful rays , but as to the unnecessary excitement, respecting her brilliant appearance (in *re* whether she was the Star of Bethlehem), it conveyed an intimation of mental extravagance which was not pleasant to dwell upon !

1888.

JANUARY.

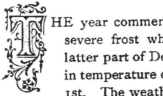HE year commenced with a continuance of the severe frost which had prevailed during the latter part of December, but a considerable rise in temperature occurred during the night of the 1st. The weather continued mild to the 12th, when cold weather returned and continued, for the most part, to the end of the month. The high temperature on the 10th and 11th was very remarkable and exceeded any instance which I had previously recorded for January. On the former day the highest temperature in the shade was 58°·4, and on the latter 57°·2. The sky was absolutely cloudless on these two days, the atmosphere perfectly calm, while the sun's rays felt so warm, for the time of year, that, for the sake of testing them, I placed my black-bulb thermometer (in vacuo) by the side of my usual instruments, and found that it registered a temperature of 89°·6! At mid-day some hundreds of bees left a neighbour's hive and settled on an adjoining cottage, for some time, before they discovered that they had made a premature exit from their home. Before sunrise on the 10th and after sunset on the 11th, some beautifully coloured tints were visible in the aqueous vapour lying above the distant horizon. In the clear atmosphere of these mornings the planet Venus, although so many weeks past the theoretical period of greatest brilliancy, shone with such intensity as to cast a shadow. During the night of the 25th a continuous gale occurred from the S.W.; the mean temperature of the month was

rather below the average. The rainfall was considerably below the average, so that the deeper springs were lower than is usual, or desirable, at this season.

FEBRUARY.

The frost which prevailed during the latter part of January continued during the first three days of this month, after which the weather was comparatively mild for the time of year until the 15th, when the wind backed to the N.E. and the frost returned, and continued, for the most part, to the close of the month. On several occasions this cold wind blew with almost the force of a gale, particularly during the nights and early mornings, so that the temperature felt much colder than the thermometer indicated. The amount of precipitation was 1·87 inches and consisted chiefly of snow, which fell more or less on nine days. In some exposed places it had drifted to the depth of three feet or more.

MARCH.

The mean temperature of this month was rather more than four degrees below the average, while its general character was cold, wintry and unusually sunless, with an excess of N E. wind. Snow fell, more or less, on six consecutive days, which is a very unusual circumstance in a spring month. The average night temperature was one degree below the freezing point, as shown by a thermometer protected from radiation, while frost occurred to a greater or lesser extent on twenty occasions. A heavy gale passed over on the morning of the 11th and stormy weather prevailed on the 17th, 18th and 24th.

O

APRIL.

It may be safely affirmed that this was the coldest April which had been experienced in the South of England during the last half-century. Its mean temperature was five degrees below the average. The weather was bitterly cold during the first ten days, with an almost constant prevalence of N.E. wind, frequent slight falls of snow and nightly frosts, together with a remarkable deficiency of sunshine. The daily highest temperature was very low for the time of year and only reached 60° and upwards on three occasions, viz., on 16th, 28th and 30th. Rainy weather prevailed from 15th to 23rd; nevertheless the total rainfall for the month was more than half-an-inch below the average. A solar halo, slightly prismatic, was visible for a time about 11 a.m.; and I saw, for the first time this season, three butterflies on the wing, viz., G. Rhamni, V. Urticæ and V. Io; this latter being a remarkably fine specimen. The 24th had been fine and pleasant during the morning, but during the afternoon a cold N.E. wind set in with such a great decrease of temperature that the highest temperature recorded for the 25th was only 44°·7. The cuckoo was not heard in this immediate district before the 28th, which was much later than usual

MAY.

The mean temperature of this month was somewhat below the average, but the departure therefrom was much less than in the two previous months. The rainfall was again below the average of many years and fell only on eight days. There was a decided increase in temperature on the 8th, so that so late as 8 p.m. it remained for some time at 60°! The morning of the 19th was hot and almost sultry, and between 3 and 4 p m thunder was heard to the S.E About 7 p.m a thick fog came up from the sea, with a great decrease of temperature Thunderstorms were prevalent in this district on the 21st during the afternoon and evening. The remainder of the month was fine, for the most part, and a shower fell during the night of the 29th. Sawerthal's comet was very well seen here on the night of the 12th, with its small bright nucleus and narrow tail.

JUNE.

This month was cold and wet for the first month of summer. The 25th was the hottest day, when the temperature in the shade rose to 80°, for the only time during the entire summer The mean temperature was nearly two degrees and a half below, while the rainfall, which occurred on fifteen days, was considerably above the average. On the 2nd and 3rd there was a remarkable display of the Cirrus cloud over the South of England. Just before sunset, on the latter day, a thick fog advancing from the sea was beautifully illuminated, of a dark pink colour, by the rays of the setting sun. The weather on the 8th was very showery, which, in former days, would have been considered an augury of a wet harvest, according to the old distich,

> "If on the 8th of June it rain,
> It foretells a wet harvest men sam "

A heavier rain occurred on the 9th, which was most acceptable to the growing crops. On the 12th there was another great display of the Cirrus cloud as well as on the 13th. A very heavy shower fell during the afternoon of the 28th, when nearly half an inch of rain fell in about fifteen minutes. At the close of the month vegetation generally was in a very backward and sad condition from the previous wet and sunless weather.

JULY.

With the exception of the very cold month of July, 1879, the mean temperature of this month was lower than I have recorded for any July. If, however, I refer to the mean daily maximum temperature for July, 1888, I find that it was even *lower* than that in July, 1879. At Crowborough the rainfall was the largest amount which I have ever registered, for this month, during the last eighteen years. This sunless month may be described as having had only one cloudless morning (13th), while the average daily amount of cloud, at 9 a.m., was as much as 9·5 (an overcast sky being represented by 10·0). On the 6th, a thunderstorm passed away to the eastward, and some rain and hail fell here. A considerable quantity of hail or snow must have fallen on the hill to the north of Beachy Head, as I noticed its whitened appearance so late as 8 a.m., the sky being densely overcast. An unusual darkness prevailed on the 15th; a dense cloud rested on the hill and I observed frequent faint flashes of lightning, but no thunder in consequence of immediate earth contact. I have previously observed this phenomenon on more than one occasion. On the 17th, this district was again visited by a thunderstorm, and there was considerable electrical disturbance on the two following days. On 22nd, about 10.45 p.m., a rather severe thunderstorm occurred, and with such heavy rain that more than one inch fell in about 45 minutes.

AUGUST.

This, the last month of summer, proved more season-able than either June or July, and the temperature, during the day and night, was warmer than any other month, nevertheless the mean was two degrees and a half below the average of many years. The temperature fluctuated very much, and chiefly in consequence of the frequent variations in the direction of the wind; the S.W. was the most prevalent. There was not much electrical disturbance after the 1st, but thunder was heard on the 15th and a slight thunderstorm occurred on the 30th. The greater portion of the hay crop was secured during the first fortnight, but a very considerable quantity would be in very bad condition and absolutely useless for fodder. During the thunderstorm on the 1st, at Rotherfield, a valuable team of horses was struck by lightning; one was killed instantaneously and the others were injured.

SEPTEMBER.

The mean temperature of this month was, within a fraction of a degree, equal to the average of many years, although still warmer weather would have been very desirable for the harvest; yet the general condition of the air was an agreeable change after the very humid weather of the previous three months. It was by far the driest month of the year, as the rainfall was scarcely equal to one-third of the average. Vivid lightning was visible to the eastward during the evening of the 9th, which was followed by rain during the night, and a cold shower of rain and hail on the 10th. From the 10th to the 28th, the air was very dry and no precipitation occurred. On the 24th distant thunder was heard in the

N.W , and about 4 p m. on the 27th a very fine prismatic solar halo was visible for some time. Its diameter was 35 degrees

OCTOBER

This month was unseasonably cold, and the mean temperature nearly four degrees below the average. On the 4th some showers of rain and hail fell, causing a considerable decrease of temperature and such a severe frost during the night that many half hardy plants were much injured and in some instances killed. Slight frost occurred again on the 7th. The rainfall was an inch and a half below the average The month passed without any gale or even stormy weather.

NOVEMBER.

This was the first month in the year in which the mean temperature exceeded the average, the excess was considerable and amounted to 3° 4. So high a temperature had not been recorded for November since 1881 There were only two frosty nights during the entire month. The only gale occurred on the 27th, and was from the S.E. The rainfall was frequent and heavy at intervals, and the month's total an inch and a half above the average of many years A great and sudden decrease of temperature occurred on the 6th, and the highest temperature for the day was upwards of 18 degrees lower than on the 5th. At midnight of the 17th a very fine prismatic lunar corona was visible. About 7 p m of the 26th a very loud and continuous peal of thunder was heard. The lightning struck a house near Cross-in-Hand. The electric fluid passed down a chimney and knocked down the family, who were seated around the fire, but without seriously injuring anyone. Lightning was visible again over the S E. horizon on the evening of the 27th, and a rainbow was visible at mid-day on the 28th.

DECEMBER.

The mean temperature was also above the average Some slight frosts occurred during the third week, but the weather, upon the whole, was mild and dry with a considerable amount of southerly wind, and more than the average quantity of bright sunshine. The rainfall was about half-an-inch less than the average and fell on 15 days The heaviest rain was recorded during the afternoon of the 25th. The early morning of the 18th was foggy, but before 9 a.m. it subsided from the top of the hill, but enveloped the whole of the surrounding country, presenting the curious appearance, occasionally observed here, of a horizontal layer of fog in every direction A moderate gale passed over on the 21st, and the weather was very stormy and wet on the 27th The following flowers were in bloom on the 25th —Roses, African marigolds, several varieties of polyanthus, wall-flowers, violets, and some scarlet geraniums in a sheltered situation.

1889.

JANUARY.

THE mean temperature of this month was about one degree below the average, although the frost was not at any time severe. The lowest temperature in the shade was recorded on the morning of the 6th, and that of terrestrial radiation on the 5th, which was followed by a brilliant day and night. Thick rime accumulated on the trees and shrubs. A faint lunar halo was observed on the night of the 19th, and during the following week the weather became colder, with frequent but not severe frost at night. The last day of the month was particularly mild and pleasant for the time of year The prevailing wind was the N.E. The rainfall was not much above a third of the average.

FEBRUARY

Was colder than January and its mean temperature fully two degrees below the average. On the morning of the 12th the temperature in the shade fell to 18°·2, which proved to be the most severe frost during the winter. Frosty nights were frequent and very clear on several occasions. Northerly winds were the most frequent. Rainfall was somewhat above the average and snow fell in trifling amounts on eleven days. A rather heavy gale from S.E. passed over on the afternoon of the 13th, and a prismatic lunar corona was observed at 9 p.m. on the 14th.

MARCH

Began with very cold weather and sharp frosts occurred very frequently to the 17th, when the weather became much milder, with occasional showers, to the end. The total rainfall was about equal to the average. A brilliant prismatic lunar corona was observed on the night of the 16th, which was followed by mild weather and variable winds. The reading of the barometer was low on the morning of the 20th, viz., 29·039 inches at sea level. The nights of the 11th and 22nd were remarkably favourable for astronomical observations

APRIL.

Although the mean temperature of this month was considerably below the average, yet it was warmer than the corresponding month of last year. The weather was, upon the whole, very sunless and ungenial and, as a consequence, vegetation was very backward for the time of year. Rain fell more or less on twenty days. The prevailing wind current was N. or N.E. on twelve days, which much conduced to a low mid-day temperature. Several thunderstorms occurred along the borders of Sussex and Kent, while that on the 9th was very severe. The lightning struck Cowden Church as well as several oak trees in that neighbourhood. I noticed that many flashes were of the globular form. The rain was very trifling here, but we had a continuous hail shower for upwards of an hour, which caused such diminution of temperature that the maximum on the 10th was only 44°·7. A rather severe gale came on from the S.W on the 23rd and a slight thunderstorm with rain and hail showers occurred on the 25th.

MAY

Was a warm and very genial spring month, while both the day and night temperature was considerably above the average. I observed a lunar halo at 9 p.m. on the 8th. Lightning was visible to the westward on the 24th and 25th. On several days a dense haze pervaded the landscape. The night of the 22nd was a very brilliant one for astronomical observation, with that exquisite telescopic definition which frequently obtains here during the spring months.

JUNE.

Little need be said of this month but that it was upon the whole exceedingly dry, warm and pleasant. The temperature was high both day and night. There was an extraordinary prevalence of a north-easterly current of wind on 19 days, 13 of which were consecutive, viz , from 16th to 28th, both inclusive. Frequent thunder was heard in the S.W. during the afternoon of the 6th On the 7th, during the greater part of the afternoon, I observed some magnificent masses of cumulo-stratus cloud, highly-electrified, extending in a continuous line along nearly the entire length of the contiguous borders of Kent, Sussex and Surrey, from which very heavy peals of thunder rolled almost incessantly for nearly two hours, while here the sun shone brilliantly all the afternoon The rain and hail of this storm was very heavy at Tunbridge Wells and its vicinity, while the damage occasioned thereby was greater than on any instance on record in that neighbourhood. I was credibly informed that many of the hail-stones were the size of pigeons' eggs, and that Mr. Young, of Barden Mill, picked one up which weighed nearly or quite half-a-pound! The effect of this ice storm was so great that the highest temperature of the 8th was just twenty degrees lower than on the 7th. It is worthy of record that the S.W. wind, which is generally so prevalent over the S.E of England, was entirely absent throughout the month.

JULY.

The fine weather of June continued to the 6th of this month, when a rather sudden decrease of atmospheric pressure indicated the approaching change which arrived on the following day, and rain fell daily (13th and 19th excepted) during the succeeding twenty-two days to the amount of 4·30 inches. Although this heavy rainfall was very beneficial to vegetation generally, yet it interfered very much with that portion of the hay harvest which had not been completed during the latter part of June. The first and last weeks were fine and pleasant; notwithstanding which the mean temperature of the month was about two degrees below the average. On the 23rd lightning was very vivid and frequent on the S.E. horizon, and on one occasion I noticed three separate flashes pass down towards the sea, simultaneously, and apparently about a quarter of a mile apart.

AUGUST.

The mean temperature was about one degree below the average and a large quantity of rain fell during the first three weeks, which very much delayed the ingathering of the harvest. The total was nearly one inch above the average of many years There was an entire absence of thunderstorms. The highest temperature in the shade was only 79° on the 1st and 79°·3 on the 30th and 31st. The S.W. wind was more prevalent than had been observed for many months. The evening of the 7th was very favourable for the observation of the occultation of Jupiter by the Moon. In consequence of first contact happening in bright sunlight I could not be certain of the exact time, but disappearance took place 16h. 12m. 18s , L.S.T. The planet, when in contact with the moon, assumed a peculiar green colour, but its limb was quite bright to the moment of disappearance. Re-appearance occurred at 17h. 5m. 56s., L.S.T., and last contact at

17h. 7m. 58s., L.S.T., the planet was then of a somewhat greener colour than at disappearance; this greenish colour continued for upwards of an hour. The limb of the moon was very sharp and black as it passed over the disc of the planet. The belts were dark on emersion, but perfectly distinct close up to the moon's limb. The evening of the 28th was also very favourable for an observation of Davidson's Comet, which I then saw for the first time; its appearance was that of a bright, somewhat oval nebulosity, with a nearly central condensation.

SEPTEMBER.

Although this was a very fine, dry and pleasant month, yet the mean temperature was scarcely equal to the average, but this may have been due in part to the great prevalence of N.E. wind during a full third of the month. The readings of the barometer were very uniform, above the average, and exceeded 30 inches on 20 days at sea level. The total rainfall was little more than a third of the average of many years. Severe thunderstorms occurred in various parts of the Kingdom on 2nd, and the places more especially visited in the counties of Sussex and Kent were the neighbourhoods of Tunbridge, Sevenoaks, Edenbridge and Rye. Considerable damage was done there by the lightning and torrents of rain. The lightning, as seen from my Observatory, was magnificent, and it exhibited for the most part a tint closely resembling that of the ordinary electric light; only a slight shower fell here about 9 p.m. This month was particularly favourable for astronomical observations, as no less than 15 nights were remarkably clear.

OCTOBER.

The mean temperature was rather more than one degree below the average; a condition caused by a low mid-day temperature, for the nights were much warmer than usual and the month passed away without any frost even on the surface of short grass. In a long series of years the average rainfall in October is the largest for the year, and in the present instance it fully maintained its character, for there were only seven dry days and the total quantity was nearly double the average of many years. At Crowborough the amount was 8·09 inches, which has been only once exceeded during the last 19 years, viz., 8·30 inches in 1882. The temperature of the Dew Point was only $2°·7$ below that of the air at 9 0 a m A rainbow was observed at noon on the 4th and again at the same hour on the 9th, which is a certain sign of an approaching wet season. During the night of the 19th a heavy gale prevailed from the S W. and another on the 26th from the N.E.

NOVEMBER.

The heavy rains of October continued to the 3rd of this month, on which day nearly an inch of rain was registered, but for three weeks from this date no more rain was registered, although during that time the weather was frequently gloomy and damp, notwithstanding the long continuance of an anticyclone. The mean temperature was above the average both day and night and no trace of frost was observable until the 26th. On the 27th a gale came on from the northward with a slight fall of snow, and this was only the fifth time during the month that any precipitation was recorded.

DECEMBER.

In consequence of some rather severe frosts during the first and last weeks, the mean temperature was much below the average. Frequent rain occurred from the 12th to the 24th, but the total quantity for the month was nearly an inch below the average of many years An unusual amount of fog and a generally misty condition of the atmosphere prevailed during a great part of the month and, as a consequence, the temperature of the Dew Point at 9.0 a.m. was only one degree below that of the air. An Aurora was visible early in the evening of the 10th, but the sky soon became overcast and not much was seen of it. The month ended with sharp frost and a cold wind from the southward.

1890.

JANUARY.

HE year commenced cold and frosty until the afternoon of the 3rd, when a sudden increase of temperature occurred, and very little frost was recorded during the remainder of the month. Its mean temperature was about 1°·5 above the average, with a great prevalence of westerly winds, very dense fogs and the atmosphere more frequently saturated with moisture than I have observed for some years past. Rain fell more or less on 24 days, but the total quantity was not more than about half-an-inch above the average. Gales, more or less violent, came over on the 5th, 9th,

18th and 26th, whilst that on the 23rd reached the force of a hurricane during the afternoon. The barometer at 9 a.m. on this day had fallen to 28·745 inches at sea level.

FEBRUARY.

The mean temperature was one degree below the average and the night temperature, both in the shade and on the grass, was below the freezing point. The general character of the weather throughout the entire month was, upon the whole, seasonable and pleasant. Rain fell on six days and the total quantity was nearly an inch below the average of many years. From the 9th to the 12th, both inclusive, the sky was almost cloudless both day and night and telescopic definition remarkably good. At the close of the month a few primroses were in bloom in sheltered situations.

MARCH.

The frosty weather which prevailed during the two last days of February became very intense during the first four days of this month. On the morning of the 3rd the temperature in the shade fell to 15° 8 ; on the grass to 9°·6 ; and on the following morning to 16°·2 in the shade, and on the grass to 8°·7. These were the lowest temperatures which had been recorded in March since the year 1845. The mean temperature was rather more than one degree above the average in consequence of the warm weather, frequent rain and westerly winds which prevailed during the last ten days. On the morning of the 4th, and when there was no visible cloud, some beautiful snow crystals fell occasionally, which, when lying upon the frozen snow, refracted the sun's rays with great brilliancy. S.W. winds were the most prevalent after the first week.

APRIL.

The fine weather which prevailed at the close of last month continued very steadily to the 6th. The days and nights were for the most part brilliant and almost cloudless; but the N E. wind caused slight frosts at night, particularly on the 5th During the second week the temperature was much lower and sharp frost occurred almost every night, with snow showers occasionally. Some lightning and thunder with a hail shower occurred about noon on the 8th. Lightning was visible to the S.E. on the evening of the 16th. The third week was warmer, with frequent showers. The remainder of the month was fine and dry, nevertheless the mean temperature for the month was about two degrees below the average and the rainfall half-an-inch in excess.

MAY

Was, upon the whole, a fine and pleasant month. The mean temperature was above and the rainfall rather less than the average. A splendid sunset was visible on the evening of the 10th, when some long lines of Cirrostratus cloud were beautifully illuminated by a deep crimson tint for a considerable distance along the horizon, both east and west of the setting sun. On the evening of the 15th the Comet was well seen, having a bright nucleus with a short but broad tail, very well defined On the evening of the 19th, some vivid lightning was seen along the eastern horizon, between 9 and 10 o'clock.

JUNE.

This was a very gloomy, cold, unseasonable month. The mean temperature was as much as 3°·5 below the average of the last seventeen years. A slight frost occurred on the grass in the early morning of the 1st. The rainfall was 3·26 inches; a quantity three-quarters of an inch above the average. It was not, however, the actual amount of rainfall, but the number of days upon which it fell, which rendered the weather so unfavourable for the hay harvest, more especially during the last week; confirming the old precept that it is not wise to commence haymaking during the Midsummer week. Thunderstorms visited this district on the 12th and a severe gale of wind with heavy rain on the 30th. The morning of the 17th was not very favourable for observing the partial solar eclipse, but a very good observation of last contact was obtained.

JULY.

The general character of this month was for the most part similar to that of June, more especially during the first half of it. The mean temperature was three degrees below the average and summer heat, in the shade, was only once registered during the entire month, viz., on the 16th. The rainfall was rather more than a fourth greater than the average of twenty years. A thunderstorm occurred in the vicinity of the Hill in the early morning of the 11th, which was the only instance of electrical disturbance.

AUGUST.

Although this month was somewhat finer than June and July, yet we had very little true summer weather.

P

The highest temperature occurred on the 5th and 6th, when the maxima were 76°·5 and 76°·8 respectively, but only on three other days did it reach 70° in the shade The first week was tolerably free from rain and there was a great improvement in the amount of sunshine. The mean temperature of the month, however, was about one degree and a half below the average and the rainfall one inch in excess, and fell, more or less, on sixteen days. The wind blew very generally from the westward.

SEPTEMBER.

This was by far the most pleasant month of the year and had the highest mean temperature. Many days and nights in the second and third weeks were brilliantly clear and most favourable for astronomical observations The rainfall was less than an inch, therefore the deficiency was nearly two inches and a half below the average. With the exception of a slight shower on the 2nd no rain fell until the 17th, when a slight thunderstorm visited this locality. This spell of fine weather was of incalculable benefit to the farmers in the S.E. of England, where much of the late harvest and the whole of the hop-picking was completed in a far more satisfactory manner than could have been anticipated.

OCTOBER.

The fine weather during the first three weeks was a most agreeable continuation of that of the preceding month; nevertheless, although the night temperature during this time was higher than usual, yet the month's mean was scarcely equal to the average. The rainfall was less than half the average quantity. The amount of cloud was less than usual in October, while from the 8th to 17th, both inclusive, the sky was almost cloudless both day and night with the exception of the 15th, which was a windy, showery day. The entire month passed away without any gale.

NOVEMBER.

During the first twenty-four days of this month the weather was unusually mild and the mean daily temperature was upwards of three degrees higher than the average of 17 years, but the severe frost on the last six days so reduced this excess that at the close of the month the mean temperature was half a degree *below* the average. On several days in the second and third weeks the air was almost oppressively warm, in consequence, perhaps, of its great humidity, while thrushes were singing at intervals, as in early spring. The total amount of rain and product of melted snow, for the entire month, was about equal to the average of 20 years in this locality. The following are some particulars of the great and sudden change of weather from unusual mildness to intense frost, which prevailed during the last six days. The 24th was a densely overcast and dark day, but during the evening the wind veered suddenly to the northward with a rapid decrease of temperature, which was in fact the commencement of the great frost which continued for several subsequent weeks. The morning of the 25th was fine and frosty, but about 4 p.m. snow commenced falling and the individual flakes were of larger size than I ever remember to have seen. They were comparatively few in number, but each flake upon reaching the ground was the full size of a halfpenny. The frost was more severe on the 26th, while heavy snow commenced falling early in the morning and continued

P 2

throughout the day, so that by sunset it was about a foot deep upon the level. There being no wind accompanying the snowfall, the evergreen trees and shrubs were much loaded by it and were leaning in all directions, to their great detriment. On the 27th the frost was still more severe and increased to still greater intensity until the afternoon of the 28th, when at 2.30 the temperature in the open air was 14°; at 4 p.m., 11°; at 5 p.m., 10°; but at 10 p.m. it had risen to 13°. A self-registering thermometer, also exposed to the open air, gave a record of 8°·6, while another in Stevenson's screen recorded 11°·3 as the minimum in that position. I believe that the lowest temperature occurred between 4 and 5 p.m. Another instrument lying just above some grass, swept of snow, recorded 3°·2 as the minimum of terrestrial radiation. The 29th was a dull day with hard frost and a little granular snow fell occasionally. The 30th was a finer morning and day, but with hard frost until the afternoon, when the temperature was above the freezing point for the first time since the 25th. The following table gives the highest and lowest temperature recorded during the six days :—

	25th.	26th	27th	28th.	29th.	30th.
Highest Temperature in the Open Air .	41·0	31·0	29 0	27·0	31·2	39·8
Lowest ,, ,, ,, ...	27·4	21·8	19·9	13 6	8·6	21·0
,, ,, of Radiation .	27·0	20·0	17·6	8·2	3·2	12·5
Highest ,, in the Shade ...	39·2	29 0	26 2	25 3	27 8	35 2
Lowest ,, ,, ,, ...	29·4	25·2	22 3	15·1	11·3	24 0
Melted Snow in Inches of Water.	0·68	0·48	0·10	—	0·03	—

The mean temperature of the six days in the screen was 25°·8. The low readings on the morning of the 29th occurred, as I have before stated, in all probability between 4 and 5 p.m. of the 28th; but in accordance with established rule the minima readings taken in the morning, from self-registering instruments, are recorded for *that* day, being in fact the minima of the preceding twenty-four hours. I have thus given these particulars of this severe frost for two reasons; in the first place, on account of the greatest intensity having occurred during the *daytime*, and, secondly, because such severity is unprecedented in the month of November in our meteorological annals since the introduction of trustworthy self-recording thermometers.

DECEMBER.

The severe frost which commenced on November 25th continued with varying severity during the whole of this month. The temperature fell to, or below, the freezing point *on every night*. From the 1st to 11th, both inclusive, although the highest temperature during the day was above 32°, yet it never reached 40°, while from 11th to 31st there were fifteen days wherein the maximum in the screen was below 32°, and on two separate occasions for five days consecutively. The mean temperature was 28°·4, or nearly four degrees below the freezing point and no less than 8°·2 below the average of the last seventeen years on Crowborough Hill. So far as I have been able to ascertain, this was the lowest mean temperature for December in the S.E. of England on record. I have lately seen it stated that December, 1788, was as cold or colder than now, but the most trustworthy records of that month registered a mean of 30°·4, or two whole degrees warmer. Again, December, 1796, was a very cold month and its mean temperature was 31°; from which time no long continued severity of frost in December is on record until December, 1844, when I registered a mean of 31°·4 at Uckfield. These are therefore the only three previous instances of the mean temperature for December having been below 32° since the year 1786. As is usual in cold December, the rainfall was much below the average. The total quantity was only 0·74 of an inch; the average of the last twenty years at Crowborough being 3·47 inches.[1] Although the frost was so continuous, yet its intensity was at no time so great as might have been expected, thus confirming previous observation that severe frosts are less intense on the summit of a hill than on much lower ground. On the 15th some beautiful snow crystals fell in very considerable numbers. More snow fell on the 20th, which yielded ·22 of an inch of water; but with the exception of some granular snow on the 30th, no more fell to the end of the month. At 10 p.m. on the 25th a fine prismatic halo surrounded the moon—the red and yellow colors being well defined.

1891.

JANUARY.

THE severe frost, which commenced so suddenly on November 25th, 1890, continued with but little cessation to the 19th of this month inclusive—a period of 56 days, or exactly eight weeks. This was the longest frost which we have had for many years. The mean temperature in the shade during this interval was as low as 28°·6, or nearly

$3°$ 5 below the freezing point, while the mean temperature of the first nineteen days of this month was $29°·9$, which is seven degrees below the average temperature for January during the last seventeen years at Crowborough. The mean temperature of the entire month was only $33°·6$. The increase of temperature on the 20th occurred rather suddenly in the early morning; the wind had veered to the S.W. and rain fell for some hours during the succeeding night During the greatest severity of the frost snow crystals fell in considerable numbers and in great variety.

FEBRUARY.

The weather during the whole of this month was of a remarkable character. In the first place it was absolutely dry and anti-cyclonic throughout. The reduced readings of the barometer were never below thirty inches at 9 a.m., while, secondly, as regards the drought, an absolutely rainless month had not occurred in Sussex since July, 1842. The month was, for the most part, pleasant for the time of year, and the sky unusually free from cloud, there having been fourteen cloudless mornings and sixteen cloudless nights, thus completely setting aside the old adage for February. The mean temperature in the shade was $40°·5$, or rather more than two and a half degrees above the average of the last seventeen years. The mid-day warmth of the last two days, both in the shade and in sunshine, was so unprecedentedly high that I have thought it might be interesting to give the following details.

	27th.	28th
Highest temperature in the shade ...	$60°$ 5 ...	$66°$ 6
,, ,, ,, sunshine	64 0 ...	68·0
Solar radiation (in Vacuo) bright bulb	73·1	73 8
,, ,, ,, black bulb.. ..	105 0	103 6

This was a higher temperature than was recorded in the shade during the two subsequent months of March and April.

MARCH.

The unusual warmth which prevailed during the latter part of February gradually decreased on the 1st and 2nd of this month, but the drought continued to the 6th. On the second night the wind veered to the westward with a further great decrease of temperature, insomuch that at 9 a.m. on the 3rd it was 14° colder than at the same hour on the previous day. On the 9th a severe gale came on with increasing severity all the afternoon, accompanied by a driving snow fall (quite a blizzard), while from 9 to 10 p.m. it blew quite a hurricane, and the snow was so extremely small that it penetrated into every available crevice before midnight. By the morning of the 10th the snow had been driven into deep rifts, which varied in depth from one to five feet. Snow fell again during the night of the 10th, and the wind having entirely subsided, it lay very heavily on the evergreen trees and shrubs. Very cold weather continued throughout the month, yet its mean temperature was only 1°·2 below the average. Several showers of pelletiform snow fell on the 26th, with some electrical display about 2 p.m. to the southward. These pellets were rather larger than peas. They were very soft, without any particular nucleus, and remained quite stationary upon reaching the ground and house-tops. The rainfall was much above the average.

APRIL.

The cold weather of the previous month continued for the most part throughout this month, so that its mean temperature was considerably more than two degrees below the average. Throughout the entire month the air was most ungenial and very unfavourable for vegetation, which advanced very slowly, so that the spring season was more backward than for many years past. It was a very dry month and the rainfall was about one-fourth of the average of the last twenty-one years. At the close of the month the injurious effects of the late great frost, upon certain shrubs and flowers, became apparent. The Portugal and common laurel were *not* injured.

MAY.

This month was remarkable for the great variation in its temperature. The first half was fairly warm and more genial than for many weeks past. The 16th was a remarkable day for the time of year, some rain had fallen during the previous night, but in the course of the afternoon snow and hail showers were frequent, which caused such a decrease in temperature that at 7 p.m it was only one degree above the freezing point; more snow fell during the evening, after which the clouds dispersed and a sharp frost ensued in the early morning of the 17th. The greatest cold registered in the air was $29^\circ\cdot5$ and on the grass $26^\circ\cdot1$. The evergreen trees and shrubs were much loaded with snow, which, however, soon disappeared after sunrise. From the 17th to the 28th the weather continued cold and unseasonable, with rain, more or less, every twenty-four hours. Notwithstanding the great variation in temperature, the mean for the month was little more than one degree below the average of seventeen years. The rainfall was one inch and a half above the average, which was a welcome amount after the long drought which commenced on February 1st.

JUNE.

Although this month was fine, upon the whole, and its mean temperature above the average, yet there were considerable alternations, while on several days during the second week, owing to the prevalence of northerly and easterly winds, the air was unseasonably cold and cheerless. Rainfall occurred on nine days and the total amount registered was somewhat below the average. A N.E. gale prevailed on 6th, 7th and 8th, with cold rain at intervals, from which time to the 22nd the weather continued dry and warmer both day and night. During the nights of the 22nd, 23rd and 24th nearly one and a half inches of rain fell, and on the early morning of the 25th a thunderstorm passed away to the S.E.

JULY.

Gloomy and unseasonable weather prevailed, for the most part, throughout this month, and its mean temperature was below the average. The great deficiency of sunshine had a most unfavourable influence upon vegetation. The only really warm days were the 16th and 17th, when the temperature rose to 76° and 78° respectively The rainfall was above the average, but this excess was due to the heavy thunderstorm on the morning of the 27th. Electrical disturbance was observed also on the 8th, 17th, 30th and 31st.

AUGUST.

This was another very unfavourable summer month, and a very low temperature was observed throughout, with frequent and heavy rains, much westerly wind and very small amount of sunshine. The mean temperature was two degrees below the average and the rainfall nearly double the average of the last twenty-one years on Crowborough Hill. The total amount was 5·79 inches, of which no less than four inches fell during the last twelve days. Electrical disturbance was observed here on the 3rd, 10th, 13th, 21st and 23rd. A fine solar halo was seen on the 30th. During the storm of the 23rd Uckfield Church was struck by lightning and sustained considerable damage.

SEPTEMBER.

The weather of this month was, for the most part, a pleasant change, which enabled a considerable portion of the late harvest to be secured in a fairly good condition. Hop picking was carried on with but little interruption. The mean temperature was nearly two and a half degrees above the average, and the highest day temperature in the shade for the whole year occurred on the 11th, viz., 78°·5. The rainfall was only one and a half inches. The prevailing winds were from S. to S.W. A slight thunderstorm occurred on the 21st. During the night of the 10th a strong auroral light was visible, due north.

OCTOBER

Was a very mild, stormy, wet month. Its mean temperature was nearly two and a half degrees above the average, while the rainfall was more than twice the average of the last twenty-one years at Crowborough Hill. Moreover, it was the heaviest October rainfall in Sussex during the last half century, with the single exception of October, 1865. The month passed without a trace of frost until the last morning, when the temperature of the air fell to 30°, and that of radiation to 22° 6. On the evenings of September 30th and October 1st the phenomenon of Will-of-the-Wisp was seen over the low ground in Crowborough Warren; its appearance is a certain indication of an approaching wet period, and the higher the gentleman ascends the more stormy and wet will the weather be Gales of more or less violence prevailed on the 11th, 13th, 15th, 21st and 22nd. On the 17th a thunderstorm passed to the westward, with some very vivid lightning.

NOVEMBER.

The first half of this month was much overcast, the temperature low and the rainfall heavy; nevertheless, the total fall for the entire month was rather below the average. A violent gale, which increased to the force of a hurricane, occurred during the night of the 10th, and continued more or less violent till late in the afternoon of the 11th. This was the most severe gale which had occurred in this county for several years past, evidence of which was shown by the number of trees completely blown down and a still larger number partially uprooted. The corrected reading of my barometer at noon was 28·557 inches, which was the lowest point observed here since December 8th, 1886.

DECEMBER.

This month was very mild and rainy to the 15th, with an almost constant westerly wind From the 17th to the 25th the weather was much colder, but without any precipitation. It was the warmest December since 1880 The rainfall was about an inch above the average and fell more or less on twenty days. Gales of more or less violence occurred on the 3rd, 7th, 10th and 13th. Notwithstanding the unsettled weather there was a considerable amount of sunshine, more particularly from the 19th to the 24th, both inclusive, and during the month there were twelve clear nights for astronomical observations.

1892.

JANUARY.

THE year commenced with very seasonable weather, the temperature being lower than is usual with such a great preponderance of westerly wind. Sharp frosts were frequent during the first three weeks, but the lowest temperature in the shade was only 21°·8 on the 10th, the temperature of radiation falling to 12°·2 on the same morning. Snow showers were frequent on the 6th and 7th, but during the night of the 8th the fall was much heavier and measured about five inches in depth on the level. Some rain fell on the night of the 16th, which was followed by frost the next morning, so that trees, shrubs and good radiating surfaces were encased by a thin coating of ice.

FEBRUARY.

During the first fortnight of this month the weather was, for the most part, mild and pleasant; but during the third week some rather severe frosts occurred, with frequent snow showers, while that on the evening and night of the 17th attained a depth of about five inches.

Although very mild weather prevailed again during the last week, yet the mean temperature of the month was one and a half degrees below the average of 17 years. The rainfall was about a third below the average, although snow or rain fell more or less on 18 days.

MARCH

Was a very cold month, with a great prevalence of N.E. wind, and the mean temperature was as much as $3°\cdot7$ below the average. Snow fell frequently; nevertheless, the melted snow and rainfall did not equal the average by nearly three-quarters of an inch. The only mild weather occurred from the 16th to the 21st, both inclusive. On the morning of the 22nd the wind veered suddenly from E. to N.E., accompanied by a great decrease of temperature, the maximum for that day being 17° below that on the 21st.

APRIL.

At the very commencement of this month the weather became very warm and pleasant after the cold winds and low temperature of the previous month. During the first six days the temperature was abnormally high, and the daily maximum had not been so high at this particular date since the year 1848. Very brilliant and almost cloudless weather prevailed during the first eleven days, after which time a very sudden decrease of temperature occurred, with a very cold N.E. wind, so that on the 13th the highest temperature was only $39°\cdot2$, after having been as high as $73°\cdot5$ in the shade on the 4th. On the night of the 15th a severe N.E. gale came on with almost continuous snowfall for upwards of twelve hours, which attained a depth of about seven inches on the level and to more than two feet in the drifts on exposed situations. The mean temperature was 1°·5 above the average.

MAY.

The mean temperature of May was slightly above the average and, upon the whole, was a very fine and pleasant spring month, as rain fell on only four days during the first three weeks; the month, indeed, would have been very dry but for the heavy thunderstorm on the 25th. Just before sunset on the 10th the upper segment of a bright prismatic solar halo was visible, the diameter of which must have been about 35°. On the morning of the 13th the air was remarkably dry, as at 9 a m., when the dry bulb was at 63°·6, the dew point was 45° 1. A severe thunderstorm passed over on the night of the 25th, the lightning was of bluish colour and almost incessant; short but heavy showers of rain and hail fell.

JUNE.

The weather during the greater part of this month was ungenial, with rain, more or less, on 16 days, while the total amount was about half-an-inch above the average of the last 22 years at Crowborough. The mean temperature was nearly two degrees below the average, and there were but two summerlike days throughout the month, viz., the 10th and 28th. During the third week the night temperature was very low for the season, and in some districts actual frosts occurred to such an extent as to seriously injure garden produce. After the fine warm day of the 28th, a severe thunderstorm came on in the evening, and very similar in character to that of the previous month. It approached from the S.W., and being opposed in its course by an easterly current, continued for upwards of two hours. The lightning was almost incessant, with occasional peals of thunder, which was particularly loud and of unusually long continuance.

JULY.

This month was unseasonably cold, damp and sunless, with a considerable amount of easterly wind. The rainfall, however, was below the average, although the amount of cloud was as much as 6·7 (0·10), which was most unfavourable for the ripening of the cereal crops; and much hay was spoilt by frequent showers. On the 24th a thick fog prevailed till nearly noon. During the evening of the 29th very vivid lightning was seen over the Channel, which continued, I think, during the greater part of the night. A slight thunderstorm passed over the Hill in the early morning of the 30th.

AUGUST.

This was the warmest month of the year, nevertheless the mean temperature was below the average and the rainfall considerably in excess. The most prevalent winds were from the westward. The 17th was a very warm and pleasant day and some heavy masses of electric clouds were passing along the Channel during the afternoon and evening. The 18th was also a warm and rather sultry day, and distant thunder was heard to the S.W. between 6 and 7 a.m. On the 23rd a thunderstorm passed over with some short but heavy showers; the lightning was very vivid and some flashes were distinctly double, *i.e.*, that the second flash occurred about half a second after the first. The weather was rather finer at the close of the month.

SEPTEMBER.

The weather of this month was of a variable character. There were a few brilliant days, but, upon the whole, gloomy days were the most prevalent. The mean temperature was below the average, as was also the rainfall; the wind was chiefly from the westward. The 20th was very warm and sultry; distant thunder was heard in the early morning and a somewhat heavy thunderstorm occurred over the Channel during the forenoon. The 26th was also a warm day, when thunder was heard again to the southward. Vivid lightning was seen to the eastward during the evening of the 28th, which was followed by a stormy, showery day here

OCTOBER

Was a very cold and wet month, although no actual frost was registered in the screen. The mean temperature was as much as four degrees below the average, and the rainfall two inches in excess. A very heavy rain was recorded in this county on the 4th, viz., 1·45 inch. Easterly winds were very prevalent at intervals. The readings of the barometer were lower than at any other period of the year, and the average temperature of the dew point was only three degrees below that of the air.

NOVEMBER.

The atmosphere during this month was exceedingly gloomy, mild and rainy, with the lower stratum of cloud frequently resting upon the Hill. There was a remarkable exemption from frost. Nevertheless the readings of the barometer were high for the time of year, and the month passed away without any particular gale. The rainfall

Q

was rather more than half-an-inch greater than the average of 22 years at this Observatory.

DECEMBER.

The mean temperature was quite two degrees below the average, and from the 1st to the 11th frost occurred more or less on every night. The weather then became milder to the 22nd inclusive, after which a cold period commenced and continued to the close of the month. On the morning of the 21st eleven degrees of frost occurred on the surface of short grass and nearly eight degrees in the screen. The last fortnight was remarkably dry and the winds were chiefly from the eastward.

_____

1893.

JANUARY.

THE frost which commenced on December 23rd continued to the 18th of this month, a period of 27 days, and was more remarkable for its continuance than for its severity. The lowest reading in the screen was $18°·2$ on the morning of the 3rd. During the last thirteen days the temperature was much higher and on two nights only did it fall below the freezing point. The mean temperature of the month was $33°·5$, which was three degrees below the average and the lowest since 1881. Snow fell several times during the first seventeen days, but the depth never exceeded four inches. The rainfall and melted snow amounted to 2·67 inches, which was about 0·75 inch less than the average. On the 5th a bright solar halo was visible from 11 a.m to 1 p.m. On the 11th some beautiful snow crystals fell in considerable quantity.

FEBRUARY

This month was mild and very wet. The temperature was 1°·5 and the rainfall nearly two inches above the average. Slight frost occurred during the first and third weeks, but never more than four degrees below the freezing point. The wind was chiefly from the westward with gales, more or less severe, on 9th, 14th, 21st and 26th. Snowstorms passed over on 22nd and 23rd. A bright Aurora was visible on the evening of the 7th. At 4 p.m on the 21st the lowest reading of the barometer was 28 738 inches, which was the lowest reading during the month.

MARCH.

On the second day of this month commenced the most severe drought which had occurred in the South of England during the last half century. The mean temperature of this month was nearly six degrees above the average; consequently it was the warmest March for many years past. Throughout the month the amount of sunshine was quite phenomenal, while the brilliancy of the nights for astronomical observations was almost continuous during the latter half of the month The air, as might be expected, was remarkably dry, the temperature of the dew point having been on several days as much as 15° to 20° below that of the air. The winds, for the most part, fluctuated between west and north-west.

APRIL.

This was the driest month throughout the drought, while the brilliancy of the sky, both day and night, exceeded even that of the previous month. The wind was chiefly from the eastward, while the dryness of the air on many days was excessive. The temperature in the shade was never abnormally high, with the exception of the 17th, but it was decidedly above the average during the third and fourth weeks. The mean temperature for the entire month was six degrees above the average. The only rainfall was a slight shower on the morning of the 17th. A brilliant solar halo was visible at 10.30 on the 19th. At the close of the month vegetation generally was in a very exhausted condition. Many of our spring flowers came very prematurely into bloom and through lack of moisture soon faded and disappeared. Nevertheless, some seed of the annuals quickly ripened and falling, soon germinated with the rains of July and flowered in the autumn, a circumstance which I do not recollect to have ever previously observed. The lilac came into full bloom, which is very seldom observed before the latter part of May in this locality

MAY.

During this month also the drought continued, for the rainfall was little more than a fifth of the average, and came in such driblets that it was scarcely sufficient to lay the dust in the roads. Brilliant weather continued, for the most part, both day and night, consequently the mean temperature was five degrees above the average. Throughout the month the temperature at night was high for the season. The wind was extremely variable. If the drought was so serious at the end of April it was, of course, still more so at the close of this month. Many shrubs and trees, planted in the previous autumn, perished. The pastures were parched and brown, while here and there scarcely a green blade was to be seen except under the shade of trees and hedges. The wheat was the only crop which looked fairly well.

JUNE.

The drought may be said to have continued during the first three weeks of this month also, for the trifling showers which fell on the 4th and 6th very quickly evaporated from the parched soil, so that it was not until the early morning of the 23rd that a really refreshing shower fell. The mean temperature of the month was nearly three degrees above the average. The weather was very hot on the 19th, viz , 88° in the shade ; while a thermometer (with a blackened bulb in vacuo) indicated 142°·5. This was the warmest day since August 11th, 1884. The wind was chiefly from the eastward and the air very dry, thus on the 17th, at 9 a m., the temperature of the dew point was as much as 30° below that of the air ! The rainfall for the month was about half the average.

OBSERVATIONS UPON THE GREAT DROUGHT DURING THE SPRING MONTHS OF 1893.

The drought which prevailed during the late spring and first three weeks of summer was, I think, without any doubt, the most severe and protracted over the South and South-East of England, of which we have any satisfactory record during the present century.

As we have no evidence that rain gauges were employed for any statistical purpose until the latter half of the seventeenth century, we have no means of ascertaining how far ancient records are reliable with respect to the severity and continuance of the droughts mentioned by them.

Mr. G. J. Symons, F.R.S., has given, in his "Annual British Rainfall" for 1887, a very comprehensive list of droughts which are supposed to have occurred in the British Isles since the third century, some of which are, to a certain extent, confirmed by successive historians. A very remarkable one is recorded by the Venerable Bede, who states in his "Ecclesiastical History," B iv., C. xiii., that about the year 678 there had fallen no rain in the province of the South Saxons for three years, and the people were brought into such misery by reason of the famine which ensued, that often forty or fifty men, being spent with want, would go together to some precipice or the sea shore and there hand in hand either perish by the fall or be swallowed up by the waves. The chief sources of information respecting severe droughts in former times are "The Saxon Chronicle," Holinshed's, Stow's and Short's "Chronicles," &c.

With respect to the rainfall at my Observatory on Crowborough Hill the following are a few particulars of the late drought as compared with other spring seasons since the year 1870. During this period the mean aggregate rainfall of the months of March, April and May was 6 89 inches, but for 1893 the amount was only 1·05 inch,* which is 15°/₀ of the average. This shows a rainfall deficiency at Crowborough of 5·84 inches, which in weight of water represents a loss to the land of 590 tons per acre. Little wonder, then, that field crops were so exhausted, while some disappeared altogether!

* This includes the rainfall on March 1st.

Although some of our wells were dry, yet the two public springs have well maintained their ancient character of being inexhaustible; otherwise our population would have been in great straits for the important element.

JULY.

This month also had a mean temperature above the average and so was also the rainfall, notwithstanding which the amount of moisture was no more than sufficient to revive vegetation without having any beneficial effect upon the springs and wells, which had been almost exhausted for several weeks. The only real summer weather occurred during the first week, after which time the weather was much cooler and showery. The only heavy rain fell on the 19th. On the 8th some very large hailstones fell a short distance to the westward. A gale came on during the night of the 19th and continued till nearly noon of the following day. During the latter part of the month this locality, and I believe the county generally, had to endure a great plague of wasps, but although some hundreds of nests were destroyed, yet their number scarcely diminished.

AUGUST.

Notwithstanding the remarkably fine weather which prevailed during the spring this month was, upon the whole, the most genial of the year. Its mean temperature was upwards of three and a half degrees above the average of twenty years. It was a very dry month, as the rainfall was little more than one-fourth of the average, while the dew point temperature at 9 a.m. was more than eleven degrees below that of the air. The winds were chiefly from S.E. to W. The hottest period occurred during the third week, in which the highest daily temperature in the shade ranged from 72° to 87°. Some electrical disturbance was observed on the 9th and 18th. Altogether, the weather was most favourable for harvest operations. The plague of wasps continued throughout.

SEPTEMBER.

The fine summer weather which had prevailed during the previous month continued to the 15th and at this period vegetation generally gave indications of lack of moisture, for less than three-quarters of an inch of rain had fallen during the previous five weeks. The mean temperature was somewhat below the average, in consequence of the gloomy wet weather which prevailed during the last fortnight. The rainfall was half-an-inch above the average. The brilliant skies on fifteen nights were most favourable for astronomical observations.

OCTOBER.

The mean temperature of this month was rather more than two degrees above the average of many years, while the temperature at night more resembled that of September, or even the latter part of August. The rainfall was above the average, which was due to the very heavy rain on the 11th, which exceeded two inches. This was the heaviest rain on any day since September 3rd, 1884. Sharp frosts have sometimes occurred towards the end of this month, but not a trace of frost was observed until the last morning, when the temperature fell to 29°·5. Distant lightning was seen on the 9th and 30th. Both solar and lunar haloes were frequent.

NOVEMBER.

This month was cold and showery with a great prevalence of N.E. wind, which reduced the mean temperature to more than two degrees below the average. The rainfall was more than an inch below the average of many years. On the 18th, a severe gale with snow came on from the N.E., which was followed by several frosty nights and a low day temperature. In consequence of the high wind on the 18th the precise depth of snow could not be ascertained, but it must have been more than was indicated by the gauge. The month ended in very gloomy, damp weather.

DECEMBER.

The mean temperature of this month was slightly above that for November, but nearly three degrees higher than the average. Upon the whole, it was the warmest December which had been observed here for several years. Gales more or less severe occurred on the 8th, 12th, 13th, 19th and 20th. On the latter day the reading of the barometer reduced to sea level at 4 p.m., 28·735 inches; this was the lowest since November 11th, 1891. On the morning of the 30th the reading was very high, viz., 30·801 inches at 9 a.m, so that during the month the readings ranged upwards of two inches. Fourteen nights were very favourable for astronomical observations. The rainfall was below the average.

With respect to the total rainfall of this dry year, I will remark that, with the exception of 1884, it was the driest year during the last 23 years at Crowborough, and that it was as much as 8·60 inches below the average.

1894.

JANUARY.

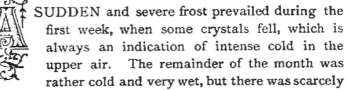SUDDEN and severe frost prevailed during the first week, when some crystals fell, which is always an indication of intense cold in the upper air. The remainder of the month was rather cold and very wet, but there was scarcely any return of frost. The rainfall was heavy on the 25th, and the total for the month exceeded the average by two inches and a quarter. On the 17th a beautiful prismatic corona surrounded the moon at 9 p.m. On the 19th a gale came on from the westward and less severe ones on the 22nd and 27th.

The mean temperature was equal to the average of 23 years.

FEBRUARY.

This month was mild, with frequent slight rains, but the total for the month was below the average. The mean temperature exceeded the average by rather more than one degree. With the exception of three days during the second week the readings of the barometer were high.

On the evening of the 28th I noticed, about 8.45 p.m , a brilliant display of the Aurora Borealis, extending from almost due east to N.W. At different points were patches of pink cloud, while nearer the horizon were some patches of white cloud visible, which by degrees slowly shifted away to the eastward and appeared alternately brighter and paler as they passed along. The patches of pink cloud were considerably higher than the general mass of the Aurora. At ten o'clock the whole phenomenon had much diminished in extent and brilliancy.

MARCH.

The first week of this month was fine and pleasant, but during the second week the weather was gloomy, damp and showery, with a gale on the 11th. From the 15th to 31st inclusive no rain fell, but the temperature was rather low for the season on account of the great prevalence of northerly and easterly winds The last week was remarkable for brilliant and almost cloudless skies. The mean temperature was upwards of three degrees above the average and the total rainfall half-an-inch below it.

APRIL

The drought which prevailed during the last 17 days of March continued during the first 13 days of this month, thus constituting an absolute drought of 30 days. The general character of the weather much resembled that of the corresponding period of 1893. The mean temperature was very high and as much as five degrees above the average of 21 years On the 13th vegetation generally was in a drooping condition, so that the refreshing shower of the 14th was most welcome. A considerable amount of rain fell during the last eight days, which was of essential benefit to all growing crops. The total for the month was slightly above the average

MAY.

A cold month The mean temperature was two degrees below that of the previous month and nearly three degrees below the average. The weather was frequently gloomy and showery, but the rainfall for the month was below the average In common with most parts of the kingdom a frost occurred on the morning of the 21st, but it amounted to only one degree in the screen. It was much more severe on the lower grounds in this neighbourhood—even to the extent of ten degrees! The upper leaves of the potato haulm and the strawberry blossom were only slightly injured here. At Buxted, on the S. side of us, and Tunbridge Wells, to the N., an immense amount of damage was done in gardens, and even the oak trees were almost stripped bare of their young and tender foliage, from which they did not recover until about the middle of July.

JUNE

During the first three weeks the weather was gloomy, cold and showery, with an unusual amount of N.W. wind. The mean temperature was slightly below the average and the rainfall also. The weather improved considerably during the last week and the sky was almost cloudless from 25th to 30th inclusive. These few days and the two first of the following month comprised the only suitable weather for hay-making throughout the summer.

JULY.

With the exception of the 1st, 2nd and 6th days the weather throughout the month was gloomy and wet. Nevertheless, the mean temperature was nearly equal to the average. On the night of the 6th a heavy thunderstorm passed over. The lightning was of a peculiar character, consisting of double flashes, having an interval of about half a second between them. The greater portion of it was like sheet lightning, passing from cloud to cloud without earth contact. Thunder was only heard at intervals. Very heavy rain fell during the nights of the 10th and 29th, the amount exceeding an inch in both instances. The total rainfall was nearly two and a half inches above the average.

AUGUST.

This month was also very gloomy and wet, although the total rainfall was not equal to the average. The mean temperature was somewhat below the average and its daily range unusually small for the season. Some distant electrical disturbance was observed on the 25th and 26th, but there was not any thunderstorm in this immediate locality. During the last week a very considerable breadth of hay was still lying in the fields, not dry enough to be stacked.

SEPTEMBER.

This month was for the most part gloomy and cold, with some heavy rains at intervals, while the total amount exceeded the average of twenty years by about an inch The mean temperature was as much as two and a half degrees below the average. There was a most unusual prevalence of easterly winds, for, with the exception of five days, they blew persistently between the northerly and south-easterly points. Haymaking was not finished by the end of the month and hop-picking was much interrupted by the frequent rains.

OCTOBER.

The mean temperature was above the average and there was not a trace of frost—a most unusual circumstance in this month. During the first nineteen days the rainfall was considerably below the average, but from the 20th to 31st, both inclusive, rain fell more or less every day, and frequently to a large amount, so that the total for the month was above the average of this, the wettest month of the year. Strong gales from the westward occurred on the 24th and 27th North-easterly winds were the most prevalent and the sky was much covered by cloud, so that haymaking had to be *finished* during the first week, which, I should think, must be the latest time on record.

NOVEMBER.

The chief feature of this month was the continuous rain during the first sixteen days, which, added to that of the last twelve days of the previous month, amounted to the very large quantity of 10·58 inches in the twenty-eight consecutive days. It was a very mild month and the mean temperature was more than three degrees above the average. This month also passed away without a trace of frost. It was the warmest November since the year 1881. The last fortnight was comparatively fine, pleasant and very mild for the season.

DECEMBER.

This was another very mild month and its mean temperature was more than two degrees above the average With the exception of a slight frost on the morning of the 4th, none occurred until the last week. Heavy gales were recorded on the 21st and 28th. Rain fell more or less on sixteen days, but the total for the month was considerably below the average of twenty-four years. Notwithstanding the great depression of the barometer on the 21st and 29th, the readings for the month exceeded the average. At 9 a.m. on 28th my barometer reading was 30·616 inches (reduced to sea level), and at the same hour on the following morning it had fallen to 29·524 inches.

———

1895.

THE GREAT FROST OF JANUARY AND FEBRUARY.

THE severe frost of January and February, 1895, having been the most protracted since the great frost of 1814, I trust that the following particulars respecting it, as it occurred on Crowborough Hill and its neighbourhood, may be of interest for future reference.

The month of November, 1894, was very mild, without a trace of frost, while its mean temperature was more than three degrees above the average of 22 years. December was also very mild, with a mean temperature of more than two degrees above the average The temperature in a Stevenson screen, at a height of four feet from the ground, fell to 25°, from which date to January 13th, inclusive, frost, more or less severe, occurred on every night.

The succeeding eight days (14th to 21st, both inclusive) were comparatively mild, with frequent rains, and no frost was registered. This constituted a very decided break in the otherwise long continuous frost. During the early morning of the 22nd there was a return of frost which henceforth was continuous to February 18th, inclusive. It was during this period that the cold assumed its greatest severity (January 25th excluded). The mean temperature of these 27 days was as low as 25°·2.

The frost may be said to have gradually lessened in severity from February 19th to March 8th, both inclusive, as from this latter date the temperature in the screen did not fall to the freezing point at any time during the remainder of the month.

This frost was far more severe in the neighbourhood of Crowborough than on its summit. Thus, at Buxted Park, as I have elsewhere stated, the temperature fell to 4° below zero; at Groombridge, to 4°; at Tunbridge Wells, to 4°; at Kidbrooke Park, near East Grinstead, to 9°. At Hedgecourt Lake, near East Grinstead, the ice attained a thickness of 13 inches. This lake is between 60 and 70 acres in extent and on one day during the frost a gentleman drove his four-in-hand coach round it and did a couple of miles on the ice without the slightest fracture being occasioned.

The mean temperature of the whole period from December 30th to March 8th, both inclusive, was 29°·7, the mean maximum 34°·3 and the mean minimum 25°·2, but if we exclude the mild weather which prevailed from January 14th to 21st, we shall find that the mean temperature from December 30th to March 8th was only 28°·6, the mean maximum 33°·4 and the mean minimum 23° 8.

The following table will give the daily highest and lowest temperatures from December 30th, 1894, to March 8th, 1895, both inclusive. The small letter ˢ indicates that the precipitation was snow.

TABLE I.

1894-95. December / 1895 January

1894-95 Dec.	Maximum	Minimum	Precipitation
30	35·0	30·0	
31	32·4	25·0	ˢ04
Jan 1	33·4	25·5	ˢ10
2	38·0	27·7	ˢ06
3	33·1	30·8	ˢ02
4	34·0	28·0	ˢ06
5	33·4	30·5	
6	34·9	27·1	·01
7	31·8	25·6	ˢ02
8	33·8	27·5	
9	30·0	28·2	ˢ39
10	35·0	24·2	·11
11	28·0	23·2	·17
12	36·0	22·1	·03
13	38·0	25·0	·11
14	40·0	35·0	·01
15	39·5	35·2	·09
16	42·0	35·3	·62
17	41·8	38·0	·27
18	40·1	32·2	...
19	44·3	34·1	
20	48·6	38·0	
21	36·6	36·2	

1895 Jan	Maximum	Minimum	Precipitation
22	36·4	27·1	ˢ17
23	39·8	26·8	ˢ08
24	39·0	23·8	ˢ09
25	36·3	34·8	ˢ04
26	31·5	22·0	ˢ02
27	31·0	21·2	ˢ01
28	26·0	22·2	
29	30·4	20·0	ˢ05
30	29·2	20·5	
31	30·2	22·4	ˢ16
Feb 1	27·8	18·8	
2	30·3	21·0	ˢ07
3	29·6	16·6	ˢ04
4	32·8	22·5	
5	25·8	21·0	ˢ03
6	21·8	14·7	ˢ16
7	19·6	12·8	
8	27·6	13·0	
9	30·1	18·0	...
10	26·0	19·1	...
11	29·0	21·8	
12	33·3	18·1	
13	34·3	21·3	...

1895 Feb	Maximum	Minimum	Precipitation
14	24·3	19·0	
15	29·0	18·1	
16	31·0	23·5	
17	34·6	21·0	
18	33·0	24·2	
19	35·9	28·0	·30
20	35·3	26·1	ˢ20
21	38·2	31·5	
22	38·2	32·5	:
23	40·0	31·4	:
24	43·8	32·6	·04
25	31·8	29·2	ˢ03
26	37·0	25·7	·06
27	38·3	27·8	
28	42·4	28·8	·18
March 1	40·4	27·0	:
2	37·2	30·1	:
3	34·0	22·4	
4	35·9	23·8	
5	37·3	27·0	
6	38·9	29·6	
7	35·6	29·2	:
8	41·5	30·8	·07

R

The mean temperature of February was 27°·4, which was the lowest mean monthly temperature recorded in Sussex during the last fifty-three years.

Had it not been for the mild weather which prevailed during the third week of January, the severe cold might be said to have been continuous for the long period of 69 days, or nearly ten weeks, but, setting this aside, it was certainly the most remarkable frost since 1814; nevertheless, it should be understood that its chief feature was its long continuance rather than its intensity.

Snow fell frequently in January, but in small quantities; the heaviest fall occurred on the 12th, when quite a blizzard of wind and snow passed over; the snow being very small penetrated into every crevice of the house roofs. On the 23rd quite a hurricane with fine snow, lightning and thunder occurred, when the District Church was struck by lightning and slightly damaged. In February snow fell on five days only and rain once. Snow *crystals* fell on many days, more particularly on January 28th and 30th, in various forms and without any visible cloud; also on February 1st, 2nd, 8th, 14th and 15th, but on the 6th and 7th they again fell in considerable quantities without any visible cloud.

MARCH.

The mean temperature of March was slightly above the average of 22 years and the rainfall just equal to the mean of 25 years. A sudden and great decrease of temperature occurred between the 22nd and 23rd. The maximum on the former day was 61°, but on the latter only 47°. A very fine prismatic lunar corona was visible near midnight of the 5th.

APRIL.

The mean temperature was slightly above the average as was also the rainfall. The weather was very variable in its character, while a considerable amount of fog and mist were prevalent at intervals, with a great interchange of north - easterly and westerly winds. The cuckoo appeared on the 10th, a swallow on the 11th and the nightingale on 21st.

MAY.

The mean temperature was nearly three degrees above the average, and, notwithstanding the great prevalence of N , N E. and easterly winds, it was a very pleasant month and remarkably dry, the rainfall amounting to only 0 06 of an inch, which was the least amount recorded in this county for any month of May during the last fifty-three years. On several days the temperature in the shade was very high, more particularly on the 13th, 14th and 30th. On the mornings of the 17th and 18th a sharp frost occurred in many parts of Sussex, but the lowest temperature recorded here was $35°·2$ in the screen and $34°·2$ on the grass

A very brilliant solar halo was visible here from 9 to 10 a.m. on the 12th. Frequent lightning occurred during the evenings of 25th, 30th and 31st.

JUNE

Was a very fine summer month, although its mean temperature but very slightly exceeded the average. It was also a very dry month and vegetation suffered rather severely on account of the great drought of the previous month. This drought may be said to have commenced on April 28th and it continued to July 17th—a period of 81 days—the total amount of rain which fell was only 0·68 of an inch.

At the close of this month the rainfall since January 1st had only been 7·97 inches, which was little more than *half the average* for the same period during the last 25 years.

JULY.

July was fine and pleasant to the 17th, when rainy weather commenced and continued to the 28th inclusive, so that the month's total of rainfall was exactly equal to the average. The mean temperature was more than two degrees below the average.

AUGUST.

The rainy weather, which commenced on July 18th, continued, for the most part, to the 14th of this month, during which time (four weeks) 5·86 inches of rain had fallen, which proved to be of immense benefit to vegetation generally. From the 14th to the close of the month the weather was again very fine and pleasant, the temperature having been above the average both by day and by night. The warmest day was the 22nd, with a maximum temperature of 77° in the shade during the day and a minimum of 63°·4 during the night.

SEPTEMBER

This month was very remarkable for its high temperature, frequent cloudless skies and drought. Its mean temperature was higher than either of the summer months, while the great heat which prevailed during the last week was quite abnormal and exceeded any previous instance, so late in the month, of which we have any satisfactory record. The mean temperature of the entire month was 62°·3, which is nearly four and a half degrees above the average of many years. The only previous instances of such great heat in September, at all comparable, occurred in the years 1843 and 1865, but in both these instances much earlier in the month

In consequence of the recurrence of drought during this month the deficiency in the rainfall since January 1st had increased to 9 36 inches, notwithstanding the welcome showers of July and August. The most prevalent winds were from the S E. and S W. It was an exceedingly fine month also for astronomical observations, the sky having been cloudless on 21 nights !

OCTOBER.

With this month came a very great decrease of temperature The usual difference between the mean temperature of September and October has been rather more than seven degrees, but in this instance it amounted to sixteen and a half degrees, which, however, was, in part, due to the fact that the mean temperature of October was nearly three degrees below the average of the last 22 years. The rainfall was half an inch below the average.

During the last week frost occurred on every night, but the lowest temperature in the screen was only 27°·3. Brilliant lightning was visible over the Channel during the evenings of 24th and 25th A little snow fell on the early morning of the 29th.

NOVEMBER

Was a mild month and its mean temperature was nearly four degrees above the average and the rainfall nearly two inches. The sky was much obscured by cloud, mist and fog, while gales of wind were prevalent on the 5th, 10th, 15th, 24th and 25th.

DECEMBER

Was also a mild month, but a few slight frosts occurred occasionally. The lowest temperature in the screen was 29° on the 28th. The rainfall was nearly an inch above the average, and it was very heavy (1·33 inch) on the 16th. Strong gales occurred on the 5th and 12th and the month closed with very mild weather and N.W. wind.

1896

JANUARY.

HIS was a very mild month and its mean temperature was more than two degrees above the average. The rainfall was about equal to half the average quantity, although the wind was very prevalent from the westward. On the morning of the 9th the reduced reading of the barometer was as high as 30·927 inches, which was the highest I have recorded since January 18th, 1882. Very little frost occurred, and but one slight fall of snow, during the night of the 8th.

FEBRUARY.

This was, upon the whole, another mild month, but in consequence of the cold weather which prevailed during the last week its mean temperature only slightly exceeded the average.

It was a very dry month, notwithstanding its mildness, for the total rainfall amounted to only one-seventh

of the average. The most prevalent wind was from the
N.E. The barometer remained very high, and this month
also passed away without any gale. Notwithstanding
the drought, the weather was often very dull, with some
fog at intervals Although the winter was so mild, yet
it was not so warm as the winters of 1882-83 and 1883-84.

MARCH.

The weather was again very mild throughout this
month, with scarcely a trace of frost, which was a very
unusual circumstance in the first of the spring months.
Its mean temperature in the shade was almost four
degrees above the average, and was therefore nearly as
warm as the corresponding month in 1893. Rain fell
more or less on twenty days and the total was nearly an
inch above the average.

A great many sulphur butterflies (Gonepteryx Rhamni)
appeared on the 21st and also the Vanessa Urticæ.

APRIL.

The mean temperature of this month was 1°·5 above
the average. The drought, which had been prevalent in
February, returned during the second week and continued for the most part to the second week in June.
The readings of the barometer were high and the most
prevalent wind was from the N.W. About one o'clock
on the 1st the Hill was enveloped for about half-an-hour
in an extraordinary darkness, which finally cleared off
and the sequel was a brilliant starlight evening and
night. On the 12th some smart showers of snow and
hail fell, with wind squalls from the N.W. A lunar halo
was visible during the evening of the 21st and a solar
halo on the following morning.

MAY.

For the last twenty-six years this has been, upon the average, the driest month of the year, and in the present instance it fully maintained its character, the total rainfall not having been more than one-fifth of the usual amount. There was an extraordinary prevalence of N.E. wind; a very high barometer; a low Dew Point, and the lowest relative humidity of any May during the last twenty-one years. At the close of the month vegetation generally stood in urgent need of some soaking showers, for, with the exception of the shower on the 21st (0·21 inch), scarcely any rain had fallen.

THE DROUGHT.

With the exception of the month of March the five preceding months were remarkably dry. The total rainfall was only 6·55 inches, whereas the average for Crowborough Hill during the past twenty-six years has been 12·23 inches. This great deficiency, added to that of 6·71 inches for the year 1895, shows a total deficiency of 13·26 inches during the seventeen months ending May 31st, 1896, and fully exercised a great strain upon the water supply throughout the county, for the actual loss was at the rate of 1,340 tons of water per acre.

JUNE.

The severe drought may be said to have terminated during the first week of this month. The welcome change was heralded by a brilliant chromatic solar halo, which was continued from 10 a.m. till noon on the 2nd. It was followed by a shower during the night. Rain also fell on the 4th, 6th and 7th. On the early morning

of the 10th heavy rain commenced and continued
throughout the entire day and part of the night. This
great rainfall was followed by some very fine weather
and rain was only registered twice during the remainder
of the month. Its mean temperature was rather more
than one degree above the average and variable winds
were prevalent. A slight thunder shower occurred on
the morning of the 4th and again during the afternoon
of the 24th.

JULY

Was a fine summer month, with frequent brilliant weather
and only an occasional rainfall, the amount of which was
little more than one-third of the average. Its mean
temperature was exactly equal to that of the last 23
years. Although the weather was so fine, yet the heat
was never oppressive, while the maximum temperature
in the shade only exceeded 80° on the 14th and 21st.
Distant thunderstorms were observed on the 15th. A
sudden and very great decrease of temperature occurred
on the 16th, when the maximum in the shade was twenty
degrees lower than on the previous day. At the end of
the third week the air had again become very dry, so that
vegetation was once more drooping until there occurred
the refreshing shower (0·54 inch) on the 26th.

AUGUST.

The weather during this month was showery and cold,
while its mean temperature was more than four degrees
below the average. Although rain fell more or less on
14 days, yet the total amount was nearly one inch below
the mean of 26 years. N.E. and N.W. winds were
unusually prevalent. Thunderstorms occurred in this

district on the 19th, 25th, 26th and 27th. On the 26th the lightning struck some cottages at Brede, which were burnt to the ground. Very vivid lightning was seen over the English Channel about midnight of the 31st.

SEPTEMBER.

This month was remarkable for its low temperature and very heavy rainfall. Its mean temperature was two and a half degrees below the average, while the amount of rainfall was the largest for this month within living memory.

There were only six days without rain, while on the 12th 1·20 inch fell during the twenty-four hours, ending at 9 a.m. on the 13th, and still more (1 29 inch) fell on the 24th. By far the most prevalent wind was the S W., of which there had been a decided deficiency in several previous months A severe thunderstorm passed over on the 8th, with heavy rain. The church steeple of Lamberhurst was wrecked by the lightning. Thunderstorms also occurred on the 9th and 12th with heavy rain.

During the night of the 22nd a heavy gale came up from the westward and quite a hurricane prevailed during the night of the 24th. It was preceded and accompanied by a great fall of the barometer. The lowest reading observed by me was 28 873 inches at 9 a m of the 25th, which indicated a fall of 1·097 inch since the same hour on the previous day.

OCTOBER.

This was another wet and cold month, while its mean temperature was as much as four degrees below the average. Rain fell more or less on twenty-two days and gave a total of rather more than one inch above the mean for this, which is usually the wettest month of the year. It was distributed very irregularly over the county; thus at Thorny, near Chichester, the total was only 3 08 inches; at Horsham, 3·86 inches; at Lewes, 5·36 inches, and· at Selmeston Vicarage, 6 56 inches. South-westerly winds were the most prevalent, accompanied, on several days, by low barometric readings. Thunderstorms with vivid lightning occurred on the 5th, 25th and 26th.

A heavy snow shower fell in the early morning of the 19th, which was followed by a heavy precipitation of rain, sleet and snow for several hours. The sky was for the most part densely overcast both day and night during the first three weeks. The last few days were clearer and very little rain fell after the 26th.

NOVEMBER.

Although this was a pleasant month, for the season, on account of there having been more sunshine than usual, yet its mean temperature was rather more than three degrees below the average The weather was also rendered more agreeable by the small amount of rainfall in comparison with that for the two preceding months, only 1·73 inch having fallen, whereas the average of 26 years is 4·27 inches With the exception of hoar frost on the morning of the 7th the temperature in the screen did not fall below 32° until the 28th. Stormy winds were prevalent on the 8th and 14th. The month closed with brilliant weather and hard frost.

DECEMBER.

The first half of this month was mild, but very rainy. The third week was frosty. On the fourth a strong gale came up from S.E., accompanied by an even lower reading of the barometer than on the 24th of September, viz, 28·724 inches (reduced to sea level).

Such a severe gale seldom occurs from the S.E. in the South of England. The night of the 13th was also stormy, with rain from S.E. From the 16th to 20th, both inclusive, a very thick hoar frost continued, when the trees and shrubs were beautifully decked with rime, which continued throughout those days. A little snow on the night of the 20th.

During the last week the weather was milder again, with daily rains and a densely overcast sky.

The mean temperature was nearly one degree and the rainfall one and a half inches above the average.

—

1897.

JANUARY.

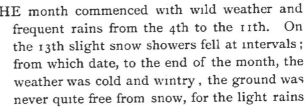

HE month commenced with wild weather and frequent rains from the 4th to the 11th. On the 13th slight snow showers fell at intervals; from which date, to the end of the month, the weather was cold and wintry, the ground was never quite free from snow, for the light rains on the 29th and 30th, which fell occasionally, were not sufficient to effect an entire thaw.

Vivid lightning was visible over the English Channel during the evening of the 22nd, while on the 23rd a severe gale from the N.E. prevailed with continuous small driving snow all day and evening, which accumulated in deep drifts in various places and obstructed traffic. The actual depth upon the level could not be ascertained by the rain gauge on account of the strong wind, but the average estimated depth was five inches, which yielded o 56 of water. This was the most severe blizzard which has occurred in this county since January, 1881. The mean temperature of the month was $2°·5$ below the average, as was also the precipitation of rain and snow. The most prevalent winds were from N.W. by north to N.E.

FEBRUARY.

This was a mild winter month and its mean temperature exceeded the average by nearly three degrees The weather was, however, very gloomy and damp from cloud resting on the Hill more frequently than I ever remember at this locality, which is, for the most part, remarkable for the dryness of its air during the winter months.

After the 1st scarcely any snow fell, but there were frequent rains during the first fortnight, and the total quantity for the month rather exceeded the average. Westerly winds were the most prevalent. A lunar halo was observed at 8 p m. on the 16th

MARCH.

The most remarkable feature of this month was the heavy rainfall during the first seventeen days, and the total for the entire month was more than five inches. This was the heaviest March rainfall which had occurred in Sussex during the last fifty-four years. Westerly winds were again the most prevalent, and not one degree of frost was recorded. The readings of the barometer were low in consequence of the frequent heavy rains and the gales which accompanied them. The lowest corrected reading here was observed at 9 a m on the 3rd, viz , 28·887 inches.

APRIL

Although scarcely any frost occurred this month yet in consequence of the low day temperature the air was generally cold and ungenial for the season. Its mean temperature was $2\frac{1}{2}°$ below the average. N.E. winds were the most prevalent, except during the second and third weeks. Vivid lightning was visible to the northward during the afternoon of the 7th, while on the 15th, between 2 and 3 p m., a heavy thunder shower passed over the Hill. The lightning was very vivid and the peals of thunder unusually prolonged Heavy hail fell, the stones being of very uniform size and about the size of marbles. The ground for a time was quite covered by them and presented a remarkable appearance They were soft, considering their size, and no damage was done to glass houses. The cuckoo came to us on the 15th, but the swallow not until the 23rd.

MAY.

Another dry May ! for very little rain fell until the last six days of the month. It was also a cold month and therefore very ungenial for all kinds of vegetation. During the third week bitterly cold N.E. winds reduced the mean temperature to fully three degrees below the average. The readings of the barometer varied but slightly. By the end of the third week the soil had

From a Photograph by Wynter, Seaford.

A REPRODUCTION (FAC-SIMILE SIZE) OF SOME HAILSTONES WHICH FELL become very dry, but it was not until the 26th that all nature was refreshed by frequent showers.

On the evening of the 30th of this month a more memorable thunderstorm passed over a portion of this county than has happened within living memory. Although it occurred at a distance of nearly twenty miles from my house yet its elevated position enabled me to watch the progress of the storm for a considerable time.

Soon after three o'clock very heavy electric clouds appeared over the South Downs, near Newhaven, and for some time remained almost stationery. A rather strong easterly wind was blowing over Crowborough Hill in the direction of the storm, which seemed to prevent its advance in our direction; this wind at last increased in force and apparently drove the advancing clouds upon the main mass of the storm. Soon after 6 p.m. a line of Nimbus cloud, two or three miles in length, of a whitish appearance, exhibited a well-defined edge on its northern side and any further advance of the storm in our direction was checked. After passing over Seaford and Selmeston it rapidly increased its pace and finally disappeared to the eastward. While passing over Selmeston, accompanied by a furious wind, it struck the Vicarage with great force; hailstones measuring $1\frac{1}{2}$-inch by $\frac{3}{4}$-inch dashed through no less than 25 panes of glass and spread over the floor.

JUNE.

The mean temperature of this month was high, although there were but few really hot days, but I think this was due to the rather high night temperature, which gave a shorter range than usual. The only hot days were the 23rd and 24th. A great decrease of temperature occurred on the 25th, when the highest temperature in the shade was 18° less than on the previous day. The N.E. wind was even more prevalent than on the previous month. The rainfall was much below the average, and but for the very welcome rain during the night of the 8th the May drought might be said to have continued to the 15th. On the 6th a heavy thunderstorm passed to the north of Crowborough Hill, where the lightning and thunder was almost continuous for the space of two hours. Lightning was visible southward during the evening of the 26th and again on the 28th.

At 11 p.m. on the 13th a brilliant chromatic lunar corona was visible for a considerable time.

JULY.

This must also be considered to have been a dry month, for the total rainfall was not equal to half the average, while had it not been for the plentiful rain on the 21st vegetation would have again been sadly parched.

The mean temperature was exactly equal to the average of twenty-four years.

The winds were very variable and somewhat similar to those which prevailed in May. The air on many days was very dry and the temperature of the Dew Point was as frequently as much as twenty degrees lower. A thunderstorm occurred on the 21st and lasted two hours, while thunder showers were frequent in this district on the 26th and 27th.

AUGUST.

The mean temperature of this month was slightly above the average, as was also the rainfall, whereby vegetation was much benefited after the comparatively dry weather of the two previous months By far the most prevalent wind was from the S.W., while there was a remarkable absence of wind from due S. and N. Violent squalls of wind with lightning and showers occurred during the afternoon of the 8th. Thunderstorms were also observed in this district on the 19th and 25th.

SEPTEMBER.

The mean temperature of this month was nearly two degrees below the average; nevertheless, it was, upon the whole, a fine and pleasant autumnal month. The rainfall was very slightly in excess and fell in frequent showers. The only heavy rains occurred on the 5th and 29th. The wind was very unsettled, but chiefly from the S.W. The month passed away without any gale. Slight thunderstorms occurred on the morning of the 17th and during the evening of the 29th. A very dense haze spread over the landscape during the third week and distant objects were rendered quite invisible.

OCTOBER.

The weather during this month was of such an exceptional character that a few additional remarks are thought necessary respecting it. The principal feature was the remarkable drought, which I find from examination of my journal was without precedent for this month during the last fifty-four years.

The rainfall in October is usually the heaviest of the year, but in this instance it was not a tenth of the average for Uckfield, and not a ninth of that for Crowborough. The former extends over a period of fifty-four years and the latter twenty-six years.

S

The following are some records of rainfall in various parts of Sussex reported to me

	Inch.			Inch
Crowborough	0·36	Selmeston Vicarage	.	0 30
Uckfield	0·38	Eastbourne ...	.	0 28
Buxted Park	0 40	Horsted Place		0 40
Forest Lodge	0 45	Isfield Place		0 29
Lewes	0 22	Winchelsea ...		0 13
Brighton	0 42			

So far as I know at present the heaviest rainfall (0·67) occurred at Horsham, a rather heavy shower having fallen there on the 25th. Not only was it a dry month, but it was conspicuous for a genial and calm condition of the air on many days with an unusual prevalence of wind from the S E

Its mean temperature was nearly two and a half degrees above the average, and was therefore the warmest October since 1861, with the exception of 1886, which was also a very warm month. There was an entire absence of frost throughout, while on four occasions only did the night temperature fall below 40°. The readings of the barometer were unprecedentedly high. Forest trees continued in full foliage and more than fifty of our summer flowers were in bloom during the last week.

NOVEMBER.

It is probably without precedent, during the present century, that the months of October and November, which are usually the *wettest* months, should be, with the exception of May and July, the *driest* of the year. The *general* features of these months were also very similar, viz., a deficient rainfall; very high readings of the barometer; a mean temperature considerably above the average and an unusual prevalence of S.E. wind.

The 1st was a brilliant cloudless day, when the highest temperature in the shade reached 58°·8, while a black bulb thermometer (in vacuo), placed in free air at four feet from the ground and in the full rays of the sun, recorded a temperature of 102°·1 On the 14th the temperature in the shade was 58° and on the 18th 57°·1

Not a trace of frost was recorded until the 26th, when the thermometer fell to 29°·3, which proved sufficient to destroy many flowers which had kept in fairly good bloom throughout October and to this date.

The last four days of the month assumed a different character. On the 27th the barometer commenced falling rather rapidly and some heavy rain fell during the night. The concluding three days were also rainy and stormy, while on the 29th a strong N.E gale continued for many hours. This northerly gale was not of the same violent character here as it was along the coast line of Sussex and Kent, as well as in various districts throughout the entire kingdom

DECEMBER

This, the first of the three winter months, maintained a relatively higher temperature than the two previous months, for its mean was as much as three and a half degrees above the average. A slight frost occurred on the mornings of the 4th and 22nd. The barometric depression which commenced during the last days of November continued, with frequent rains, during the first fortnight. The rainfall recorded for the 7th was exactly one inch, and the total amount for the month considerably exceeded the average. The S W. was the most prevalent wind, and gales from that quarter occurred on the 10th, 15th and 27th. During the night of the 15th frequent lightning and thunder accompanied the gale. From the 16th dry weather again prevailed until the 26th, when stormy and wet weather was experienced to the end of the month. The temperature of the whole year was only half a degree above the average, but there was a deficiency in the rainfall of nearly five inches and a quarter, which represents a loss to the soil of 530 tons of water per acre.

CHAPTER VI.

ON PROGNOSTICS OF ATMOSPHERIC CHANGES AS RECORDED BY VARIOUS ANCIENT AUTHORS; ALSO SOME MISCELLANEOUS LOCAL OBSERVATIONS, OLD PROVERBS, &c.

BEFORE entering upon this subject I will remark that there are probably few persons engaged in out-door pursuits or occupations who would not gladly avail themselves of trustworthy indications of important changes in the weather. Our insular position precludes, for the most part, any hope of foretelling what may be the general character of ensuing seasons, but the case is different when we allude to variations which are about to occur in the course of a few hours or days.

In order to prevent any disappointment, in reference to the result of our prognostics, it should ever be remembered that it is not desirable to place too much reliance upon any single prognostic. Upon this point the old philosopher Aratus has recorded—" Do not neglect any of these signs, for it is good to compare a sign with another sign; if two agree, so much the better, but be assured still more by a third." In addition to the indications given by philosophical instruments, the careful observation of many natural phenomena connected with the habits of animals, as well as the behaviour of various flowers and plants, give such valuable notice of atmospheric changes as will amply repay those who will pay due attention to the subject Moreover, our natural curiosity excites a constant desire to know what is about to happen, and renders some persons ready to observe, and to watch, those circumstances from which experience has taught them to anticipate certain results. Many weather prognostics are as valuable now as they were two thousand years ago and ought to have been familiar to every age. It is difficult to understand why certain animals should become so extremely sensitive to the approach of decided change of weather. Some of them exhibit symptoms of uneasiness long before there are any visible signs, and often, too, when they have not the opportunity of going abroad Hence it appears probable that any important change of weather is preceded by an indefinite alteration of the electrical condition of the atmosphere, the precise nature of which we are unable to determine In the wonderful economy of nature we cannot fail to notice that plants as well as animals exhibit certain prognostics. Some plants expand or contract their flowers or leaves according to the amount of existing moisture, while others are solely affected by the particular hour of the day.

It will be convenient to arrange the following prognostics in a classified manner —

1. PROGNOSTICS OF SEASONS.
2. FROM SCIENTIFIC INSTRUMENTS
3. FROM SUNRISE AND SUNSET
4. FROM THE RAINBOW.
5. FROM SOLAR AND LUNAR HALOES

6. FROM THE HABITS OF ANIMALS
7. FROM BIRDS
8. FROM INSECTS, &c
9. FROM PLANTS
10. MISCELLANEOUS PROGNOSTICS

Prognostics of Seasons.

ITH reference to prognostics of seasons, I will merely observe that there are very few upon which reliance can be placed. The following, however, need not be altogether discarded:—

From whatever quarter the wind blows at the quarter days there is a probability of it being the prevalent wind during the ensuing quarter.

Whenever the latter part of February and beginning of March are dry there will be a deficiency of rain up to Midsummer Day.

Whenever the weather during the month of May has been cold and wet, the following September will be warm and dry, and *vice versâ.*

If the months of October and November are cold, January and February have occasionally been mild and *vice versâ.*

A very hot and dry summer is sometimes succeeded by a winter of great severity.

When there have been many fogs during the month of March there will be some sharp frosts in May.

When the spring has been very wet, the latter part of summer and the beginning of autumn will be fine and dry.

If at the fall of the leaf many of them linger on the branches, it rather indicates a cold winter to follow.

When wasps build their nests high on the bank of a stream you may expect a wet summer, but if they place them near the usual level of the water a dry summer is indicated.

Aratus alludes to a prognostic of a severe winter from the habits of the wasp.

When the swan builds her nest much above the level of the water expect a wet season, and *vice versâ*.

When during the spring you observe that more swifts than swallows have arrived, expect a hot and dry summer.

If the feathers of water fowl be thicker and stronger than usual expect a cold winter.

The *early* appearance of fieldfares, woodcocks, snipes, wild ducks and other winter birds indicates a cold winter.

> If there's spring in winter, and winter in spring,
> The year won't be good for anything.

If the ice will bear a goose before Christmas it will not bear a duck after

An unusually fine day in autumn or winter is called a "Weather Breeder" in this county.

> This maxim never forget,
> To sow dry and set wet,
> One for the mouse, one for the crow,
> One to rot, and one to grow.

When there are plenty of nuts expect a hot and dry harvest.

> Observe when first the nuts begin to bloom,
> And flourishing, bend the tender branch ; if these
> Prove fruitful such shall be thy corn's increase,
> And, in great heat, huge harvests shall be found :
> But if with swelling leaves the shades abound,
> Then shall thou thrash a chaffy stalk in vain.

A serene autumn denotes a windy winter,
A windy winter a rainy spring,
A serene summer a windy autumn,
A rainy spring a serene summer.　　　　　BACON.

When the cuckoo comes to the bare thorn,
Sell your cow and buy your corn ;
But when she comes to the full bit (good keep)
Sell your corn and buy your sheep.

When the sand doth feed the clay,
England woe and well a day ;
But when the clay doth feed the sand
Then all is well for old England

If January has never a drop
The barn will need an oaken prop.

Winter's thunder and summer's flood
Never boded Englishman good

If the grass grow in Janiveer,
It grows the worse for it all the year

Who in January sows oats
Gets gold and groats,
Who sows in May
Gets little that way.

PROGNOSTICS FROM PHILOSOPHICAL INSTRUMENTS.

TANDARD and carefully tested instruments are most essential for the investigation of all natural phenomena; especially is this the case with reference to an instrument in such general use as the barometer. The words which are engraved on the dials of wheel and aneroid barometers are of little use, except at sea level, for a correction has to be made for every increase of elevation above it.

In the south-east of England certain directions of the wind must be taken into consideration with respect to the rising and falling of the barometer. It occasionally happens that approaching rain from the S. is driven back by a sudden change of wind to the N.W. or N., and, on the contrary, dry weather from the N. is suddenly changed by rain out of the S., whatever may have been the barometric indications.

When wet weather happens soon after the falling of the barometer expect but little of it, and, on the contrary, expect but little fair weather when it proves fine shortly after the barometer has risen.

In wet weather, when the barometer rises much and high, and so continues for two or three days before wet weather is quite over, you may expect a continuance of fair weather for several days

In fair weather, when the barometer falls much and low, and thus continues for two or three days before the rain comes, you may expect much rain and probably high winds.

Long foretold long last,
Short notice soon past.

A sudden and considerable rise of the barometer, after several hours of heavy rain, accompanied by a drying westerly wind, indicates more rain within thirty hours and a considerable fall of the barometer.

Should the barometer continue low when the sky becomes clear after a heavy rain expect more rain within twenty-four hours.

When, after a succession of gales and great fluctuations of the barometer, a gale comes on from S.W., which does not cause much, if any, depression of the instrument, you may consider that more settled weather is near at hand.

During the summer months, if you should observe a simultaneous increase of pressure and temperature, expect several days of find weather, and if small patches of cirrocumulus cloud should appear, at a great elevation, the rise of temperature will be considerable.

> If woolly fleeces strew the heavenly way
> Be sure no rain disturbs the summer's day.

After heavy rains from S.W., if the barometer rises upon the wind shifting to the N.W., expect three or four days fine weather.

During the winter months heavy rain is indicated by a decrease of pressure and an increase of temperature.

Sudden and great fluctuations of the barometer at any time of the year indicate unsettled weather for several days, perhaps a fortnight.

If the barometer falls two or three-tenths of an inch in four hours expect a gale of wind.

If you observe that the surface of the mercury in the cistern of the barometer vibrates upon the approach of a storm you may expect the gale to be severe.

In frosty weather a falling barometer indicates a thaw, it seldom falls for snow.

In summer, when the barometer falls suddenly, expect a thunderstorm, and if it does not rise again upon its cessation the weather will probably continue unsettled for several days.

In summer, when a thunderstorm happens, which occasions but little or no depression of the barometer, and more especially when the electric clouds are at a considerable elevation, you may assume that the storm is very local, and will have little effect either upon the temperature or the general state of the atmosphere.

When the barometer rises considerably, and the ground becomes dry, although the sky remains overcast, expect fair weather for a few days. The reverse may be expected if water is observed to stand in shallow places, notwithstanding the barometer may read upwards of thirty inches.

When the barometer falls considerably, but the weather continues mild and the wind moderate, you may be certain that a violent storm is raging at a distance. Under these circumstances the barometer has often been unjustly considered a false prophet, but it should be borne in mind that the instrument is very sensibly affected by storms which are two or three hundred miles distant. These storms affect a large atmospheric area, and rain will generally ensue in the course of three or four days.

In winter the rising barometer indicates frost when the wind is E. or N.E., and should the frost and increase of pressure continue, expect snow.

The barometer falls lower for high winds than heavy rains, and should the decrease of pressure amount to one inch in the course of twenty-four hours, expect a very severe gale.

The range of the barometer in this latitude is rather more than two inches. The readings seldom exceed 30°·800 as a maximum and 28°·800 as a minimum at sea level.

MY EQUATORIAL TELESCOPE.

Hoc sub pace vacat tantum : juvat ire per ipsum
Aëra, et immenso spatiantem vivere cœlo,
Signaque et adversos stellarum noscere cursus.—MANILIUS.

i.e.,

Fit task alone for peaceful leisure !   Rise
We then through yielding air and mount the skies,
There live and range ; learn all the signs and prove
How in their adverse course the Planets move.

If the temperature increases between 9 p.m. and midnight, when the sky is cloudless, expect rain, and if during the continuance of a long and severe frost the temperature increases between midnight and sunrise, expect a thaw.

The greater the difference between the lowest temperature of the air at four feet from the ground and that of terrestrial radiation *under a cloudless sky*, the less will be the probability of the existing state of weather continuing, and *vice versâ*.

HYGROMETER.

Consider that when a great difference exists between the readings of a dry and wet bulb thermometer the greater will be the probability of fine weather, and *vice versâ*

It not unfrequently happens that the symptoms of approaching changes in the weather are indicated by the hygrometer before any barometric depression has occurred.

TELESCOPE.

However clear and starlight the night may appear to the naked eye, yet if, with a moderately magnifying power applied to the telescope, the discs of the moon and planets appear ill-defined and surrounded by much atmospheric tremor, expect both wind and rain. Observe also that the greater the tremor the sooner will the change of weather occur. This prognostic must not be regarded when the wind is easterly, as the atmosphere is then peculiarly unfavourable for any astronomical observations.

A peculiar haze sometimes occurs which obscures the smaller stars, but is, nevertheless, extremely favourable for astronomical definition. This haze may be considered to be an indication of approaching fine weather for a few days.

PROGNOSTICS FROM SUNRISE AND SUNSET.

HEN the first rays of daylight rise considerably above the horizon it is called a "high dawn," which will probably be succeeded by wind and rain in the course of the day; but if the first rays of daylight keep near the horizon it is called a "low dawn," and is an indication of a fine day.

When the sun at rising assumes a reddish colour, and shortly afterwards numerous small clouds collect, the whole sky will soon become overcast, and rain may be expected in the course of a few hours.

If clouds disperse about two hours after sunrise expect a fine day.

When clouds (especially cumuli and cumulo-strati) are tinged on their *upper* edge of a pink or copper colour, and situated to the eastward at sunset, or to the westward at sunrise, expect wind and rain in about forty-eight hours—seldom much earlier.

If at sunrise some reddish looking clouds are seen close down upon the horizon, it must not always be considered as an indication of approaching rain. The probability of rain under these circumstances will depend upon the character of the clouds and their height above the horizon. I have frequently observed that if they extend 10° rain will follow before sunset; if 20° or 30° rain will fall before two or three p.m., but if still higher and near the zenith rain will fall within three hours.

When the sun rises or sets of a golden yellow colour, with disc ill defined and rays extending 4° or 6°, a strong wind and much vapor exist at a considerable elevation, and rain usually occurs within twenty-four hours, which will continue for some time if there are any opposing currents, whether direct or lateral.

When the sun sets with disc well defined, red, large, shorn of rays and its brilliancy much diminished by haze, expect fine weather for a day or two.

Or—

> The evening red and the morning grey
> Is a sure sign of a fine day.

> An evening red and a morning grey
> Helps the traveller on his way;
> But an evening grey and a morning red
> He must put on his hat, or wet his head.

In summer time, when the sun at rising is obscured by a mist which disperses about three hours afterwards, expect hot and calm weather for two or three days.

Pliny mentions several prognostics to be derived from observations made at sunrise and sunset, from which I have selected the following out of his eighteenth book, upon all of which I consider some reliance may be placed :—

If the sun rises clear and not fiery red it is a sign that the day will be fine If the sun's rays are red both at its rising *and* setting much rain may be expected. If red-tinted clouds are about the sun at its setting a fine day may be expected on the morrow.

Prognostics from the Rainbow.

 H EN the rainbow appears broad, with the prismatic colours very distinct, and green or blue predominating, expect much rain the succeeding night. If the red colour is conspicuous and the last to disappear, expect both rain and wind.

Whenever you observe the rainbow to be broken in two or three places, or perhaps only half of it visible, expect rainy weather for two or three days.

If, soon after the bow is formed, the colours become more and more distinct and highly coloured, expect short but heavy showers, which will be followed by wind, amounting almost to a gale, if the wind should happen to be S.W. or S W. by W.

The rainbow, after a long drought, is the precursor of a decided change to wet weather, and it happens also that a perfect bow, after an unsettled time, is a precursor of fair weather.

If the rainbow forms and disappears suddenly, the prismatic colours being but slightly discernible, expect fair weather next day.

When a perfect rainbow shows only *two* principal colours, which are generally red and yellow, expect fair weather for several days.

If a rainbow appears to the westward expect much rain, but if to the eastward there is a probability of fair weather. For the like reason, when a rainbow is formed in an approaching cloud, expect a shower, but when in a receding cloud, fine weather. This is consistent with the old adage:

A rainbow in the morning
Is the shepherd's warning,
But a rainbow at night
Is the shepherd's delight.

A double bow is occasionally seen, but a triple one very rarely. Opposite to whichever part of the bow the prismatic colours first disappear, wind and rain may be expected.

A rainbow at noon usually brings much rain. Seneca says:

A meridie ortus magnam vim aquarum vehit.

PROGNOSTICS FROM HALOES.

OLAR and lunar haloes are usually considered to indicate wet weather, but an attentive consideration of their sequences leads to the belief that such a result can only be relied upon during the summer months. In autumn, winter and spring they are followed about equally by fine and wet weather. I have observed that the larger the halo, whether solar or lunar, the greater the probability of rain within 36 hours.

Whenever a solar or lunar halo exhibits strongly marked prismatic colours rain will certainly follow within four days, and in all probability to a considerable amount. Rain more frequently follows a lunar than a solar halo. Parhelia or mock suns, and paraselenæ, or mock moons, very seldom occur, but are generally followed by fair weather; the reason for which

T

is that they are formed when both atmospheric pressure and the elevation of the clouds are considerable.

PROGNOSTICS FROM THE APPEARANCE OF AN AURORA BOREALIS.

Brilliant displays of this phenomenon have occasionally been observed in the South of England. They are almost invariably followed by very stormy weather, after an interval of from 10 to 14 days.

PROGNOSTICS FROM ANIMALS.

WHEN cattle do not leave off feeding till long after dusk, expect rain the next day.

When cattle, sheep, deer, rabbits and hares eat greedily in the early morning, expect rain before noon.

When cattle lick one another against the hair, expect rain.

Et Boves cœlum olfactantes, seque
Lambentes contra pilum.—PLINY, B. xviu. c. 35.

When cattle lift up their noses and sniff the air, expect rain.

Aut bucula cœlum
Suspiciens patulis captavit naribus auras.—VIRGIL, G. 1, 375

When cattle run to and fro more than ordinary, kicking and extending their tails, a storm frequently follows.

In Gay's first pastoral occurs the following :—

We learnt to read the skies
To know when hail will fall or winds arise,
He taught us erst the heifer's tail to view,
When stuck aloft that showers would straight ensue.

The " British Apollo " has the following :—

> A learned case I now propound,
> Pray give an answer as profound—
> 'Tis why a cow about half an hour
> Before there comes a hasty shower
> Does clap her tail against the hedge

When asses bray more than usual and mules rub their ears, expect rain.

> When the old donkey blows his horn
> Expect much rain —perhaps a storm

When sheep leap upon all four legs and butt one another, expect rain.

When goats wander towards the hedgerows and eat leaves (particularly the oak) instead of grass, expect rain ; also when they utter their peculiar cry.

When dogs wander about fields, biting grass and tossing it about, also when the hound stretches out his legs and rests his belly on the ground, expect rain.

When foxes bark and utter shrill cries, expect a violent tempest of wind and rain within three days. What has been said by the ancients respecting wolves applies to foxes in this country. Aratus, Homer and Theophrastus particularly mention this prognostic.

When swine wallow in the mire or run about the farm yard tossing up wisps of straw, expect rain.

Swine are also very uneasy at the approach of wind.

When cats lie upon the side, with the upper part of the head upon the ground, or when they scratch the bark and clamber up trees, or appear more restless than usual, rain will soon appear.

When mice and rats run about in the daytime and crawl up fences, expect rain.

When weasels and stoats are seen running about during the forenoon expect rain before sunset.

When cattle quit their pasture unwillingly expect rain shortly.

If cattle are seen to lie down during a shower it will soon cease.

If sheep or cattle turn their backs to the wind expect changeable, showery weather.

Moles.—When they are more active than usual expect rainy weather. They very seldom appear above ground unless a period of warm weather is at hand. They have a remarkable instinct of leaving pastures subject to floods before the event arrives.

Hedgehogs.—

> Observe which way the hedgehog builds her nest,
> To front the North, or South, or East or West;
> For 'tis, as common people say,
> The wind will blow the quite contrary way.
> If by some secret art the hedgehog knows
> So long before which way the winds will blow.

Horses.—If horses are seen to roll from side to side upon the ground expect windy, wet weather.

Tortoise.—

If attended to it becomes an excellent weather glass; for as sure as it walks elate, and as it were on tiptoe, feeding with great earnestness in a morning, so sure will it rain before night.—GILBERT WHITE

Squirrels.—Squirrels lay up a large store of food before wintry weather.

Deer.—Fight before rains.

PROGNOSTICS FROM BIRDS.

WALLOWS.—When they fly about after insects on a summer's evening, at a great height, expect fair weather for several days, but when they fly very low, and upon passing over a pond occasionally strike the water with their wings, expect rain.

Aut arguta lacus circumvolitavit Hirundo.—VIRGIL, G. 1, 377.

Hirundo tam juxta aquam volitans ut pennâ sæpe percutiat.—PLINY, B. xviii. c. 35.

Peacocks.—When they are unusually vociferous, expect rain

> When the peacock loudly bawls
> Soon we'll have both rain and squalls

Moor Hens.—When they fly at night to a distance from their usual water, and utter discordant cries during their flight, expect rain.

Pheasants are very active before rain, but when they roost near the *stems* of large trees in preference to the outer boughs, expect both wind and rain before sunrise.

Thrush.—When this bird perches itself upon the topmost bough of a tree and remains there for some time, singing loudly, expect rain. In some counties this bird is called the "storm cock."

Rooks and Crows indicate rain when they do not fly far from home, and alight in the most sheltered places; when they become clamorous upon their return home, some alighting on trees, others on the ground beneath them, moreover, frequently changing places the one with the other, and apparently quarrelsome ; also when they fly very low and slowly, and at other times drop suddenly from a great height; when near water they walk along the edge, sprinkling themselves.

> How the curst raven, with her harmless voice,
> Invokes the rain, and croaking to herself,
> Struts on some spacious, solitary shore.

Et cum terrestres volucres contra aquam clangores
Dabunt, perfundentes sese, sed maxime cornix —PLINY, B. xviii. c 35.

> Cras folus nemus
> Multis, et alga littus inutili
> Demissa tempestus ab euro
> Sternet aquæ nisi fallit augur
> Annosa cornix—

i.e ,

> To-morrow furious winds shall spread
> The troubled shore with useless weed,
> And fill the woods with scattered leaves
> Unless the cawing crow deceives ;
> The crow, that still foretells the rain
> And storm, and never caws in vain.—HORACE, B. iii., Ode xvii.

The continual prating of the crow, chiefly twice or thrice quick calling, indicates rain and stormy weather.

But the raven sometimes indicates the approach of fine weather, as Virgil has told us, *i.e.* (Georgic, 1, 410) :—

> Then thrice the Ravens rend the liquid air,
> And croaking notes proclaim the settled fair.
> Then round their airy Palaces they fly
> To greet the Sun ; and seized with secret joy,
> When storms are overblown, with food repair
> To their forsaken nests and callow Care.
> Not that I think their breasts with heavenly souls
> Inspired, as Man ; who destiny controuls
> But with the changeful temper of the skies,
> As rains condense, and sunshine rarifies ,

So turn the species in their altered minds,
Composed by calms and discomposed by winds, ·
From hence proceeds the Birds' harmonious voice,
From hence the Crows exult and frisking Lambs rejoice.

Plovers.—When Plovers fly high and then low, making their plaintive cry, expect fine weather.

Land Birds are observed to bathe before rain.

Owls hoot both in fine and wet weather, but in the latter instance they are much more clamorous

Noctua in imbre garrula —PLINY.

Herons.—When they fly at a great height indicate the approach of fine weather, says Lucan, *i.e.* ·

When watchful Herons leave their wat'ry stand,
And mounting upwards with erected flight,
Gain on the skies, and soar above the sight.

Sparrows.—When they chirp incessantly at daybreak, or roll in the dust, or forsake their roost among evergreens, and seek shelter under the eaves of stacks, barns or houses, expect rain

Larks.—When the rise *before they sing*, at dawn, with an overcast sky, expect rain; but when they fly very high, singing *as they rise*, expect a fine day.

Landrails.—When they are clamorous after sunset, and croak almost incessantly till after midnight, expect fair weather.

Woodpeckers utter peculiar cries before rain.

Doves roost later than usual before rain.

Starlings.—When they congregate with rooks, expect rain.

Cocks.—When they cry often at mid-day, or between 9 p.m. and midnight, expect a change of weather, and that suddenly

If the cock crows on going to bed
He's sure to rise with a watery head.

If the cock moults before the hen,
We shall have weather thick and thin ;
But if the hen moults before the cock,
We shall have weather hard as a block.

Hens.—When the hen goes to roost with her head covered with dust, or when she rolls in the dust and finally gathers her brood under her wings, expect rain. When she runs about uttering hoarse cries and much excited, "Good men expect a storm both within doors and without."

Magpie.—In the spring months the appearance of a single magpie indicates rain, for the mate is at home to keep the nest dry.

Geese.—When they fly suddenly from a considerable distance to a pond, uttering discordant cries, or when they rub their heads under their wings and appear restless, you may expect rain.

Seagulls.—When they appear in this neighbourhood, flying at a considerable height, and usually against the wind, expect rain.

Cum medio celeres revolant ex aquore mergi
Clamoremque—ferunt ad littora —VIRGIL, G. I, 361.

Swans.—When they fly indicate rough weather.

Pigeons wash before rain, and if they return home slowly it will probably rain very shortly.

Cuckoo.—When this bird is heard in the low lands rain may be expected, but on high land fair weather.

Guinea Fowls are very noisy before rain.

Quails.—When they are heard in the evening you may expect fine weather.

Blackbird.—When the shrill voice of this bird is heard in the early morning you may expect rain before night.

PROGNOSTICS FROM INSECTS AND REPTILES.

EES.—When they do not go far from their hive, or not at all, or return late to the hive, expect rain; but when they finish their work at an early hour, expect fair weather the following day.

Wasps and Hornets—When they fly in great numbers during the evening, foretell fine weather the next day; but if on a dull day they frequent their nests more than usual, expect both rain and wind.

Ants.—When, during the summer months, you perceive the ants removing their eggs from the nest, and the winged ants helping them, expect sudden rain or thunderstorm, also expect rain if they should disappear suddenly under ground. A celebrated naturalist relates that he one day observed these little creatures, after having brought out their corn at eleven o'clock in the forenoon, removing the same, contrary to their usual custom, before four in the afternoon. The sun being then very hot and the sky clear, he could perceive no reason for it; but half-an-hour after his surprise ceased. The sky began to be overcast and there fell a heavy shower of rain, which caused all this bustle in the community. Were we minutely to examine into the economy and management of these wonderful artificers, many other and equally curious facts might be gleaned relative to the weather, for—

> Wise as we are, if we went to their school,
> There's many a sluggard and many a fool
> Some lessons of wisdom might learn,

They don't wear their time out in sleeping or play,
But gather up corn in a sunshiny day,
And for winter they lay up their stores
They manage their work in such regular forms
One would think they foresaw all the frost and the storms,
And so brought their food within doors —WATTS

Flies and Gnats.—When they appear in large numbers and greedily bite cattle, expect rain ; but when they play up and down in the open air, expect fair weather.

Spiders.—When the terminating filaments of the common garden spider's web are very long, and but few of them, the weather will probably be fine and calm for about a week or ten days. On the contrary, when the weather is likely to become windy and wet, the terminating filaments, on which the whole is suspended, will be very short   If spiders are very indolent rain will ensue, though their great activity during rain is a strong proof of its short continuance, and that it will probably be followed by several days' calm and fine weather.   If spiders' webs are watched they will generally be found to have undergone some alterations every day.   After a cloudless night in summer you may occasionally see spread over the lawn innumerable small, and nearly circular, spiders' webs, laden with dew.   This is an almost infallible sign of approaching fine weather. When, after a long drought, you observe in hedges some very densely woven webs, *funnel shaped*, there will be a change of weather within *three days.*

Leech.—The leech possesses remarkable meteoric properties, which are very interesting to observe   The best method is to place an ordinary medicinal leech in an upright half-pint bottle, with the mouth covered over with fine linen.   If the weather is likely to remain calm and fine the creature will lie motionless and rolled up in a somewhat spiral form at the bottom of the bottle. If it rains either before or after noon it will creep up to the top of the bottle and there remain till the weather is settled. If we are to have wind the leech gallops through the water with amazing swiftness, and does not rest till it blows hard. It is very remarkable that however fine the weather may be, and to our senses there is no particular indication of a change, yet if a storm of rain and thunder is approaching, its body is almost continually without the water, and discovers great uneasiness in violent throes and convulsions. In frost as in fine summer weather it lies constantly at the bottom, and in snow as in rainy weather, it ascends to the very mouth of the bottle.

Worms.—When the common garden worm forms many "casts" rain or frost will follow according to the season of the year. When they appear in the daytime expect rain, but when early in the evening it indicates a mild night, with heavy dew and two days' fine weather. There is a small, reddish worm, which, when it becomes luminous at night, indicates the near approach of a thunderstorm It sometimes leaves a phosphorescent trail upon the ground.

Glow-worms, when they shine more brightly than usual, indicate rain within 48 hours, more especially when they remain luminous a short time *after midnight.*

Snails—When they crawl up evergreens and remain there during the whole day, expect rain

Toads and Frogs—When the former croak much in the water, and the latter under stones, expect rain. If frogs appear yellow fine weather may be expected, but if more brown than usual expect rain.

Snakes.—When in hot weather you see the trail of a snake across a dusty road you may expect rain soon—perhaps a thunderstorm.

Bats flying around the house of an evening indicate fine weather.

PROGNOSTICS FROM PLANTS.

HE meteorological indications afforded by some of our indigenous plants will be found to repay us for the study which we may be disposed to bestow upon them. Moreover, the vegetation of the earth is a calendar worthy of the observation of everyone. Linnæus attached great importance to such observations, and advised his countrymen carefully to consider at what time each tree expanded its leaves and blossoms, for it would teach them when annual plants should be sown. Of the several plants which possess meteorological properties the common chickweed (Stellaria media) is an excellent outdoor barometer. When the flower expands fully no rain will happen within four hours or more, and should it continue in that state no rain will disturb the summer's day. When it partly conceals its flowers the day will be showery; but if it entirely shuts up rain will surely and soon follow. The purple sandwort (Arenaria rubra) expands its beautiful pink flowers only when the sun shines, but closes them before the coming shower. The germander speedwell (Veronica chamædrys) closes its blue petals before rain, and opens them again when it has ceased. The pimpernel (Anagallis arvensis) closes its flowers before rain ; at noon, however, it always closes its flowers till about seven the next morning, hence it has been termed the poor man's weather glass.

> Of humble growth, though brighter dies,
> But not by rural swains less prized,
>   The trailing stems allure,
> Of Pimpernel, whose brilliant flower
> Closes against the approaching shower,
> Warning the swain to sheltering bower,
>   From humid air secure.

If the flower of the Siberian sow thistle keeps open all night it will certainly rain on the next day. The goat's beard (Trajopogon pratensis) keeps its flowers closed in cloudy damp weather. The common dandelion (Leontodon taraxicum) contracts its down before rain. It is also a correct sun dial, as it closes its flowers about five in the afternoon and opens them again at seven in the morning.

The wood sorrel (Oxalis acetosella) folds up its leaves at the approach of night, or a shower, while the blossom droops its head towards the ground.

> Flowers shrinking from the chilly night
> Droop and shut up , but with fair morning's touch
> Rise on their stems all open and upright.—MONTAGUE

The convolvulus folds up its leaves and closes its flowers on the approach of rain.

The great white oxeye (Chrysanthemum leucanthemum) closes its flowers before a storm.

> There gay chrysanthemums repose,
> And when stern tempests lower,
> Their silken fringes softly close
> Against the shower.—A. S.

If the African marigold does not open its flowers in the morning, about seven o'clock, expect rain that day.

The gentian (Gentiana pneumonanthe), which grows so beautifully on Ashdown Forest, closes up both flowers and leaves before rain.

The trefoil (Trifolium Arvense) is known to enlarge its stalk, which becomes more upright, while the leaves droop, before rain.

> When the leaves show their under sides,
> Be very sure that rain betides
>
> The frost in the winter will be long and strong
> If the leaves on the trees remain very long.

When the odour of shrubs and flowers is very perceptible, expect rain.

> When the mulberry tree is in full leaf
> There will be no frost to give you grief

Apple blossom in reference to the making of cyder :—

> " If your blossom comes in March,
> You need not for your barrels sarch ,
> If they come in Aparill,
> You may perhaps some barrels fill ,
> But if your blossom comes in May
> Look out for barrels every day."

Besides foretelling changes in the weather many plants close and open their petals at certain hours of the day. Linnæus has enumerated forty-six plants which possess this kind of sensibility , he divides them into three classes. (1) Meteoric flowers, which less accurately observe the hour of folding, but are expanded sooner or later, according to the cloudiness, moisture and pressure of the atmosphere. (2) Tropical flowers, which open in the morning and close before evening every day , but the hour of expanding becomes earlier or later as the length of the day increases or decreases. (3) Equinoctial flowers, which open at a certain and exact time of the day, and for the most part close at another determinate hour. Several of these, which are indigenous to our country, have been prettily enumerated by Mrs. C. Smith :—

In every copse and sheltered dell,
Unveiled to the observant eye,
Are faithful monitors who tell
How pass the hours and seasons by
The green-robed children of the spring
Will mark the periods as they pass,
Mingle with leaves Time's feathered
    wing,
And bind with flowers his silent glass.
Mark where transparent waters glide,
Soft flowing o'er their tranquil bed ;
There, cradled on the dimpling tide,
Nymphea rests her lovely head
But conscious of the earliest beam
She rises from her humid nest,
And sees reflected in the stream
The virgin whiteness of her breast.
Till the bright day-star to the west
Declines, in ocean's surge to lave,
Then, folded in her modest vest,
She slumbers on the rocking wave
See Hieracium's various tribe
Of plumy seed and radiate flowers,
The course of time their blooms
    describe,
And wake or sleep *appointed hours*
Broad o'er its imbricated cup
The Goatsbeard spreads its golden
    rays,
But shuts its cautious petals up,

Retiring from the noontide blaze.
Pale as a pensive cloistered nun
The Bethlehem star her face unveils,
When o'er the mountain peers the sun,
And shades it from the vesper gales.
Among the loose and arid sands
The humble Arenaria creeps ;
Slowly the purple star expands,
But soon within its calyx sleeps.
And those small bells so lightly rayed
With young Aurora's rosy hue,
Are to the noontide sun displayed,
But shut their plaits against the dew.
On upland slopes the shepherds mark
The hour, when, as the dial true,
Cichorium to the towering lark
Lifts her soft eyes serenely blue
And thou, "wee crimson-tipped flower,"
Gatherest thy fringed mantle round
Thy bosom at the closing hour,
When night-drops bathe the turfy
    ground ;
Unlike Silene, who declines
The garish noontide's blazing light ;
But when the evening crescent shines,
Gives all her sweetness to the night.
Thus in each flower and simple bell
That in our path unbroken lie,
Are sweet remembrancers who tell
How fast their winged moments fly.

MISCELLANEOUS PROGNOSTICS.

HEN distant objects are seen distinctly during the summer months it is an indication of coming rain, but during the autumnal, winter and early spring months it is as often a precursor of fine weather as of wet.

When distant sounds are heard distinctly. I consider that much more reliance may be placed upon this than upon the previous prognostic, particularly when the sound has a metallic origin, as railway trains, church bells, firearms, &c.

When rain commences before seven a.m it usually ceases about noon, and when it commences at noon it frequently continues for several hours, especially when the wind is from S.E. or E.

When small dark clouds (broken nimbi) appear against a patch of blue sky there will be rain before sunset.

When the sky becomes gradually overcast and the sun or moon shines less and less till quite obscured, a six or eight hours' rain may be expected, more especially when there are opposing currents of wind.

When you observe greenish tinted masses of composite cloud collect in the S.E. and remain there, apparently stationary, for several hours, expect a succession of heavy rains and gales.

When ash coloured masses of cumulo-stratus and cirro-stratus cloud collect over the sea, extending in a line from S.E. to S.W., expect rain, and probably wind, on the second day.

When you observe long lines of cirro-strati clouds, *slightly contracted in their centre*, extend along any part of the horizon, expect heavy rain the following day.

When large masses of cumulo-strati cloud collect simultaneously in N.E. and S W., with the wind at E., expect cold rain or snow in the course of a few hours; the wind will ultimately back to N.

> When clouds appear like rocks and towers
> The earth's refreshed by frequent showers.

When clouds float in different currents of wind the upper current will ultimately prevail. It will indicate fine weather if from N.E., wet if from S.W.

When the South Downs look *blue* and near after heavy rain, a gale may be expected within 30 hours.

When, on a cloudless summer day, you perceive a white, flocculent mist lying upon the summit of the South Downs (*i.e.*, from Mount Harry to Lewes Race-course), expect *very hot* weather within three days. (This is a very sure prognostic.)

When mists (stratus) form on low grounds immediately after sunset and disappear before midnight, expect rain within 24 hours; but when they continue all night and disappear *after* sunrise, expect fine weather for two or three days.

When you observe smoke from the chimney of a lone cottage descend (flop down) immediately upon the roof and pass along the eaves, expect rain within 24 hours.

When a carriage wheel rotates rapidly along a dusty road it raises three ridges of dust; if the central ridge lies flatter than the others, expect rain within 36 hours.

If, shortly before sunset, the upper parts of cumulus clouds become tinted of a pinkish colour when situated along the southern and eastern horizons, expect both wind and rain.

If, before sunrise, the same appearances present themselves on the western and south-western horizons, both wind and rain may be expected and particularly the former.

The higher the clouds, the finer the weather.

When the soot from a wood fire falls frequently from the chimney expect rain.

If dew lies long upon the grass after sunrise expect fair weather, but the early disappearance of dew indicates rain.

In summer evenings when, although the sky is cloudless, yet no dew is found three hours after sunset, *nor at any period of the night*, expect rain the next day.

When there have been hoar frosts on three consecutive mornings rain usually follows. Rain also succeeds a single hoar frost when the crystals are very long and readily melt, notwithstanding the temperature may have been several degrees below freezing point.

When the landscape looks clear, having your back towards the sun, expect fine weather, but when it looks clear, with your face towards the sun, expect showery, unsettled weather.

Other prognostics may be observed from an attentive consideration of the formation, change and dispersion of clouds; the study of which becomes extremely interesting to those who watch their sudden, but regular and wonderful transformations, and particularly with respect to the Cirrus cloud, for if its terminating filaments point upwards expect rain soon to follow, but if downwards fine weather is probable.

In the preface I alluded to the fact that Virgil had borrowed much of his weather lore from Aratus, in proof of which I will here insert, as a conclusion to this subject, the following metrical translation* of a certain portion of his first Georgic :—

> All that the genial year successive brings,
> Showers, and the reign of heat, and freezing gales,
> Appointed signs foreshow ; the Sire of all
> Decreed the omens of the varying moon ;
> Decreed what sign the southern blast should bring ;
> That hinds, observant of the approaching storm,
> Might tend their herds more near the sheltering stall.

PROGNOSTICS I., OF WIND.

> When storms are brooding—in the leeward gulf
> Dash the swelled waves, the mighty mountains pour
> A harsh, dull murmur, far along the beach
> Rolls the deep rustling roar ; the whispering grove
> Betrays the gathering elemental strife
> Scarce will the billows spare the curved keel
> For swift from open sea the cormorants sweep
> With clamorous croak, the ocean dwelling coot
> Sports on the sand ; the hern her marshy haunts
> Deserting, soars the lofty cloud above.
> And oft when gales impend, the gliding star
> Nightly descends athwart the spangled gloom,
> And leaves its fire-wake glowing white behind.
> Light chaff and leaflets flitting fill the air,
> And sportive feathers circle on the lake.

PROGNOSTICS II., OF RAIN.

> But when grim Boreas thunders ; when the east
> And black winged west roll out the sonorous peal
> The teeming dykes o'erflow the wide champaign,
> And seamen furl their dripping sails. The shower,
> Forsooth, ne'er took the traveller unawares !

* See Howard's "Climate of London."

U 2

The soaring cranes descried it in the vale
And shunned its coming; heifers gazed aloft
With nostrils wide, drinking the fragrant gale;
Skimm'd the sagacious swallow round the lake,
And croaking frogs renewed their old complaint.
Oft, too, the ant, from secret chambers, bears
Her eggs—a cherished treasure—o'er the sand,
Along the narrow track her steps have worn.
High vaults the thirsty bow; in wide array
The clamorous rooks from every pasture rise
With serried wings The varied sea-fowl tribes,
And those that in Cayster's meadows seek,
Amid the marshy pools, their skulking prey,
Fling the cool, plenteous shower, upon their wings,
Crouch to the coming wave, sail on its crest,
And idly wash their purity of plume.
The audacious crow with loud voice hails the rain,
A lonesome wanderer on the thirsty sand.
Maidens that nightly toil the tangled fleece
Divine the coming tempest.   "In the lamp
Crackles the oil, the gathering wick grows dim."

PROGNOSTICS III., OF FAIR WEATHER.

Nor less, by sure prognostics, may'st thou learn
(When rain prevails), in prospect to behold
Warm suns and cloudless heavens around thee smile.
Brightly the stars shine forth; Cynthia no more
Glimmers obnoxious to her brother's rays;
Nor fleecy clouds float lightly through the sky
The chosen birds of Thetis, halcyons* now,
Spread not their pinions on the sun-burnt shore,
Nor swine the bands unloose and toss the straw.
The clouds descending settle on the plain,
While owls forget to chaunt their evening song.
But watch the sunset from the topmost ridge.
The merlin swims the liquid sky sublime,
While for the purple lock the lark atones,
Where she with light wing cleaves the yielding air,
Her shrieking fell-pursuer follows fierce—
The dreaded merlin; where the merlin soars,
Her fugitive swift pinion cleaves the air,

* Kingfishers.

And now, from throat compressed, the rook emits
Treble or fourfold, his clear piercing cry ,
While oft, amid her high and leafy roosts,
Bursts the responsive note from all the clan,
Thrilled with unwonted rapture , oh ¹ 'tis sweet,
When brightening hours allow, to seek again
Their tiny offspring and their dulcet homes.
Yet deem I not that heaven on them bestows
Foresight, or mind above their lowly fate ;
But rather, when the changing climate veers,
Obsequious to the humour of the sky ,
When the damp south condenses what was rare,
The dense relaxing—or the stringent north
Rolls back the genial showers, and rules in turn,
The varying impulse fluctuates in their breast ;
Hence the full concert in the sprightly mead,—
The bounding flock—the rook's exulting cry.

PROGNOSTICS IV., THE MOON'S ASPECTS.

Mark with attentive eye the rapid sun,
The varying moon that rolls its monthly round ,
So shalt thou count, not vainly on the moon ,
So the bland aspect of the tranquil night
Will ne'er beguile thee with insidious calm
When Luna first her scatter'd fires recalls,
If with blunt horn she holds the dusky air,
Seamen and swains predict th' abundant shower.
If rosy blushes tinge her maiden cheek
Wind will arise ; the golden Phœbe still
Glows with the wind. If (mark the ominous hour ¹)
The clear fourth night her lucid disk define,
That day, and all that thence successive spring,
E'en to the finished month, are calm or dry ;
And grateful mariners redeem their vows
To Glaucus, Inöus, or the Nereid nymph.

PROGNOSTICS V., THE SUN'S ASPECTS.

The sun, too, rising, and at that still hour,
When sinks this tranquil beauty in the main,
Will give thee tokens ; certain tokens all,
But those that morning brings, and balmy eve
When cloudy storms deform the rising orb,
Or streaks of vapour in the midst beset,

Beware of showers, for then the blasting south
(Foe to the groves, to harvests and the flock),
Urges with turbid pressure from above.
But when beneath the dawn's red fingered rays,
Through the dense band of clouds diverging, break,
When springs Aurora, pale from saffron couch,
Ill does the leaf defend the mellowing grape;
Leaps on the noisy roof the plenteous hail,
Fearfully cracking. Nor forget to note,
When Sol departs, his mighty day-task done,
How varied hues oft wander on his brow;
Azure betokens rain; the fiery tint
Is Eurus' herald, if the ruddy blaze
Be dimm'd with spots, then all will wildly rage
With squalls and driving showers; on that fell night
None shall persuade me on the deep to urge
My perilous course, or quit the sheltering pier.
But if when day returns, or when retires,
Bright is the orb, then fear no coming rain;
Clear northern airs will fan the quiv'ring grove.
Lastly, the sun will teach th' observant eye
What Vesper's hour shall bring;—what clearing wind
Shall waft the clouds now floating;—what the south
Broods in his humid breast. Who dare belie
The constant sun?

CHAPTER VII.

SOME RECOLLECTIONS OF THE DISTRICT OF CROWBOROUGH SIXTY YEARS AGO.

BEFORE bringing to a conclusion my remarks upon the Topography and Climatology of Crowborough Hill, it has been suggested to me that I should give a few brief particulars respecting the condition and aspect of the district as they existed upwards of sixty years since, and I trust that the following remarks, the result of personal observation, may be of some interest to both present and future residents in the locality. I will premise that so long ago as 1841 I occasionally practised my profession among many of the poor inhabitants of the district, and poor indeed they were, at the above date. Their little houses were few and far between, while their mode of life was necessarily thrifty in the extreme. Some obtained a livelihood by cutting litter off the otherwise barren Common, while indulging, to a certain extent, in poaching, smuggling, and sundry other lawless transactions. Even at this distance from the coast a severe affray would occasionally occur with the revenue officers and frequently with a certain amount of bloodshed.

I have heard it stated that it was considered scarcely safe to pass over Crowborough Hill at night without a pair of pistols. As might be expected the bulk of the people were absolutely lawless and would not allow the slightest interference with their accustomed habits and pursuits.

The area of Crowborough has been too frequently designated " The Forest," which has proved a very misleading term   During my various local explorations I have never been able to find the slightest trace of the growth of large trees of any kind; not a root, of any size, was ever found, while the general appearance of the surface would warrant the conclusion that the ground had never been upturned for any extensive planting purposes, with the exception of certain portions of what is now called " Crowborough Warren," respecting which I shall have more to say presently.   In former times the term "Forest" was applied to Lancaster Great Park, situated to the westward of the summit of Crowborough Hill.

I have an old map, now very scarce, which mentions what was included within the boundaries of the Park, as well as all the various gates by which this once Royal Chase was entered. As it so closely approximates to the district of Crowborough I will here insert the names of these gates, some of which still remain, while others must have been swept away and most probably forgotten.

TARTING then from the most southerly boundary of the Park and proceeding eastward we come to Lampool Gate, in the Parish of Maresfield, then Tyes Gate, Old Land Gate, Barnes Gate, Pound Gate, Crowborough Gate, Heave Gate (on the southern slope of the Hill), Boxes Gate, Newnham Gate (this gate must have been on the summit of the Hill and just beyond Hanover Hall, probably, too, on the same site as the present entrance gate to Crowborough Warren); Frayer's Gate. From this point, and proceeding westward, we come to Reads Gate, Chuckhatch Gate, New Bridge Gate, Coleman's Hatch Gate, Shepherd's Gate, Quabrook Gate, Plaw's Gate, High Gate, Kilbrook Gate, Claypits Gate, Mudbrook Gate, Maller's Gate. We now turn to the southward and find Legshill Gate, Plawhatch Gate, Footbridge Gate, Cowler's Gate, Chelwood Gate, Brabies Gate, Stone Gate. We now arrive at Nutley, in the Parish of Maresfield, where the main London road forms the boundary on the western side of the Park. Here we find Prickets Hatch Gate, Courtland Gate, Upper Horny Gate, Lower Horny Gate, and from thence to Lampool Gate, from whence we started.

The only residence mentioned is Old Lodge, which appears to be surrounded with a ring fence on the top of Black Hill. The date of this map is 1747 and a photographic copy, which I took of it some years since, may be seen in the Library of the Sussex Archæological

Society at Lewes. The chief part of the present Crowborough Warren was within the boundaries of the Park, which, at the date mentioned above, was a portion of the large area of waste land extending from Crowborough towards Forest Row and East Grinstead. My father informed me that early in the present century a city gentleman of the name of Howis purchased of the Lord of the Manor of (I think) Duddleswell that portion of the Park called Crowborough Warren He enclosed this land, partly by hedges, partly by banks, and made large plantations of both deciduous and evergreen trees, extending over several hundred acres, the larger portion being of the coniferous kinds, for which the soil was found to be admirably adapted. Mr. Howis must have been a man of great mental energy and bodily activity It was said of him that he would leave London, on horseback, about two or three o'clock in the morning and, upon arrival at Godstone, would change his horse and continue on his journey to Crowborough for breakfast. He would then occupy his time in superintending the formation of various enclosures, the building of a residence, various mills and out-buildings, &c. In the evening he would leave again for London on horseback.

From Mr. Howis's executors I believe the property passed into the possession of a Mr. French and from him to the late Mr. Ramsbotham.

Y way of comparison with the present rate of building at Crowborough it may perhaps be deserving of mention what were the various dwellings in existence near the main road leading from the Crow and Gate to Boar's Head sixty years ago, and these I will endeavour to point out as far as my memory serves me after the lapse of so many years.

I purpose commencing with the Crow and Gate Inn. Proceeding northwards there was a small cottage on the left of the road, now called Little Warren. The next house on the same side of the road was the little public-house called the Blue Anchor, which was the resort of various smugglers, poachers, and other lawless inhabitants of the district. After passing the Blue Anchor the next cottage* was one exactly opposite the entrance to the Grange, while some hundred yards further on was Hanover Hall,* a small but prettily-built cottage, the property of Mr Newnham, of Maresfield Park, and the gate, which went by his name, was at about the same site as the present entrance to Crowborough Warren. From Hanover Hall to the Cross I do not think there was any other house, unless Horn Read was in existence, but of this I am not sure. From the Crow and Gate to the Cross there was not any house on the eastern side of the road, with the exception of the cottage adjoining the Wilderness property, which had just been built.

Crowborough Cross consisted of the present inn and several detached houses. A miserable little grocer's shop occupied the site of the present Post Office. I was

* Both pulled down a few years since.

informed by an old inhabitant that no butcher's shop
existed and what little meat was required could only be
obtained at the village of Rotherfield. After passing
the Cross there was no house on either side of the road
until you came to a small house on the southern side of
the road, near Steel Cross, where a branch Post Office is
now established. Between Steel Cross and Boar's Head
was a house (now pulled down) which was occupied by
the local shoemaker, while exactly opposite to this was
an ancient dwelling, owned and occupied by a well-
known family of the name of Lockyer.

A little farther on the road was an old public-house
which was for many years kept by a very eccentric widow,
who, for the purpose of attracting the beer-drinking
people of the neighbourhood, was in the habit of dress-
ing in a great variety of colours; wearing a fool's cap
with long feathers inserted in it; often pretending to be
tipsy, but, at the same time, perfectly well aware of what
she was about. Leaving this house to the right we soon
came in site of the well-known Boar's Head Rock, which,
at our date, stood prominently out upon its base, but is
now so nearly hidden by trees that it has to be searched
for. On the opposite side of the road was, and still
remains, a nice farmhouse. Returning to the southern
side of the hill and near the present golf house no direct
road existed which would lead to South View. There
was only a footpath which led to an old public-house
across the Common and near some yew trees, which was
in a better condition then than it is at present. On the
side of the path leading up to the house was a long
border planted with Solomon's Seal, and upon my asking
why such a large quantity was grown I was told that

"it was very good stuff for the cheps when they got a fighting and give one another a black eye I bruise a root and rub some of the juice on the part and there was no mark in the morning to show what they had been about."

Passing along, there were some rude huts which even now exist, on either side of Preston Lodge, while there were no other houses, to the best of my recollection, on either side of the road, as far as the Cross, unless it was one in which dwelt the village schoolmaster, a very quaint old man who delighted to tell a visitor how on one 1st of April he sent a *cunning* neighbour of his to the blacksmith's shop for "*some straight hooks which he had ordered.*"

Entering what is now called Church Road, from the main road, a small cottage existed on the site of the present Isfield Lodge and another on the opposite side of the road near the corner, at which you turn to the left for the direction to the Cross. The only other houses from this point to Jarvis Brook were—one near the church—the cluster of cottages adjoining the White Hart Inn—another opposite the inn, and three more before you come to Jarvis Brook, viz., one on the left and two on the right hand side of the road.

In former days the road across the brook was in a very unsatisfactory condition ; a swamp existed on either side inhabited chiefly by frogs, hence it obtained the name of "Frogs Hole"

So much, then, for Crowborough and its neighbourhood more than half a century ago.

I will now recount a few of my medical experiences in the district at about the same date.

HE first annoyance in starting from Uckfield to Crowborough, on a dark winter's night, was the old turnpike gate and the trouble which often ensued in arousing the keeper from his slumbers. After giving a good shout I heard spoken in a gruff voice, "Coming." Some minutes would elapse before I heard anything more than a *snore*, upon which I got off my horse and kicked at the door until the man called out, " I *be* a-coming," and at last the gate was opened, but I generally extracted a promise that it should be left unlocked until my return. Upon one such occasion I found on my arrival that my attendance was required for a poor woman who, with her husband and family, was living in a conical hut, on the open Common, into which I was obliged to crawl upon my hands and knees in order to enter the establishment.

Notwithstanding this miserable arrangement the woman appeared quite contented and soon recovered. On another occasion I entered a room where the mother and several girls were in bed ; and I was told there were three boys lying on mattresses overhead between the ceiling and the roof.

Experiences like these are long retained in the memory and with the following instance I will conclude them :

One very wintry night I was called upon to attend a person at Crowborough whose illness was of such nature as required my constant attendance at the bedside ; while thus engaged I felt my feet getting very cold and, upon looking down, I found they were surrounded by snow which had drifted through a broken window This, however, was not the only inconvenience experienced by the household, for in consequence of the inclement weather my horse was brought into the kitchen where, being left to its own devices, it found out the bread crock and devoured its contents.

It is probable that, at the present day, few people have any idea of the distress which the very poor of the parishes of Buxted and Rotherfield had to endure. I once went into a cottage, when the people were at dinner, and found them eating some turnip rinds; upon asking them what else they had the reply was, "Nothing; we had the turnips yesterday, but to-day we have only the rinds" There was no bread in the house. To drink, they had only some hot water stained with tea, for it really was nothing more.

During my frequent visits among them I scarcely ever heard that a clergyman visited them, even in time of sickness, nor were any clubs established to assist them in time of need An occasional visit from the relieving officer was the only semblance of relief. The present generation of poor may be well satisfied that they live in better times, and it may truly be said, as of old, " Tempora mutantur; nos et mutamur in illis "

VALE.

The Old Bridge at Uckfield

T page 143 is given a photograph of the Old Bridge at Uckfield. It was a very picturesque structure, built about the middle of the 17th Century It was removed, I believe, in the interest of the railway company and principally on account of its massive supports being placed in the midst of the stream, which, in times of heavy rains, were a serious impediment to the rapid flowing down the river of the large volume of water which had passed through Hurstwood and Buxted Park from the southern slopes of Crowborough Hill and intermediate ravines. About the year 1797* a very melancholy accident occurred on the bridge.

In consequence of continued rains so large a quantity of water flowed down to Buxted Park that it carried away a wooden fence, which, becoming fixed on the eastern side of the bridge, caused an immense accumulation of water behind it. This obstruction suddenly gave way and such a weight of water was thrown against the bridge as to carry away its stone parapets and, with them, several persons who were watching the rise of the flood. One of these persons, a village schoolmaster, who lived in the adjoining old house, was unfortunately drowned. Upon the recovery of the body it was taken to the "Bell" Inn to await an inquest. I was informed

* See "Sussex Archæological Coll," Vol. XII., p 2.

INDEX.

FARNCOMBE & CO., LEWES.

BIBLIOLIFE

Old Books Deserve a New Life
www.bibliolife.com

Did you know that you can get most of our titles in our trademark **EasyScript**™ print format? **EasyScript**™ provides readers with a larger than average typeface, for a reading experience that's easier on the eyes.

Did you know that we have an ever-growing collection of books in many languages?

Order online:
www.bibliolife.com/store

Or to exclusively browse our **EasyScript**™ collection:
www.bibliogrande.com

At BiblioLife, we aim to make knowledge more accessible by making thousands of titles available to you – quickly and affordably.

Contact us:
BiblioLife
PO Box 21206
Charleston, SC 29413

Printed in Great Britain
by Amazon